TO LORNA

JOHN FORD
BAROQUE ENGLISH DRAMATIST

In this discerning study, John Ford is presented as the English baroque dramatist *par excellence.* An introductory essay defines the concept of literary baroque by
distinguishing between the baroque style and several related stylistic phases—
renaissance, mannerism, classicism, and rococo. Drawing on parallel examples
from visual art and literature, the author suggests that Ford is a baroque dramatist
in much the same way that Crashaw is a baroque poet or Bernini a baroque sculptor. The remaining chapters demonstrate in detail the close relationship between
Ford's plays and the baroque tradition in art and literature.

Dr. Huebert relies on the theory of baroque literature to develop a fresh
interpretation of Ford's plays. He locates a baroque resonance in Ford's intensely
emotional treatment of such major themes as love and death. He argues that in
matters of design, Ford showed a decided preference for the "open" form typical
of the baroque style; as a poet, he abandoned the strictly logical guidelines of
renaissance rhetoric in favour of a verbal practice based on psychology.

Although this approach to Ford stresses those qualities that make his plays
distinctive and unusual, it does not isolate his drama from its local environment.
In a discussion of selected plays by Massinger, Fletcher, Shirley, and Otway, the
author illustrates the continuity of the baroque tradition in English drama.

Concluding with a brief essay in criticism, Dr. Huebert lays to rest the view of
Ford as a "decadent" follower of Shakespeare, and establishes beyond doubt his
integrity as a dramatic artist.

Ronald Huebert is Assistant Professor of English at Dalhousie University, Halifax,
Novia Scotia.

JOHN FORD

BAROQUE ENGLISH DRAMATIST

Ronald Huebert

McGill-Queen's University Press

Montreal and London

1977

© McGill-Queen's University Press
International Standard Book Number o 7735 0286 6

Legal Deposit fourth quarter 1977
Bibliothèque nationale du Québec

Design by Anthony Crouch MGDC
PRINTED IN GREAT BRITAIN
AT THE UNIVERSITY PRESS, CAMBRIDGE

CONTENTS

ILLUSTRATIONS   ix
PREFACE   xiii
ABBREVIATIONS   xvii

CHAPTER ONE
Poets and Painters Curiously Compared
An Essay in Definition   1

CHAPTER TWO
Love's Martyrs Must Be Ever, Ever Dying
An Essay on Themes   35

CHAPTER THREE
Turmoils Past Like Some Unquiet Dream
An Essay on Dramatic Structure   77

CHAPTER FOUR
Language Suited to a Divided Mind
An Essay on Verbal Style   129

CHAPTER FIVE

Great Men and Worthy of Report

An Essay on Massinger, Fletcher, Shirley, and Otway   163

CHAPTER SIX

Trial Now More Fortunate

An Essay in Criticism   195

NOTES   217

INDEX   237

ILLUSTRATIONS

Plates between pages 128 *and* 129

PLATE ONE
Gianlorenzo Bernini. *The Ecstasy of St. Teresa*. 1645–52.

PLATE TWO
Giovanni Bellini. *St. Francis in Ecstasy*. c. 1485.

PLATE THREE
Raphael. *The Descent from the Cross*. 1507.

PLATE FOUR
Peter Paul Rubens. *The Descent from the Cross*. 1603.

PLATE FIVE
Donato Bramante. *The Tempietto*. 1502.

PLATE SIX
Peter Paul Rubens. *The Raising of the Cross*. 1609–10.

PLATE SEVEN

Pietro da Cortona. *Santa Maria in Via Lata*. 1658–62.

PLATE EIGHT

Rosso Fiorentino. *The Descent from the Cross*. 1521.

PLATE NINE

El Greco. *The Vision of St. John the Divine*. 1610–14.

PLATE TEN

Tintoretto. *The Last Supper*. 1592–94.

PLATE ELEVEN

Peter Paul Rubens. *The Rape of the Sabines*. c. 1635.

PLATE TWELVE

Nicolas Poussin. *The Rape of the Sabines*. c. 1636–37.

PLATE THIRTEEN

Gianlorenzo Bernini. *Baldacchino*. 1624–33.

PLATE FOURTEEN

Jacques Verberckt. *Le Cabinet de la Pendule*. 1738.

PLATE FIFTEEN

Pietro da Cortona. *The Triumph of Divine Providence*. 1633–39.

PLATE SIXTEEN

Sandro Botticelli. *The Birth of Venus*. c. 1480.

PLATE SEVENTEEN

Peter Paul Rubens. *Marie de Médicis Landing in Marseilles*. 1622–25.

PLATE EIGHTEEN

Hans Holbein the Younger. *Henry VIII*. 1540.

PLATE NINETEEN
Anthony Van Dyck. *King Charles on Horseback.* c. 1638.

PLATE TWENTY
Gianlorenzo Bernini. *The Rape of Persephone.* 1622.

PREFACE

JOHN FORD'S name seldom attracts more than cursory attention, even among superbly educated and intensely curious people. There is only one reason why Ford in fact deserves a more sympathetic audience: he was a playwright of exceptional talent. *'Tis Pity*, *The Broken Heart*, and *Perkin Warbeck* are brilliant achievements, both as literature and as theatre. *Love's Sacrifice* is a less impressive work, but it certainly merits a better reception than the usual mixture of neglect and condescension. Even in the tragicomedies, where Ford was admittedly not at his best, he frequently reached a level of theatrical skill and verbal polish that few playwrights can hope to emulate.

This book is a defence of Ford's integrity as a dramatist. In order to define the special artistic practices which distinguish Ford from his more famous contemporaries, I have chosen a way of describing his style that will at first raise some skeptical eyebrows. Ford is a baroque dramatist, I am suggesting, in much the same way that Rubens is a baroque painter or Bernini a baroque sculptor. In one sense this is a cumbersome approach, because it commits me to spelling out at some length, in a preliminary chapter, just what the term "baroque" means in the context of seventeenth-century art and literature. My definition of the baroque style is of course heavily indebted to the writings of many critics and art historians, most of whom I have tried to acknowledge in the notes. The only originality I can claim is a shift in emphasis which allows the baroque style a meaningful place (alongside renaissance, mannerism, classicism, and rococo) in the most vital and most influential period of English drama. Readers who do not share my particular interest in Ford may of course take the first chapter as an independent argument, but I hope it will persuade them to look more closely at the works of a dramatist whom they might otherwise consign to the specialists.

Readers who do share my concern with Ford will notice, I believe, that calling Ford a baroque dramatist is not just an old game played with a new word. The central chapters of this book offer detailed interpretations of Ford's plays which differ in many essentials from the standard critical accounts. My aim here has been not novelty for its own sake, but rather an imaginative sympathy with the special qualities of Ford's artistic world. In a concluding essay in criticism I have tried to state precisely the relationship of my own interpretation to the work of previous critics and scholars. Again, I hope that my reliance on the writings of others has been adequately and fairly recorded.

Since there is still no reliable edition of Ford's complete works, I have used as my reference text the old-spelling reprints of the quartos by Bang and de Vocht. In all old-spelling quotations I have silently modernized usage of *i/j*, *u/v*, and long *s*. I have likewise corrected obvious typographical errors (such as the turned *u*), expanded archaic abbreviations, and modernized punctuation in a few cases where obsolete usage would interfere with meaning. Extended passages of italic type—such as songs or dedicatory poems—are silently altered to roman, but in all other cases italics in quotations are reproduced from the sources quoted. In those instances where I have translated from French or German, the original passages are given in full in the notes.

There remains the conventional but pleasant duty of acknowledging assistance of many kinds, both from institutions and from individuals. A fellowship from the Canada Council allowed me to write an earlier version of the present book. Indeed, without the provisions for travel in the Canada Council grant, I would have been unable to visit the National Gallery, the Louvre, the Borghese Museum, the Uffizi Gallery, or the many smaller museums and galleries that shaped my understanding of seventeenth-century culture. For assistance in obtaining photographs, and for permission to reproduce them, I wish to thank Fratelli Alinari (Florence), the Frick Collection (New York), Gabinetto Fotografico Nazionale (Rome), the Metropolitan Museum of Art

(New York), the National Gallery (London), la Réunion des Musées Nationaux (Paris), Roger-Viollet (Paris), and Scala Fine Arts Publishers (New York). To Dalhousie University I am grateful for the award of a Killam postdoctoral fellowship. The final result of my work on Ford owes much to the reading, thinking, and writing that I was free to do during the period of the fellowship. I should mention also that this book has been published with the help of a grant from the Humanities Research Council of Canada using funds provided by the Canada Council.

My personal debts may be acknowledged here, however inadequately. Robert F. Whitman of the University of Pittsburgh has generously supported my work with advice and encouragement; the substance and style of this book remain heavily dependent on his incisive judgment and keen intelligence. Peter Davison read an early draft of my argument, written largely while I was a special student at the Shakespeare Institute, University of Birmingham. His careful editorial eye and his critical acumen have left their mark both in fine points of detail and in the design of the whole. In reading the proofs and preparing the index, I have relied on the diligent assistance and kind indulgence of Richard Cooper and Marcia Rodriguez. Two of my teachers—Roy Wolper and Arthur Saxon—have contributed in more ways than I could easily explain. With both of them I share the privilege of having borrowed from the wisdom of the late Charles R. Crow. To this last debt I can respond only with respectful silence.

Finally, I should like to thank those colleagues, students, and friends at Dalhousie who encouraged my work through their advice, commiseration, or simply their good will. No list of names would be sufficient here to describe the congenial and stimulating environment in which I have been able to complete this book. For these many kindnesses, my special thanks.

HALIFAX, NOVA SCOTIA
1 May 1977

ABBREVIATIONS

TITLES OF FORD'S PLAYS

BH	The Broken Heart
Fancies	The Fancies Chaste and Noble
LM	The Lover's Melancholy
LS	Love's Sacrifice
LT	The Lady's Trial
PW	The Chronicle History of Perkin Warbeck: A Strange Truth
Queen	The Queen, or the Excellency of her Sex
TP	'Tis Pity She's a Whore

TITLES OF PERIODICALS

EIC	Essays in Criticism
JAAC	Journal of Aesthetics and Art Criticism
MP	Modern Philology
RenD	Renaissance Drama
SEL	Studies in English Literature, 1500–1900
ShS	Shakespeare Survey
SP	Studies in Philology
UTQ	University of Toronto Quarterly

CHAPTER ONE

POETS AND PAINTERS CURIOUSLY COMPARED

An Essay in Definition

IN ordinary speech the term "baroque" describes bizarre, extravagant, or sensational things and events. Even at this level of communication John Ford may well qualify as the most typically baroque dramatist of the English tradition. A poet who chooses witchcraft, melancholy, masochism, misogyny, and incest as major themes must have a taste for the bizarre. A playwright who directs one romantic lover to open a vein and bleed himself to death, another to enter the stage in triumph with his sister's heart on his dagger, must be partial to the extravagant and the sensational. But these baroque qualities are not to be dismissed as wild aberrations of uncontrolled fancy. At a deeper level, Ford's plays form part of a broad cultural rhythm that pulsates through Europe in the seventeenth century. This cultural phase, expressed through the art, the music, and the literature of the period, is known as the baroque style.

Traditionally, scholars have tried to understand the concept of a baroque style by contrasting it with the major preceding stylistic period—the renaissance. Heinrich Wölfflin's essays in art history are still the important starting point for this comparative exercise.[1] Wölfflin distinguishes between renaissance and baroque styles by setting up five pairs of contraries. In matters of design, he says, renaissance art shows a draughtsmanlike, linear technique; baroque art shows a more fluid, painterly technique. With respect to composition, the renaissance art work is built up out of a number of parallel plane surfaces; the baroque art work creates the impression of recessional movement and depth by stressing diagonal distances and oblique lines. Renaissance structures fit precisely into firm boundaries which have the effect of defining space and suggesting closed form; in the baroque style movement and visual energy tend to spill over the artificial structural boundaries, so baroque structures often have open form. Unity, in renaissance art, is a matter of harmony among multiple, discrete, independent parts; in baroque art one dominant theme or motif creates unity by fusing the dependent parts, by subordinating them to the whole. Renaissance art aims at absolute clarity; baroque art aims at relative clarity only.[2]

As many of his critics have noticed, Wölfflin approaches the problem of style in purely formal terms—that is, virtually without reference to subject matter.[3] On this question his theory of style in the visual arts runs parallel to the work of W. K. Wimsatt, Cleanth Brooks, and William Empson in the theory of verbal style: in both cases discussion of style is limited to the qualities of the artistic medium. If the rules of academic discipline are rigidly enforced, we will find art historians discussing the problem of style at a strictly visual level, while literary critics restrict discussion of the same problem to matters of verbal technique. If the same terms appear in these two isolated debates on style—"gothic," "high renaissance," and "rococo" for example—we shall have to interpret their double appearance as sheer coincidence. For, on a purely formal analysis of style, communication between painting and poetry is by definition impossible.

More recent developments in art history and criticism have considerably broadened the concept of style. Due largely to Erwin Panofsky's persuasive arguments, the iconographical method has brought the question of meaning or content in the visual arts back into prominence. According to Panofsky's view, the style of a work of art depends on its relationship to the body of mythology from which it springs. Thus, important clues to distinguishing between renaissance and baroque styles may be discovered by studying the respective treatment given to a common mythological figure in each stylistic phase. In a delightful essay on "Blind Cupid," to take one instance, Panofsky finds that whether blind or not, the god of love receives "allegorical" treatment in medieval art, develops a "humanistic" personality in the renaissance, and rises to a "devotional plane" in the baroque phase.[4] This change in theoretical strategy acts as an invitation for literary critics to join in the discussion about style. Anyone familiar with English literature may select examples which correspond to Panofsky's three Cupids from the amorous poetry of Chaucer, Sidney, and Crashaw. In both Prologues to *The Legend of Good Women*, the "myghty god of Love" is the patron of dignified *amour courtois*, so the narrator assures us that, contrary to popular belief, Cupid is fully capable of seeing.[5] But in the Temple of Venus scene from *The Knight's Tale*, where "Cupido" represents cupidity or sensuality, he is pictured as "blynd" in accordance with allegorical tradition (ll. 1963–66).[6] Much the same distinction operates in renaissance poetry: different kinds of love correspond to the various levels of Neoplatonic theology. In *Astrophil and Stella* Cupid is on the one hand an "image" of divine, spiritual love, and on the other a mere "boy" and a "wanton."[7] Crashaw's "Epithalamium" typifies the baroque stage in the literary progression. Here Cupid becomes a sensuous angel who presides over the ritual of defloration; he attends the maiden while she expires in "fumes"; he watches her "exhale in flames of his owne fire."[8] If literature and the visual arts are adaptations of the same body of mythology, or displacements of the same system of archetypes, then it should not be surprising to find that Panofsky's three versions of Cupid appear also in three corresponding literary phases. And on this view similarities in style between visual and literary arts are far from coincidental. A painter and a poet, broadly speaking, share a common style insofar as they adopt the same attitude toward their mythological heritage.

Since the Christian myth is the measure of all things in the seventeenth century, religious art becomes the natural touchstone of the baroque style. Bernini's *The Ecstasy of St. Teresa* (pl. 1) marks a high point in the baroque preoccupation with the most emotional aspects of religious experience, and may serve as a typical example of the baroque approach to sacred mythology. St. Teresa's lips are languidly parted, her eyes are nearly closed, her body flutters with anticipation. The angel who appears to the saint in the form of a mystical vision stands ready to plunge the flaming dart into her breast. At the same time he wears a beatific, yet almost sadistic smile. The youthfulness of this figure, the dart which he holds, and the curious expression on his face, indicate that this angel belongs to the Cupid family. Thus, St. Teresa is at the mercy of a divine, spiritualized Cupid; her love is a sacred desire for union with God, but the vehicle for expressing this love is the profane symbol of eros.

The blatant emotionalism of Bernini's statuary group is so unrestrained, so impulsive, so ecstatic, that it often baffles the ironic twentieth-century eye. "Entering those rich chapels in...Santa Maria della Vittoria," writes Aldous Huxley, "one has the impression of having opened a bedroom door at the most inopportune of moments."9 Huxley's suspicions are quite accurate, of course; the relationship between angel and saint is frankly erotic. But the naughty feeling of voyeurism is a comment only on modern prudishness, not on the quality of the religious vision. For the baroque artist no emotion is too uninhibited, no feeling is too strong, to be placed in the service of piety. Erotic sensations may express the profoundest religious feeling.10

In typical renaissance painting and sculpture, religious subjects are treated from a theological or philosophical point of view. Even when dealing with an overtly emotional theme, the renaissance artist avoids total concentration on the psychology of the moment, and stresses instead the broader framework of his humanistic faith. Bellini's *St. Francis in Ecstasy* (pl. 2), like Bernini's *St. Teresa*, focuses visual attention on a powerful religious experience. But here the resemblance stops. St. Francis, in the renaissance painting, stands bolt upright, raises his eyes heavenward, and casually extends his arms in a tranquil gesture of thanksgiving. His monk's habit flows comfortably and naturally from his shoulders, as if to reinforce the strong vertical lines of his body. St. Teresa's draperies, by contrast, wrap her reclining body in billowing undulations. There is no doubt that St. Francis is profoundly moved by his experience, but his ecstasy is calm and peaceful, not violent and overwhelming. Bellini takes pains to picture St. Francis in his chosen surroundings—among the rocks, trees, and birds of nature. In the background, a shepherd tends his flock at the outskirts of a hillside city. Even in his moment of rapture, St. Francis is entirely at one with the natural world of God's creatures, and with the equally natural world of human civilization. Again quite to the contrary, St. Teresa's baroque ecstasy sweeps her up in a cloud where only the divine light from above can penetrate, where the only reality is her subjective vision.

The same contrast between renaissance composure and baroque dynamism appears in the development of English devotional poetry. Constable and Crashaw stand at opposite ends of the stylistic scale, and furnish convenient illustrations of the two approaches to shared mythology. Constable's religious vision, here expressed in the first quatrain of a sonnet "To St. Mary Magdalen," is fairly typical of renaissance devotional writing:

Such as retyr'd from sight of men, lyke thee
    by pennance seeke the joyes of heaven to wynne;
    in desartes make theyr paradyce begynne:
    and even amonge wylde beastes do Angells see.[11]

For the renaissance poet, religious experience gains in significance to the extent that it can be integrated with the larger patterns of traditional theology and cosmology. Key words like "pennance" and "paradyce" lend point to the theological dimension. And like St. Francis in Bellini's painting, St. Mary Magdalene sees religious truth in her natural surroundings, among the beasts of the field. The purely visionary possibilities of the subject are muted in Constable's poem; angels do not come into view trailing clouds of glory, but assume instead a perfectly comfortable place beside the members of the animal kingdom. This connection rests on fundamental renaissance doctrine about the ordered universe: animals occupy an intermediate level between chaotic matter and civilized man, just as angels fill the sphere between the human world and the divine. The renaissance vision is not an idiosyncratic moment of special insight, but rather a particularly clear perception of universal truth. Such confidence in the ultimate order of the universe breeds a psychological calm and assurance; again in the spirit of Bellini's *St. Francis*, the speaker in Constable's poem hopes to "fynde heaven" in his "retyred hart."

To develop some feeling for the difference between renaissance and baroque literary styles, one need only compare Constable's sonnet to the much more turbulent realization of the St. Mary Magdalene myth in Crashaw's "The Weeper." Even the title suggests the lengths to which Crashaw goes to transform a theological exercise into a psychological drama. Still more telling, because of its obvious relationship to Bernini's statuary group, is Crashaw's "Hymn to the Name and Honor of the Admirable Sainte Teresa." The speaker of this poem sees St. Teresa's face glowing under the pressure of "a sweet & subtle PAIN." Breathlessly he describes his saint's frenzied anticipation of the moment of ecstasy:

How kindly will thy gentle HEART
Kisse the sweetly-killing DART!
And close in his embraces keep
Those delicious Wounds, that weep
Balsom to heal themselves with. Thus

When These thy DEATHS, so numerous,
Shall all at last dy into one,
And melt thy Soul's sweet mansion;
Like a soft lump of incense, hasted
By too hott a fire, & wasted
Into perfuming clouds, so fast
Shalt thou exhale to Heavn at last
In a resolving SIGH. [12]

St. Teresa longs for a burst of emotion strong enough to propel her toward heaven in a single explosion of energy. As in Bernini's sculpture, there is an unmistakably sexual resonance. Words like "kisse" and "embrace" build the erotic tension; words like "melt" and "exhale" resolve the tension in orgasmic triumph. In this instance religious feeling has no connection whatever with natural surroundings or with theological propositions; like the lunatic, the lover, and the poet, St. Teresa is alone with her vision. Neither men nor angels can explain the saint's ecstasy, Crashaw's narrator tells us. "Suffice," he says, "Thy selfe shall feel thine own full joyes / And hold them fast for ever."

It is tempting to rush at once to the sweeping conclusion that baroque art and literature are simply more emotional than their renaissance counterparts. Like all dangerous simplifications of fact, this one contains a kernel of truth. Emotional impact, in renaissance style, grows out of the system of philosophical beliefs and conventions which dominates renaissance thinking; or, to use the traditional vocabulary, pathos is strictly controlled by ethos. In the baroque style, with a new emphasis on psychology, artists tend to treat emotional experience for its own sake. The soul of man is no longer the centre of a charted universe, but rather an object for analysis, a subject for speculation, and an artistic vehicle for exploring the infinite range of human emotion.

The spectre of death will always prompt man to express his very deepest fears and yearnings. The long road from the "Lament of the Last Survivor" in *Beowulf* to Eliot's "The Hollow Men" serves ample warning that death is not the concern of any one style, or the province of any single period. Yet, because death is the focal point of many mythologies, the artist's approach to the subject is bound to provide valuable clues about his style. In general, the renaissance humanist thinks of death as the last, inevitable event of life; as a result, he faces death with Christian Stoicism, or at least with restrained sorrow. For baroque man, by contrast, death is the most highly charged emotional experience of all; he frequently longs for death, delights in its pain, revels in its sweetness.

The difference between Raphael's *The Descent from the Cross* (pl. 3) and Rubens' version of the same theme (pl. 4) tells us a good deal about the shift in attitude. In Raphael's painting the quality of mourning is sincere but subdued. Dramatic energy is built up by concentrating on the business in hand; the faithful remnant goes about the task of carrying Christ's body to the tomb, while the women busy themselves by comforting Mary. In Rubens' *Descent*, death is the occasion for emotional indulgence far more histrionic in tone. Mary Magdalene, on the right, upstages the theological content of the painting by insisting on the erotic possibilities of her relationship to Christ. Even more typically baroque in its enjoyment of the sensations of dying is Rubens' *The Raising of the Cross* (pl. 6). Here death is emphatically not accepted as a *fait accompli*. The baroque painter chooses a moment before death precisely because he is interested in the process of dying as an experience of anguish and ecstatic fulfilment. The muscular workmen heave and strain to hoist the cross into position; their concentrated physical energy induces a corresponding emotional intensity. Christ's heavenward gaze mingles the sweetness and the sorrow of death in a way unknown to the renaissance.

Artistic attitudes toward death in renaissance and baroque styles are most clearly reflected in funeral monuments and commemorative sculpture. In this specialized genre English art exhibits the progression of styles with particular clarity. Renaissance funeral monuments, according to Eric Mercer, present the deceased's family as merely a line of descendants, arranged in chronological order with the eldest son nearest his father's image. Gradually, the family begins to group itself around the effigy in more dramatic formations, with greater expressions of affection and grief. The token death's-head of the renaissance expands in size and importance, until it becomes the full skeleton, the symbol of death in all its "hideous detail." After 1625 English funeral art moves beyond the grotesque handling of death, to a new stage of "religious emotionalism."[13] This pathetic and very nearly masochistic approach to death marks the baroque style in one of its most typical moments.

A similar change, as it takes effect in the dramatic literature of the same period, has been carefully documented and analyzed by Theodore Spencer. The plays of Marlowe and Chapman conform to the renaissance view of death.

Marlowe's heroes curse death because it cuts off human life and announces eternal torment for the damned; Chapman's heroes meet death nobly because they have lived nobly. In either case the renaissance attitude prevails: man's death is the appropriate close to his life. But for Beaumont and Fletcher's tragic characters, death often appears as a moment of sweetness to be savoured with some relish. In Ford's tragedies, and to some extent in Shirley's and Massinger's, death is welcomed as a moment of consummate emotional rapture, as the ultimate release.[14] Spencer does not use the word "baroque" to describe the new trend that focuses on the unbearable sweetness of death, but in view of parallel developments in visual art, especially funerary art, the term can surely be extended to advantage.

The baroque preoccupation with psychology, according to Panofsky, signals a shift of "the very principle of reality...to the subjective human consciousness."[15] Renaissance thinkers and artists draw a clear line of demarcation between reality and illusion, and they are convinced that the distinction makes good sense. A baroque mind, like that of Descartes, dwells on the possibility that all human experience may be a diabolical illusion, and solves the problem by the most subjective appeal of all: *"je pense, donc je suis."*[16] By the standards of the renaissance, this seems like a retreat into chaos; but for the baroque thinker and artist it is a bold step into a new frontier where the passions of the human soul and the endless mirages of human experience bring into being the higher reality of visionary truth.

Wölfflin approaches the problem of reality and illusion very gingerly in his discussions of renaissance and baroque styles. He argues, for example, that the linear technique in art and architecture strives to outline reality, to present things the way they are, while the painterly technique aims directly at illusion, and presents things the way they appear to be.[17] Similarly, the absolute clarity of renaissance style is a symptom of the desire to imitate the real world, and the relative clarity of the baroque stems from the need to create vivid illusion.[18] Bramante's *Tempietto* (pl. 5) typifies the renaissance style, with its emphatic affirmation of objective reality. The regularity of the circular plan, the exact proportions of the design, make it possible to perceive this church fully and accurately from any angle of vision. But Pietro da Cortona, a typical baroque architect, leaves the impression that his church, *Santa Maria in Via Lata* (pl. 7), is much larger than its actual size. Cortona's grand façade belies the small dimensions of this church's interior. Renaissance and baroque architects here take directly opposite positions on the same problem. The very name *Tempietto* means "little church"; renaissance structures refuse to lie about their dimensions. But the baroque architect, when faced with the problem of smallness, attempts to create the illusion of grandeur nevertheless. Renaissance artists in general do their utmost to help the eye of the beholder perceive fully, accurately, and with confidence; baroque artists make a game of trying to deceive the eye.

The distinction between reality and illusion is much more than a matter of technique, for at a thematic level the contrast is implicit in the ecstasies of St. Francis and St. Teresa (pls. 2 and 1). Bellini's saint lives and breathes within the framework of the real, visible world; if the observer wishes to share St. Francis' ecstasy, he must share also in his perception of natural phenomena, which of course are the handiwork of God. Bernini's saint is swept up beyond ordinary reality on her cloud, and isolated by the golden rays of artificial light. Her world is built up not by assembling the objects and events of daily experience, but by surrendering passionately to the inspired suggestions of her imagination. The angel, the flaming dart, the cloud, the yellow light—all are part of St. Teresa's subjective trance. Bernini's group of figures and their setting are a divine illusion; they present us with the higher reality of the visionary, not the shared reality of the objective observer. It is no coincidence that the renaissance painter chooses the founder of the Franciscan order to reflect his view of the world, or that the baroque sculptor finds in the Spanish mystic the vehicle for suggesting his cosmic vision.

Renaissance poets feel free to toy with the illusion-reality distinction, precisely because the boundary between the two worlds is firm enough to function as a literary convention. Sidney, in *Astrophil and Stella*, plants broad hints to suggest that at one level he is writing about the relationship between himself and Penelope Devereaux. However fanciful or conventional this sonnet sequence may appear to be today, Sidney wants his readers to accept the veracity of his poetic assertions, at least as a record of his private emotional experience. Spenser, even more boldly, builds the *Amoretti* and the *Epithalamion* around his own courtship and marriage to Elizabeth Boyle. In the renaissance, love poetry is written with real lovers and real ladies occupying one level of love's hierarchy, and renaissance poets are anxious to establish the reality even of their fictitious creations.

These renaissance creatures are indeed "dull, sublunary lovers" when compared to the illusionary figures of baroque poetry. Herrick's kaleidoscope of nymphs escapes even speculative identification. His Corinnas, his Julias, his Electras—all of them resplendent in ambrosia and ambergris—are creatures of sheer fancy. Crashaw again typifies the baroque spirit in its purest form. He records no real experience of love, but delights in writing down "Wishes: To his (Supposed) Mistresse." Crashaw's persona admits that his lady, "That not impossible shee," is a creation of poetic vision with no foundation in the factual world. She is simply "that Divine / *Idæa*"; she has not yet taken "a shrine / Of Chrystall flesh."[19] The firm backdrop of implied reality, so characteristic of renaissance art and poetry, disappears in the illusionistic baroque world. Jean Rousset makes the point with epigrammatic terseness. "In the quarrel between appearance and reality," he writes, "those who are on the side of the baroque can be recognized by the stress which they bring to bear on appearance."[20]

A shift in the axis of reality brings with it a change in the role of the artist, or at least in the way that the artist sees his function. Renaissance theory holds up the ideal of hiding art with art, and most artists submit humbly to "the anonymity of craftsmanship." The baroque artist's ideal of "virtuosity" makes him far more conscious of cultivating a peculiar style, of perfecting a unique manner.[21] The distinction between renaissance craftsmanship and baroque virtuosity seems at first glance to weaken when confronted with the renaissance "concept of genius" and the corresponding rise in the social status of the artist.[22] The great renaissance artists are admired and emulated for their special genius, of course; but the guild-like organization of the artist's workshop suggests that he is still a craftsman, albeit a supreme master craftsman who sets the artistic standards of his day. The leading baroque artists, Bernini and Rubens, demand worship as princes of an international cultural aristocracy. Bernini's visit to the court of Louis XIV betrays numerous signs of conflict, because the baroque artist's imperious creative sovereignty refuses to take a stance of humility even in the presence of the Sun King.[23]

In conformity with the ideal of craftsmanship, renaissance architects build scrupulously regular orders, because they feel that certain mathematical proportions are inherently correct. The relationship between the height of a column and the width of the order is not a matter of personal taste, for the renaissance builder, but a universally accepted convention. Similarly, painters happily accept the newly discovered laws of perspective, and place their figures into the world of artificial space without straining for personal inter-pretation or special stylistic effects. It is impossible to argue that the angle of vision used by Leonardo in *The Last Supper* and by Raphael in *The School of Athens* is a matter of personal preference in each case. Both painters are impeccably accurate in their treatment of perspective, both choose a central point of view that results in precise symmetry of design, because both are responding to an accepted renaissance convention—a convention that underlines the stylistic unity of the period.[24]

Baroque architects refuse to be slaves of exact regularity and proportion of orders. Each architect feels free to develop a personal manner; he may modulate the distances between columns and pilasters in order to produce dramatic effects. Roman baroque architects can embrace the majesty and grandeur of Bernini, or follow the fanciful rhythms of Borromini. Roman baroque painters, too, have a stylistic choice to make; they tend to identify themselves either with the school of Caravaggio or with the school of the Carracci, rather than with their tradition as a whole. For the renaissance artist, individual style is something that emerges incidentally in the process of trying to paint well or build well. For the baroque artist, individual style is something to be advertised with each brush stroke and with each chip of marble. The ideal of stylistic unity recedes, to be replaced with the elaborately selfconscious stylistic options of the baroque.

Manfred F. Bukofzer notices a similar change from craftsmanship to virtuosity in the transition from renaissance to baroque music. Renaissance composers take style "for granted" and draw no distinctions between sacred and secular music, for the renaissance is the last period of "stylistic unity" in the history of music. Baroque composers are conscious of three different styles—the church music style, the chamber music style, and the theatre music style. In addition, baroque musicians distinguish between two practices—the *antico* and the *moderno*. The old practice continues the carefully regulated manner of Palestrina, while the modern practice follows the more liberal, expressive style of Monteverdi. A baroque composer may choose either practice, but he will be conscious in either case that he is making a stylistic choice. "The baroque era," Bukofzer concludes, "is the era of style-consciousness."[25]

"Shakespeare had an universal mind," says Dryden in his usual authoritative manner; "Fletcher a more confined and limited."[26] Though Dryden appears to be thinking purely of individual artistic differences, the distinction he draws does imply the larger notion of a change from a universally accepted style on the one hand, to an individually contrived manner on the other. Once Marlowe has announced the fitness of blank verse for popular tragedy in his Prologue to the first part of *Tamburlaine the Great*, this vehicle is simply assumed to be the appropriate style. As a rule, renaissance playwrights feel obliged to make no further comments on stylistic matters; many plays are sent into circulation with prefatory comments no more elaborate than the standard identification tags, "A Tragedie," or "A pleasant conceited Comedie," and some acknowledgment of theatrical performance. The frequency of collaborative and anonymous work by Elizabethan playwrights would indicate that the repertory companies still foster the ideals of craftsmanship inherited from the values of the guild system.[27]

Beaumont and Fletcher operate under much more pretentious artistic and theatrical conditions; as a result, their apologies and their stylistic postures are often quite complicated. Fletcher defines "tragie-comedie" at length in a message "To the Reader" which prefaces *The Faithful Shepherdess*. No less than four introductory fragments will suffice for *The Knight of the Burning Pestle*, and all four of these—the publisher's note, the open letter to the readers, the Prologue and the Induction—comment in one way or another on the style of the play. The introductory passages affixed to renaissance plays, such as *The Spanish Tragedy*, *The Jew of Malta*, or *2 Henry IV*, generally provide expository facts to be developed later in the action, or else simply whet the audience's appetite. But in baroque drama, prefatory remarks most often indicate something about the playwright's artistic stance. It is worth noting that of Ford's eight independent plays, all eight are prefaced by dedicatory epistles to friends or noble acquaintances, five are introduced by prologues, and four end with authorial comment in epilogue form. Nearly all of these passages contain references or hints that reveal Ford's stylistic selfconsciousness. The proliferation of commendatory verses, the increasing hauteur of dedicatory addresses, and the relative scarcity of anonymous plays indicate that the Caroline theatre is indeed a "coterie" environment, and also an environment in which the dramatist wishes to assume the role of literary virtuoso.

The new climate tends to free baroque artists from the traditional genre distinctions of the renaissance. Painting, sculpture, and architecture form a perfect triad of acceptable modes for the renaissance artist; but baroque visual artists, especially under the influence of Bernini, tend to ignore or blur the boundaries between the modes.[28] The Cornaro Chapel is a stunning and theatrical mixture of sculpture, architecture, and painting. *The Ecstasy of St. Teresa* stands somewhere between sculpture in the round and bold relief. In music, the coming of the opera signals the disappearance of rigid genre distinctions. Here is a hybrid form that welds music, poetry, architecture, painting, and the decorative arts into one. And the recitative style in singing fuses music and language into a single medium for dramatic expression.[29] The most famous literary instance of the mingling of genres is of course tragicomedy. Lyric poetry witnesses equally startling transformations. From Wyatt through Spenser, English renaissance poets work within reasonably well-defined genres—the sonnet, the rondeau, the pastoral, the satire. Then, with the arrival of the metaphysicals and the cavaliers, traditional genres burst open, intertwine, and regroup in formations that would baffle the best renaissance theory.[30]

C. S. Lewis tells an anecdote that admirably illustrates the anonymous craftsmanship of the renaissance artist. Once the Greeks had perfected the technique of carving in stone, he remarks, all that remained was to find the most skilful craftsmen and the most beautiful models, and bring them together.[31] Now, what happens when these superior artisans have exhausted the supply of exquisite bodies? In the Hellenistic phase, these beautiful figures gradually begin to twist and turn, slowly they form dramatic groups, and eventually their postures become quite theatrical. The anonymous craftsman has become the selfconscious virtuoso. For the renaissance artist it may well have been enough to excel in the traditional modes, once he had the techniques of perspective painting and blank verse at his disposal. For the baroque artist, far more selfconscious in his artistic stance, the comparable task was to rearrange, reshape, and recombine the forms of his renaissance heritage, in order to create new artistic illusions for the new age, in order to touch new emotional chords in new and dramatic ways.

The first step toward understanding and accepting the baroque style as an independent artistic development is to distinguish it as clearly as possible from renaissance style. As soon as this basic step is complete, we realize that seventeenth-century culture is far more complicated than such analysis will allow. Unless we account for the differences between the baroque style and some of its near relations—mannerism, classicism, and rococo—we run the risk of asking the baroque to be all things to all men. Briefly, mannerism may be thought of as a crucial transitional stage between the renaissance and the baroque; classical and rococo styles follow the baroque, each of them re-developing certain baroque tendencies in yet another format, each of them diverging from the baroque but in opposite directions.[32]

Wylie Sypher has called mannerism "the missing term" between renaissance and baroque styles. The confident assumptions of renaissance theology and cosmology come under rigorous attack in the mannerist phase, and with them the equally confident assumptions about perspective and proportion in visual design. Thus the style of mannerism, according to Sypher, belongs to a period of "doubt, bad conscience, and skepticism." Only with the new grandeur of the baroque can the doubts of mannerism be resolved, and even then resolution is achieved by means of overstatement, by means of splendid emotional gestures.[33]

Rosso Fiorentino's *The Descent from the Cross* (pl. 8) may stand for the middle term between Raphael's treatment of the subject (pl. 3) and Rubens' companion studies of the supreme Christian death (pls. 4 and 6). Raphael's mourners are sad, but their emotions fit the gentle decorum of mourning. The whole procedure depicted is an orderly and regulated matter, both in spatial and in psychological terms. Rosso's *Descent* pictures a Christ who would have shocked renaissance tastes. Instead of a body still beautiful and already peaceful in death, we have a limp, angular cadaver in pale green. Despite the efforts of four workmen on three ladders, there seems to be some danger of an accidental fall, since the workman in the upper left-hand corner is pointing anxiously toward the body and shouting angrily in the direction of his assistants. Meanwhile, the man directly below him is nearly losing his footing on the ladder. It is just this sort of ironic tension between subject and style that gives mannerist art its nervous, skeptical quality. Giuliano Briganti finds an "excessive tension" in the Rosso painting—a tension "which sometimes reduces the figures to haggard, macabre manikins."[34] One need only compare Rosso's disorganized crew to Rubens' energetic working party in *The Raising of the Cross* to understand something of the difference between mannerist and baroque styles. Rubens' muscular figures have one unified intention; all of the movement in this picture is resolved in a single upward surge.

The Vision of St. John the Divine by El Greco (pl. 9) occupies a similarly medial position between the ecstasies of St. Francis and St. Teresa (pls. 2 and 1). El Greco's particular subject is the Opening of the Fifth Seal of the sacred book which contains the mysteries of the apocalypse. In the biblical account of this event, the souls of those who were "slain for the word of God" approach the divine judge with a desperate plea: "How long, O Lord, holy and true, dost thou not judge and avenge our blood on them that dwell on the earth?" (Rev. vi.9–10). The Lamb replies saying that they must wait until other martyrs, still on earth, have also met holy deaths. No immediate solution is given in the biblical account, and no resolution is reached in El Greco's painting. Even apocalyptic figures are sketched in nervous lines, and tend to show more frustration than fulfilment. The martyrs are pictured as "weightlessly hovering bodies," suspended in the "unreal space" that characterizes the mannerist vision, elongated and distorted according to the principles of mannerist construction.[35]

"How long, O Lord?" The question perfectly summarizes the spiritual agitation that writhes through Donne's *Holy Sonnets*. Metaphysical poetry, with its tone of intellectual skepticism, is the middle term between the confidence of Spenser and the ecstatic faith of Crashaw. Even in a poem like "The Extasie" Donne cannot resist the temptation to use harsh, nervous, and intellectual images. The speaker's metaphoric vision of the love relationship borders uncomfortably on the grotesque:

> Our hands were firmely cimented
>   With a fast balme, which thence did spring,
> Our eye-beames twisted, and did thred
>   Our eyes, upon one double string.[36]

The image of cement is far too solid and coarse to suggest a love even remotely emotional. The twisted eye-beams, the horrifying needle-and-thread image, are hardly calculated to please a lady. Other examples of Donne's harsh imagery spring to mind—the twin compasses of "A Valediction Forbidding Mourning" or the battering ram of "Holy Sonnet xiv." Donne's agitated frenzies, unlike Crashaw's mystical raptures, fail to satisfy the needs of his frustrated poetic characters. The critical powers of the intellect are too strong, in the mannerist phase, to allow for emotional release.

In its treatment of form, mannerism breaks out in deliberate revolt against the regularity of the renaissance.[37] Tintoretto's version of *The Last Supper* (pl. 10) in San Giorgio Maggiore, Venice, strikes the viewer who comes to it from Leonardo's painting on the same theme as wilfully fragmented and dislocated. Leonardo's central axis and confident symmetry are wrenched into obliquity by the strong diagonal of Tintoretto's table. Christ's position as the optical centre of the picture is strongly challenged. He is much smaller and indeed much less interesting than the waiter and maid in the right foreground, who act out their little drama apparently oblivious to the cosmic events taking place near by. Christ's dignity and importance are not quite salvaged by the academic halo over his head. The lamp in the upper left foreground produces nearly as much light as Christ's halo; natural light seems to undercut divine illumination.

The baroque artist may accept some apparently mannerist principles of composition, but if he does, he manages to fuse them into a new formal unity. In *The Raising of the Cross* (pl. 6) the strong diagonal is again the most powerful line, as in Tintoretto's *Last Supper*. But Rubens' diagonal is formed by Christ's body and extended by the extremities of the cross, so there is no question about where the optical centre of attention lies. Where Tintoretto's diagonal cuts his composition into fragments, Rubens' use of the same device gives unity of form to the whole design. The man in the right foreground of the Rubens painting, though larger in size than Christ, remains visually and thematically subordinate. He turns his face dramatically inward and extends his left arm along the blade of the cross; in this way he directs visual attention powerfully back toward the principal character of the crucifixion story. Christ's body is far more brightly lit than any of the other figures—not by a halo, but by a warm, atmospheric glow. Movement in Rubens' picture is not the nervous agitation of mannerism; rather, it is a strong upward flow of vital energy that complements Christ's upward gaze and consolidates the triumphant religious meaning of the scene.

The disjointed and contrived asymmetry of the *stile coupé* in English prose is a mannerist revolt against the balanced Ciceronian cadences of the renaissance. In prose as in poetry, Donne is the master of the mannerist style. His speaker complains bitterly about the miseries of illness in the first meditation from the *Devotions upon Emergent Occasions*: "We are not sure we are ill; one hand askes the other by the pulse, and our eye asks our urine, how we do. O multiplied misery!"[38] Both sentiment and style are mannerist. The phrases are short and the images startling. Donne avoids connectives that might ease his reader from one jolt to the next. This meditation ends with the corrosive refrain on the miserable condition of man. Donne himself sets the tone of deliberate revolt when he subtitles this passage "*The first grudging of the sicknesse.*"

The loose style characteristic of baroque prose often employs mannerist fragments, but reinterprets them and blends them into a rhythmic psychological unity. Burton's prose in *The Anatomy of Melancholy* may stand for the baroque style. In the following passage Democritus Junior rings a series of verbal changes on his central theme, "*the Force of Imagination*": "I will only now point at the wonderful effects and power of it; which, as it is eminent in all, so most especially it rageth in melancholy persons, in keeping the species of objects so long, mistaking, amplifying them by continual & strong meditation, until at length it produceth in some parties real effects, causeth this and many other maladies."[39] Leaving aside the baroque implications of Burton's subject, we may notice the stylistic difference between this typical period and the corresponding passage from Donne. Burton's sentence might be reconstructed to read: "The imagination has power to cause various mental illnesses." This paraphrase would account for only the opening clause and the concluding phrase; the remainder is a series of short fragments, much like the fragments in Donne. But this time they are not sharply set off in jarring isolation. Instead they form a series of parenthetical elements within a unifying frame. The sequence of verbs and verb substitutes in this long parenthesis ("rageth," "keeping," "mistaking," "amplifying," and "produceth") forms a psychological progression which suggests the ability of the imagination to transform the delusions of madness into "real effects."[40]

In the drama, the fragmented vision of mannerism accounts for the unsettling artistic focus of plays like *The Revenger's Tragedy, Women Beware Women,* and *The Changeling*. Jacobean plays bitterly lament the past order of renaissance humanism in a tone of profound and disillusioned skepticism.[41] Bosola's famous speeches near the close of *The Duchess of Malfi* vibrate with mannerist doubt under the tension of mannerist technique. The pitiful existence of man on this degraded planet becomes, in Bosola's words, no more than a disorganized and arbitrary game played with human "tennis-balls" (V.iv.54), and the setting for this grotesque pageant is a series of "vaulted graves" (V.v.97). Such a gathering storm of pessimism corresponds to the atmospheric darkness of *tenebroso* painting:

> O, this gloomy world!
> In what a shadow, or deep pit of darkness,
> Doth womanish and fearful mankind live!
> (V.v.100–102)[42]

Bosola need not be taken as Webster's mouthpiece, of course, but his skeptical utterances and his haunting images viciously undercut any feeling of triumph that the Duchess may have inspired. Metaphors of instability, of darkness, of torment, grow more fierce and more frequent as the Duchess's death approaches; when finally she dies we feel that the last spark of goodness has left the world to its corruption. It is with considerable justification that Bosola defines the mannerist vision of chaos as "a perspective / That shows us hell!" (IV.ii.358–59).

Baroque theatre, like baroque art, resolves the mannerist doubts through powerful emotional impulses. In Rotrou's *Saint Genest*, the hero looks forward with strange ardour to the moment that will consummate his martyrdom. The world in which he lives is still thoroughly evil, but the inner experience of the martyr now triumphs over his surroundings:

> I'll court your eyes no more; from this day on
> I seek to please the heav'nly emperor.
> I'll not amuse nor sing your praise; for I
> Must join the angel choir, to win the garland
> Of eternal days. I leave this stage of clay
> To act another part—Grant I be worthy—
> Upon the martyr's altar. And so
> My part is played. I'll say no more.
> (IV.vi)[43]

Rotrou's play has none of the disillusionment of mannerism. In fact, *Saint Genest* is a *tour de force* in the art of creating illusions and sustaining them into the infinite reaches of the next world. The hero is permitted to glimpse the supreme illusion—the miraculous vision that accompanies martyrdom. If Webster has been shaken by the mannerist doubts of Montaigne, Rotrou is willing to stake everything on Pascal's leap of baroque faith.

The genre definitions of the renaissance are unacceptable to the mannerist, and simply irrelevant to the baroque artist. Thus, we have a breakdown of renaissance forms in the mannerist phase, and a reintegration of new forms in the baroque. To take dramatic forms by themselves, we notice that the distinction between tragedy and comedy erodes. Under the influence of mannerist technique tragedy and comedy draw much closer together, as both move in the direction of satire. The reduction to bathos in *The Revenger's Tragedy* and the biting ambiguities of *Women Beware Women* bring even the bloodiest scenes of tragedy to the brink of laughter. And the very same qualities in *Volpone* account for the almost tragic character of mannerist comedy. As F. P. Wilson observes, "the laughter of Jonson is rarely laughter for its own sake, and it is never sympathetic laughter."[44] The comic world of mannerism, like the corresponding tragic world, is charged with bathos and tinged with bitter irony; both worlds lie precariously near to the domain of satire.

In the baroque phase, tragedy and comedy again move toward one another, but this time both dramatic genres approach romance. Since the baroque tragic hero is frequently a martyr, his death may include an exaltation that resembles apotheosis. Thus, in Corneille's *Polyeucte* and in *Saint Genest*, death is no longer a horrible skeleton that mocks human life, but a bridge to the realm of wish fulfilment, an ecstatic moment of union for the tragic lovers. Even when a baroque hero is not technically a religious figure, the dramatist may award him the status of martyrdom. Such is the case in *Ermorderte Majestät, oder Carolus Stuardus* by the German baroque dramatist, Andreas Gryphius. At the conclusion of this secular martyrdom, Charles I reaches out to grasp the "crown of eternity."[45] A parallel transformation occurs in comedy, where plays like *The Winter's Tale* and *The Faithful Shepherdess* set the stage for the new hybrid genre of dramatic romance. The festive spirit of renaissance comedy and the mockery of mannerism are transformed in turn; baroque comic form, in Corneille's *L'Illusion comique* or in Massinger's *The Maid of Honour*, consists of romantic triumph over a potentially tragic world.

The rivalry between baroque and classical styles forms a lively episode in the history of French literature, and an even livelier debate in the history of

French literary criticism.[46] The terms of this polarity are not marshalled quite so noisily in the English seventeenth century, but they are certainly present and even obvious as opposite and equally attractive possibilities in Dryden's critical theory. Succinctly stated, the baroque is the art of expression, and classicism the art of restraint. The baroque artist always strives for an emotional climax, for psychological consummation and release. The classicist keeps the emotional content of his work, no matter how strong it may be, always under firm control. Baroque forms are stirred by powerful and dramatic movement that often surges beyond the work of art itself into a suggestion of the infinite. Classical forms are in general pictured at rest, and usually suggest a sense of permanence and immobility.[47]

Two visual presentations of *The Rape of the Sabines* mark the difference between baroque and classical styles with particular clarity. In Rubens' version of this legend (pl. 11) we have a whirlpool of human bodies pulsating vigorously in the heat of sexual combat. Then we turn to Poussin's painting (pl. 12) to find that all action and all movement have been suddenly frozen, that the moving figures have become rigid and statuesque. Rubens' picture boils with energy; Poussin's crystallizes the action. In the left foreground of Rubens' version, a Sabine lady is about to lose her footing as a Roman soldier tugs forcefully at her garment. In the right foreground another young woman is being hoisted up onto an impatient horse where the embrace of an equally impatient Roman awaits her. Instead of rendering such dramatic action in progress, Poussin gives us all of the actors neatly arranged in formal, dance-like groups. The two most prominent Sabine women in the foreground hold up their left arms in parallel gestures of dismay, while in the centre of the picture a third Sabine raises both arms. Taken together, the three groups form a perfectly regular triangle. More important, none of these women is in any danger of falling; in order to avoid imbalance the Roman soldiers plant their feet firmly and embrace the women securely. Even in a scene of erotic violence, Poussin manages to leave an impression of firmness, order, and stability.

The shopworn example of classical restraint in English literary criticism is Dryden's *All for Love*. At least partly under the influence of French literary theory, Dryden tempers and cools the passions of Shakespeare's *Antony and Cleopatra*. The grand vistas of Shakespeare's cosmic design solidify into the firm and hardened literary masonry of classical drama. In the French theatre, where the lines of battle between baroque and classical styles are more clearly drawn, the expressive outbursts of Rotrou's *Saint Genest* or Corneille's *Le Cid* are checked and disciplined by Racine. In *Andromaque* we find the great expanses of ancient mythology compresssed into one city, one palace, even one room. Instead of dynamic gestures and extravagant rhetoric, Racine provides a dignity and solidity so monumental as to produce the impression of eternal stasis.

A comparison of Herrick's "To his Dying Brother, Master *William Herrick*" and Dryden's "To the Memory of Mr. *Oldham*" furnishes a more manageable view of the transition from baroque to classical style. In typical baroque fashion, Herrick focuses attention on the moment just before death. His speaker watches death in process:

> Life of my life, take not so soone thy flight,
> But stay the time till we have bade Good night.
> Thou hast both Wind and Tide with thee; Thy way
> As soone dispatcht is by the Night, as Day.
> Let us not then so rudely henceforth goe
> Till we have wept, kist, sigh't, shook hands, or so.
> There's paine in parting; and a kind of hell,
> When once true-lovers take their last Fare-well.[48]

Movement in nature underscores the dynamic quality of this death scene, and the accumulation of verbs builds to a moment of climax. Death is a "hell" that unites these brothers in a new understanding of the true nature of their love.

Dryden's poem, by contrast, is dedicated to the "memory" of his friend and fellow poet. The point of view is retrospective. Dryden's speaker wishes to create a monument that will outlast the ravages of time, that will fix Oldham's memory and reputation in classical rest and permanence:

> FAREWEL, too little and too lately known,
> Whom I began to think and call my own;
> For sure our Souls were near ally'd; and thine
> Cast in the same Poetick mould with mine.[49]

There can be no doubt about the sincerity of Dryden's poem; somehow it shows through, despite the muted discipline of his classical couplets. But while Herrick's speaker gives full vent to his emotion, Dryden's tries to restrain feeling. Herrick's speaker begins with a direct address, a plea, an argument, and an invitation. Dryden's speaker opens with a formal apostrophe; it is clear that he is speaking not to Oldham directly, but to posterity. Herrick's breathless enjambments and short phrases call to mind the recitative style of baroque singing. Dryden's lines are nearly all end-stopped; in their formal majesty they are more like the classical fugues of Bach.

The whole question of the baroque-classical polarity has been unnecessarily complicated by theorists who postulate a late-baroque style that tends to swallow, one by one, all of the works usually considered classical. Sypher's late-baroque phase, for example, includes Poussin and Le Brun in art, along with Dryden and Racine in letters.[50] The term "baroque" is extended in this way, it appears, because the works in question are not yet fully classical. But to accept this argument is rather like agreeing to call the whole of the sixteenth century "late-medieval." Such terminology places undue stress on the notion of historical continuity, and it tends to spread out stylistic terms to cover such a huge range of disparate artistic developments, as to make them almost meaningless. A coherent theory of style should recognize the multiplicity of approaches to artistic problems in the seventeenth century. One way of suggesting this multiplicity is to see the baroque and classical styles in competition with each other: the baroque style dominates the first half of the century, while classicism gains the upper hand in the second half and fades out only well into the eighteenth century. This point of view can at least reckon with works of art that show both baroque and classical tendencies—such as Milton's *Samson Agonistes*— without extending the late-baroque phase to include an artistic practice fundamentally alien to the baroque spirit.

One further area of stylistic complexity—and a very important one for English drama—concerns the distinction between baroque and rococo. If baroque art sweeps grandly into the infinite, rococo minces gingerly toward the infinitesimal. In general, the baroque is the art of the great cathedral; rococo is the art of the drawing room.[51]

This contrast may be brought to life by comparing the *Baldacchino* in St. Peter's, Rome (pl. 13) to the *Cabinet de la Pendule* at Versailles (pl. 14). The towering, spiral columns of Bernini's *Baldacchino* are by far its most impressive feature. They propel visual attention upward into the vastness of St. Peter's dome, to create the effect of dynamic and overwhelming massiveness. The

Cabinet de la Pendule demonstrates at once that rococo art retains the spiral and curvilinear tendencies of the baroque, but here the elegant curves are miniature in size. Since they need not inspire solemnity, rococo curves can be decoratively sprinkled onto the walls in the form of gilding, stylishly added to the already curved table legs, or intricately patterned around the face, body, and legs of the clock. Chandeliers, picture frames, mirror edges, and ceiling borders— all repeat the theme of sinuous, playful curves in subtle variations. The gyrations and spirals that suggested pomp, majesty, and emotional energy in baroque art are now reduced to microscopic size suitable for decoration. In fact, a touchstone of rococo style is the proliferation of rocaille, or shell-like ornament.

Both baroque and rococo styles rely to a large extent on the seductive appeal of illusionism. The *Baldacchino* creates the illusion of soaring upward movement. And baroque ceiling frescoes, such as Cortona's *The Triumph of Divine Providence* in the Barberini Palace (pl. 15), make a studied effort of projecting the illusion of movement into infinity. Rococo interiors are no longer designed to support *trompe-l'œil* on a grand scale; instead, they frolic with the tiniest subtleties of vision and sport with the elegance of deception. The *Cabinet de la Pendule* is lavishly furnished with mirrors and other reflecting surfaces. It is easy to imagine a party of Louis XV courtiers in this room costumed *à la mode*, almost masked behind their gracious wigs, cavorting with each other and with their multiple reflections. The baroque style sets the stage for grand and theatrical events, for visions of mystical ecstasy, for dramas of ultimate conflict. Since the setting for rococo art is the social world, since its tone is "gallant or voluptuous or arcadian or even flippant,"[52] it will never aspire to the infinite with the operatic grandeur of the baroque. Inevitably, the towering mythological figures of the baroque phase become mischievous and puckish creatures in the genteel surroundings of the rococo style.

In English literature we feel something of this transformation from baroque to rococo when the grand rhetoric of Milton's early poetry fades away, and the delicate graces of Restoration comedy become fashionable. *Comus* is undoubtedly one of Milton's more baroque works; the illusionistic world of the masque becomes a vehicle for suggesting a victory which borders on apotheosis. In the following speech, the Elder Brother expounds the theme of the poem:

'Tis chastity, my brother, chastity:
She that has that, is clad in complete steel,
And like a quiver'd Nymph with Arrows keen
May trace huge Forests and unharbor'd Heaths,
Infamous Hills and sandy perilous wilds,
Where through the sacred rays of Chastity,
No savage fierce, Bandit or mountaineer
Will dare to soil her Virgin purity.

(ll. 420–27)[53]

If this poem is read in the spirit of the seventeenth century it soon becomes clear that chastity is no mere academic quibble about maidenheads, but rather a "sage /And serious doctrine" (ll. 786–87) coloured by profound emotional reactions. The "complete steel" image alludes to the armour of the Christian warrior; the savages and bandits of this passage are powerful opponents; the Lady's victory at the end of the poem is a miraculous triumph over evil.[54]

In the comic world of Sir George Etherege, chastity is a real problem only insofar as it affects reputation. The title character of *The Man of Mode, or Sir Fopling Flutter* spends all of his time and energy keeping up the appearance of the gallant, and seems to have little desire for genuine debauchery. Even Dorimant and Harriet have something of Sir Fopling's obsession with reputation. They begin their relationship by bargaining about appearances. "Put on a gentle smile," Dorimant suggests, "and let me see how well it will become you" (IV.i.131–32). But Harriet does not wish to play the game of appearances, because she fears the court critics will never grant that she is a beauty. Dorimant reassures her, and argues that social trivia may be more important than she suspects: "The Women, nay the very lovers who belong to the Drawing-room will malitiously allow you more than that; they always grant what is apparent, that they may the better be believ'd when they name conceal'd faults they cannot easily be disprov'd in" (IV.i.143–47).[55] Unchaste behaviour is now a topic for polite *causerie*, a "conceal'd fault" that cannot be proved, but which provides endless opportunities for gossip and scandal. An unusually frequent occurrence of the word "mirror" in this comedy reminds us of the flirtatious use of mirrors in rococo drawing rooms. Polite society places a high premium on appearances, and the social graces become the real virtues of the rococo style.

It is this trivial view of chastity, this rococo treatment of a formerly grand theme, that Pope satirizes with such a light touch in *The Rape of the Lock*. Ariel rallies the Sylphs and Sylphids to Belinda's defence with a tone of voice that becomes more flippant the more it aspires to the heroic:

> This Day, black Omens threat the brightest Fair
> That e'er deserv'd a watchful Spirit's Care;
> Some dire Disaster, or by Force, or Slight,
> But what, or where, the Fates have wrapt in Night.
> Whether the Nymph shall break *Diana's* Law,
> Or some frail *China* jar receive a Flaw,
> Or stain her Honour, or her new Brocade,
> Forget her Pray'rs, or miss a Masquerade,
> Or lose her Heart, or Necklace, at a Ball;
> Or whether Heav'n has doom'd that *Shock* must fall.
>
> (II.101–110)[56]

For purposes of satiric exposure, chastity takes on microscopic proportions. Virginity equals frail china in an equation that recalls Wycherley's relentless sexual punning in *The Country Wife*. Diana, who appears armed with Christian weapons in *Comus*, now divides her concern equally between "Honour" and a "new Brocade." In the rococo world, no social nuance or polite pretence can escape notice. Pope's *jeu d'esprit* gives delightful artistic form to even the most "trivial things."

To apply a concept like the baroque to the study of literature, particularly English literature, is still a hazardous undertaking, so there are ample grounds for closing this essay in definition according to the rhetorical formula, with a refutation. Lessing's argument in *Laokoon* remains the strongest and most sustained attack on the critical procedure which accepts both art and literature as objects for comparative analysis. Lessing begins by assuming the inviolability of the artistic medium, and insofar as modern skeptics share this assumption, they inherit Lessing's theoretical position. In the visual work of art, Lessing observes, beauty of form is achieved "through the harmonious interaction of multifarious parts, which are capable of being perceived simultaneously." But in literature the individual elements are "arranged one after another," not on an extended surface but in a progressive sequence.[57] Thus the crucial distinction between visual and verbal art grows out of the difference between spatial and temporal media. It follows for Lessing that a quality which is beautiful in painting need not necessarily be beautiful in poetry, and a critical judgment based on one medium should not be transferred to another. Similar objections to the comparative method occur in recent scholarly debates on the subject of literature and the visual arts. "The specific nature of criticism depends on the specific nature of the art work," Svetlana and Paul Alpers remind us. "Attempts to compare the arts characteristically come to grief on forced equations between specific features."[58]

In a restricted and technical sense we may grant the validity of Lessing's initial assumption. A painting does not literally move through the stages of a plot, and strictly speaking a poem does not have a graphically traceable outline. But Lessing achieves his aim of defining the limits between painting and poetry at a price that few modern critics would be willing to pay. The spatial nature of visual art leads him to condemn allegorical painting outright, because of the awkward fact that a painted allegory does tell a story and may do so in a real or implied temporal sequence. By the same token, Lessing bluntly dismisses all descriptive poetry, because it refuses to stay within the boundaries he has set for the verbal medium. It would appear that Lessing's theory is much more a statement of what he would like art and literature to be, than a description of what they in fact are.[59]

In any case, though the limits of the medium must indeed affect the materials which the artist can use, it does not follow that the critic's resources need be correspondingly restricted. Edgar Wind has shown that a spatial grouping— the three graces in renaissance iconography—may be profitably interpreted with reference to the temporal sequence implied in the Neoplatonic aphorism, "Amor starts from Pulchritudo and ends in Voluptas."[60] In much the same way Panofsky's iconographical studies repeatedly locate the temporal dimension of a technically spatial artifact. Conversely, Northrop Frye discusses the structure of an admittedly temporal medium (Shakespearean comedy) in frankly spatial terms. The verbal artifact can be fruitfully analyzed as "a simultaneous unity,"

Frye argues. In this sense comedy is "something that has not so much a beginning and middle and end as a center and a periphery."[61] The results of such approaches to art and literature respectively speak for themselves. Only a blind disciple of Lessing could deny that the technical limits between spatial and temporal media have been productively violated by the best efforts of modern criticism.

For genuine skeptics it is not enough to dispose of theoretical objections. Many critics who resist the use of such terms as "baroque" in literary studies base their skepticism on the practical difficulty of transposing a concept from one discipline to another. Wölfflin's five categories are usually singled out as the primary target of attack.[62] Even if Wölfflin's criteria might in theory be applied to verbal art, the skeptics argue, most attempts to do so have in fact been superficial and naïve. Critics of this negative bent take pains to rummage through the bibliography of baroque studies to find examples of Wölfflin's categories applied to literature in the most literalistic and simplistic ways possible. These convenient straw men are then dispatched to oblivion, presumably taking Wölfflin's restless ghost with them. But surely the most inspired of Wölfflin's transpositors (like Wylie Sypher and Jean Rousset) must be consulted before the theory of baroque literature is laid to rest. Even in the heat of critical debate an argument must be spelled out in its most defensible form before it can be attacked.

In addition, attempts to purge literary studies of the impurities of Wölfflin's theory have failed to discriminate between very useful, marginally useful, and totally irrelevant categories. This is a little like refusing to read Shakespeare because he believed in witches. Perhaps the whole problem can be faced more honestly by rephrasing the basic question: To what extent are Wölfflin's categories useful tools for literary analysis?

With this question in mind we may return to the initial distinction between linear and painterly style. The renaissance artist sees in outlines, Wölfflin observes; the baroque artist sees in masses. What this distinction implies for visual art may be readily grasped by comparing Botticelli's *The Birth of Venus* (pl. 16) to Rubens' paintings in the Marie de Médicis cycle (see pl. 17). Each of Botticelli's figures, each of his most intricate details, is given definite shape by clear and precise outline. Rubens' figures are slightly blurred. In the painterly style shape merges with shape; the effect is similar to that produced by a photograph taken through a lens that is held ever so slightly out of focus. The concept is certainly visual, but it may have at least limited application to verbal style. It is helpful to think of the eloquently balanced Ciceronian prose style of the Elizabethan age in terms of a sharply held focus. The *stile coupé* of Jacobean prose is often eccentrically out of focus, deliberately distorted. The loose style characteristic of Caroline prose is held just slightly, artfully, out of focus; clarity of outline is sacrificed to atmospheric effect. In renaissance prose, logic is in full control of rhetoric; in baroque prose, rhetoric becomes the servant of psychology. The transition from the explicit clarity of renaissance prose to the implied subtleties of baroque prose corresponds to the transition from linear to painterly style.

Wölfflin's second set of categories places the dominant plane surface of the renaissance in opposition to the recessional movement and depth of the baroque. Raphael's *The School of Athens* is composed with a series of plane surfaces, parallel to the picture frame, acting as a structural skeleton. Rubens' *The Raising of the Cross* abandons this regular form of composition in favour of powerful back-and-forth movement, or recession. This concept is not only purely visual, but also purely spatial. It may be helpful for theorists who try to diagnose the attitudes that lie behind artistic composition—attitudes such as craftsmanship and virtuosity. But as a stylistic comparison the plane-recessional distinction may be too firmly rooted in space to be helpfully applied to verbal media.

Renaissance forms are typically closed, Wölfflin argues in presenting his third polarity, and baroque forms are typically open. This category is not at all purely visual, as Wölfflin's alternate formulation of the distinction— tectonic versus a-tectonic structure—indicates. As soon as we admit that literary works are structures, it is no longer difficult to conceive of them as having closed or open form, tectonic or a-tectonic structure.

The ecstasies of St. Francis and St. Teresa (pls. 2 and 1) may again be compared as illustrations of closed and open form. The frame of Bellini's painting comfortably contains the subject. St. Francis' left foot, and the trunk of the tree on the far right, are both planted firmly near the base of the picture. The upper border encloses just enough sky to make the village in the background seem natural. The two trees on the right, and the one on the left, serve as natural vertical margins. As a whole, this picture leaves the impression that Bellini has shown all there is to see about St. Francis and his ecstasy. St. Teresa's vision is not so easily contained within finite bounds. The artificial shafts of golden light lead upward beyond the framing pediment, where the real source of light is concealed. *The Ecstasy of St. Teresa* has an open form; its aspiring upward movement does not stop with the artificial boundary, but continues into the mystical unknown.

In the same way literary works may be closed or open in form. Marlowe's *Doctor Faustus* ends with thundering finality. Nothing could be more terminal than eternal damnation: "*Terminat hora diem; terminat author opus.*"[63] In general, renaissance tragedies and comedies alike end with a decisive return of some political, social, or metaphysical order. But in Rotrou's *Saint Genest*, artistic form is not so conveniently closed. Maximin, smugly savouring his victory, enjoying the death of Genest, closes the play by addressing Marcelle in these suggestive lines:

> Pity not, Lady, this man's distress;
> 'Tis he who willed it, he who caused his pain,
> And then, through godless blasphemy he tried
> To fashion truth from pretence while he died.
>
> (V.vi)[64]

In fact, Genest succeeds in making reality out of illusion. In the play within the play he acts out the part of Adrien, a real Christian martyr. Now he himself has become what he pretended to be. The theatrical illusion has become the mystic's vision, the higher reality of religious truth. In the selfconscious baroque manner, Rotrou is suggesting that his play, too, is capable of transforming theatrical illusion into mysterious inner truth. Marcelle, the leading lady of Genest's troupe, has held a consistently anti-Christian position throughout the play, but when Genest dies she cannot contain her sympathy, and there is at least the hint of a deep change beginning within her soul. At any rate, the work of the church is not finished when the martyr dies, or when the audience leaves the theatre. The vision of martyrdom, precisely because of its psychological and spiritual character, leads beyond the artificial boundary of the play's conclusion.

Wölfflin's fourth category contrasts the multiple unity of renaissance art with the unified unity of baroque art. Renaissance artists achieve unity by co-ordinating independent parts, by linking them together to build up a larger whole. Baroque artists subordinate the parts of a composition to one dominant theme or motif; thus the parts of a baroque work of art lose their individuality and become subservient to the whole. In Leonardo's *Last Supper* each of the disciples is an interesting study in his own right. Unity is achieved by carefully balancing and co-ordinating each figure with each other figure, or each group with a corresponding group. In general, this renaissance method of achieving unity may be called harmony. But in Rubens' *The Raising of the Cross* (pl. 6) everything is subordinated to the central theme of Christ in his agony and triumph. The workers lose identity as individuals, and become important only insofar as they intensify the dominant theme. In baroque sculpture, the central motif may be so strong that two forms which are physically distinct become one in energy and movement. The tremendous force of erotic energy in Bernini's *The Rape of Persephone* (pl. 20) welds the two bodies into one mass, and moves them in one, continuous, irresistible spiral. The baroque method of achieving unity is not harmony, but fusion.[65]

Since the concept of unity is again a structural matter, and since unity of some sort is expected of all art regardless of medium, it should come as no surprise that Wölfflin's fourth category may be applied to literature with the best results. Sypher suggests *The Faerie Queene* and *Paradise Lost* as illustrations of multiple unity and unified unity.[66] In Spenser's renaissance form, individual episodes are captivating in themselves, although they are co-ordinated with other episodes to form a large tapestry of interwoven unity. Milton's structural method blends all episodes into the larger motif of the fall of man. A similar contrast might be drawn between Hooker's *Of the Laws of Ecclesiastical Polity* and Burton's *Anatomy of Melancholy*. In Hooker's encyclopedia each Book, each major heading, and even each subdivision has a distinct subject all to itself, with an independent argument that reaches its own conclusion. Each of these independent parts can be co-ordinated with corresponding independent parts. The result is a harmony of form that corresponds to the harmony of Hooker's universal hierarchy. But in Burton's book even the most digressive anecdotes are subordinated to the main theme of abnormal psychology. Burton's unity is of the baroque variety: it is a broad, rhythmic unity of tone and atmosphere. Hooker achieves unity through a procedure similar to architectural construction; he piles layer upon layer with the confidence of a builder who knows his trade and has measured his territory. With Burton the process is more like modelling a vessel from clay; the material is shaped and reshaped until a unified form gradually emerges out of chaos.

The last category in Wölfflin's theory claims absolute clarity for renaissance art as opposed to relative clarity only for the baroque. This distinction is intended as a general summary of the other four categories. In stylistic terms, only the linear technique will produce absolute clarity; the blurring tendency of the painterly technique aims at diffuse effects. When applied to structure, this category overlaps with the distinction between closed and open form. A closed form contains a clearly defined amount of material, within clearly defined boundaries; an open form may suggest some mysterious hidden element beyond its borders. If the absolute-relative clarity distinction adds anything new to Wölfflin's system, it does so at the thematic level. Renaissance art presents clearly discernible themes, and aims to make them clearly understood; baroque art prefers mysterious themes, and interprets them only through visions and mirages. We are back at the quarrel between reality and illusion, with Bramante, Bellini, Sidney, and Spenser on the side of reality; with Cortona, Bernini, Herrick, and Crashaw on the side of illusion.

To weigh Wölfflin's theory in the balances of an either–or hypothesis, then, may not be the wisest way of judging the possible correspondences between art and literature. Only one of his categories—the plane surface versus recessional movement distinction—is so firmly attached to plastic concepts as to be of little use in analyzing the verbal arts. The distinction between closed and open form, and the distinction between harmony and fusion, may be very useful keys to the principles of baroque literary structure. The two remaining categories—linear versus painterly style, and absolute versus relative clarity—may be of at least some help when questions of verbal style arise. It is of course true that Wölfflin's categories have been on occasion applied to literature indiscriminately, but these lapses in judgment should not be allowed to obscure the possible advantages of cautious and informed comparison.

The risks involved in adapting a term such as "baroque" to literary uses may be run in the hope of achieving positive benefits. The Caroline dramatists, the cavalier poets, and the recusant prose writers all stand in need of rescue from their cumbersome labels. The term "baroque," firmly linked as it is to the cultural climate of the seventeenth century, would be a decided improvement. By the same token, the term "mannerism" is more descriptive of the artistic tone of the early seventeenth century than phrases like "Jacobean drama," "metaphysical poetry," or "Senecan prose." Terms borrowed from art history may never be purified of all ambiguities; but at least they are anchored in the broad cultural phases of Europe, not simply tied to the lives and deaths of the English kings and queens.

Even so, the broadly comparative emphasis of the new terms is by no means a radical revision of literary history. I am suggesting no more than a slight adjustment of the critical lenses—an adjustment which receives coincidental support from the particular historical context. Indeed, the very period of Ford's major dramatic production, roughly 1625 to 1640, stands out as the most plausible period of time for the growth of an English literary baroque. The contributing historical circumstances may be briefly sketched.

The position of Charles I as the arbiter of English taste is by far the most important factor. His impact on English culture has been succinctly reviewed by Margaret Whinney and Oliver Millar: "As a patron of living artists and a lover of modern painting Charles I's achievement was to set England for a tragically short period within the orbit of most of the contemporary artistic movements on the Continent." Under Charles's direct patronage or indirect influence, many Italian and Dutch baroque artists worked for at least brief periods in England; the list of names includes Rubens, Van Dyck, Daniel Mytens, François Dieussart, Orazio Gentileschi, and Francesco Fanelli. All of these artists were active in England between 1625 and 1641. Two of them— Gentileschi and Van Dyck—served as official court painters to Charles, and several others were employed on royal projects. Van Dyck of course left the largest legacy: his famous portraits of Charles I (see pl. 19) transformed a rather unheroic king "into the cavalier with his air of languid romance and with a prescient aura of martyrdom which has surrounded the popular image of King Charles ever since."[67]

A second matter—not unrelated to the king's tastes—is his marriage to Henrietta Maria of Bourbon in 1625. If the English setting needed a symbol of the Counter-Reformation to provide an added impetus in the baroque direction, the new queen was admirably suited to the part. During Henrietta's tenure, perhaps as a result of her influence, Bishop Laud's dreams for restoring the authenticity of the English church became Archbishop Laud's practical measures.[68] The Queen's Chapel at Somerset House served as a tiny enclave of continental Catholic spirit. A Flemish artist, François Dieussart, decorated the altar of this chapel in keeping with the principles of "full baroque illusionism."[69]

Following Henrietta's audacious example, the Caroline court began to take a far greater interest in things theatrical.[70] The masque grew to its full opulence in the 1630s. The composers who set the masques to music—Nicholas Lanier, William Lawes, and Henry Lawes—travelled to Italy and imported at least an echo of the recitative style so characteristic of Italian baroque music.[71] It was under Henrietta's patronage that Crashaw would later write the greatest English baroque lyrics, and indeed it was for Queen Henrietta's men that Ford, Massinger, and Shirley wrote many of their finest plays.[72]

Two years before the royal match was celebrated, young Charles might be found in Spain, courting the favour of another Catholic princess, the Infanta. A lively record of this disastrous courtship has survived in the correspondence of James Howell. In a letter to Sir Thomas Savage dated 27 March 1623, Howell describes the enthusiastic welcome that the Spanish public gave the Prince of Wales. In order to escape from "the confluence of People," young Charles boarded a coach, "and so went to the *Prado*, a place hard by, of purpose to take the Air."[73] More probably, given Charles's interests, he saw an opportunity here to visit and admire the new masterpieces of the Spanish baroque—the paintings of Zurbarán and Velázquez. In the cultural setting of Madrid, Charles was bound to encounter an artistic milieu sympathetic to the "courtly baroque style"[74] which Van Dyck would shortly bring to perfection.

It has become a scholarly cliché to notice the native resistance of England to the baroque style, particularly in art and architecture.[75] But it does not follow from the scarcity of native baroque visual art that England stands opposed to or isolated from the baroque spirit. A peculiar convergence of circumstances during the reign of Charles I suggests quite the opposite. The king's tastes, the popularity of Van Dyck, the coming of Henrietta Maria, the Laudian movement, and the Spanish venture—all of these events help to give the Caroline court its baroque tone. One of the leading figures of this court, and a great admirer of Van Dyck and Fanelli, was William Cavendish, First Duke of Newcastle.[76] It may be significant that Ford dedicated *Perkin Warbeck* to this influential patron of the arts; dramatists, like courtiers, may be drawn into the baroque orbit. And it is tempting to suppose that Ford had a Van Dyck portrait of the "courtly baroque style" in mind when he wrote these lines:

> *Poets* and *Paynters* curiously compar'd
> Give life to Fancie; and atchieve Reward
> By Immortality of Name: So thrives
> *Art's Glory*, that *All*, what it breathes on, lives.[77]

Historically speaking, then, it would seem probable that a playwright with aristocratic pretensions might be dazzled and attracted by the new baroque spirit of the English court. And there is at least one further reason, apart from the evidence of the plays themselves, for entertaining the theory of baroque style as a possible approach to Ford's drama. A small but important handful of Ford's readers has suspected that there may be something to gain by studying him as a baroque dramatist. In the early days of baroque studies, Friedrich Wild located "a bursting forth of baroque stylistic principles"[78] in the drama of Ford and some of his contemporaries. A decade later we find Roy Daniells repeating the suggestion in almost the same terms.[79] More recently, Clifford Leech has referred in passing to the "baroque imagery" of Ford's early poem, *Christes Bloodie Sweat, or the Sonne of God in his Agonie*,[80] and Frank J. Warnke has glanced at *The Broken Heart* in a synoptic study of European baroque literature.[81] Admittedly these are cursory observations, but since each citation appears to be independent of the others, collectively they support one another with the weight of intuitive agreement.

In the pages that follow I shall argue that Ford's relationship to the baroque tradition is much more than a matter of casual parallels and adventitious connections; that in theme, in structure, and in style, Ford's eight mature plays entitle him to the distinction of English baroque dramatist *par excellence*. The term "baroque" has an ambiguous history in literary criticism, and for this reason I have tried to offer an extended definition that distinguishes the baroque as precisely as possible from those stages of style with which it is most easily confused. No doubt some of the distinctions appear dogmatic, for in the interests of clarity and concision I have avoided lingering over many exceptions and qualifications. The generalizations which I have sketched in outline will serve their purpose, however, if they develop into a fully realized picture through the process of practical criticism. It will be particularly helpful to approach Ford's plays through the lens of the baroque tradition in order to discover Ford the dramatic artist, rather than Ford the rebel, Ford the moralist, or Ford the psychologist. To study Ford as a baroque dramatist is at very least a reliable way of insisting that the artistic nature of the plays themselves should be the central concern of criticism.

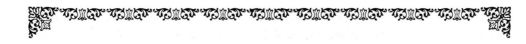

CHAPTER TWO

LOVE'S MARTYRS MUST BE EVER, EVER DYING

An Essay on Themes

SEX and death, Freud would have us believe, are the two pivotal fixed points around which human experience revolves. If we grant this assumption it is easy to demonstrate that most of our literary experience also depends on the support of these great twin themes. Dramatic experience fits the Freudian scheme with particular aptness, for the traditional action of comedy pictures man coming to terms with his sexual urges, and tragedy grows out of man's need to face the universal threat of death. Thus, to point out that Ford's favourite dramatic themes are sex and death would be simply banal, and to argue that these themes in themselves function as hallmarks of the baroque style would be clearly absurd. As so often happens, the truth lies somewhere between the banal and the absurd. In fact, Ford's drama does show a singular concentration on the themes of sex and death. Furthermore, there is an unmistakable flavour of the baroque in his presentation of the sexual experience, and in his treatment of dying. Above all, Ford exhibits his kinship with the baroque tradition through the practice of blending the two themes into one.

Annabella's death scene in *'Tis Pity She's a Whore* is the perfect point of departure for an analysis of Ford's themes, for in this crucial episode of histrionic martyrdom Fords's characteristic approach to eros and death is unusually intense. Giovanni and Annabella meet for the last time in Annabella's closet. The lovers know that they have been discovered, that they must shortly die for their sin of incest. As Giovanni prepares to sacrifice his sister's life, he urges her to prepare her soul for death:

> Pray *Annabella*, pray; since wee must part,
> Goe thou white in thy soule, to fill a Throne
> Of Innocence and Sanctity in Heaven.
>
> (V.v.2373–75)[1]

And when she lies dead before him, Giovanni refers to her body in terms borrowed from the Christian heritage of suffering and martyrdom:

> *Fayre Annabella*,
> How over-glorious art thou in thy wounds,
> Tryumphing over infamy and hate!
>
> (V.v.2419–21)

Intuitively one can sense the baroque tone of this scene: Ford's poetry is much closer to Crashaw's religious and erotic raptures than to Sidney's balanced conceits or to Donne's ironic paradoxes. And there is plenty of concrete evidence to support such a suggestion. First of all, Giovanni follows his persistent verbal habit of describing his feeling for Annabella in religious terms; as her death approaches, he is convinced that Annabella is a saint and a martyr, worthy of a throne of holiness and triumphant through glorious death. Secondly, the emotional power of the scene is generated by the ecstatic release of fundamentally irrational impulses. Giovanni makes no attempt to support his belief in martyrdom with theological arguments, for in the rapture of the moment he has left moral and rational scruples far behind. Finally, the transcendent aspirations of this death scene in no way deprive it of sensual colouring. Annabella may become a glorious martyr, but she always remains a fleshly creature; her open wounds and her bleeding heart are indeed symbols of martyrdom, but at the same time they appeal for visual, tactile, sensuous participation in the experience of dying.

Giovanni's hyperbolic worship of his sister is an attitude he shares with many of Ford's tragic lovers and tragicomic heroes. In one sense, worship of a female deity is a convention inherited from a long tradition, for the devotees of the courtly code made a religion out of love, and the Neoplatonic system of Petrarchan poetry elevated the mistress to the status of rarefied divinity. But in some important respects Giovanni's identification of Annabella with the mythology of martyrdom is characteristically baroque, and in these respects his worship of feminine divinity differs from medieval and renaissance conceits about the religious nature of love. For example, Giovanni is eager to blend erotic and religious motifs, while at the same time he rejects Christianity as a theological or moral system. The courtly lover of the Middle Ages, C. S. Lewis warns, does just the opposite. He does not blend religious and erotic motifs, because the two worlds are so completely and eternally separate. "That very element of parodied or, at least, of imitated religion which we find in the courtly code, and which looks so blasphemous, is rather an expression of the divorce between the two. They are so completely two that analogies naturally arise between them."[2] Allegory is possible only where this great gulf is firmly fixed, and one thing can be compared to another without any danger of confusing the two. The very same technique carries forward into renaissance love poetry, though here the world of Christian theology tends to be replaced by the equally fixed and never-changing realm of Neoplatonic doctrine. The great gulf still exists (this time between erotic and philosophical spheres) as the structure of Spenser's *Fowre Hymnes* shows: earthly beauty and earthly love are dealt with as analogous to but sharply different from heavenly beauty and heavenly love. The very concept of the Neoplatonic ladder of love implies that the various stages can be clearly distinguished and separated.

In Ford's dramatic poetry, the erotic world and the religious world mingle, intertwine, and become almost indistinguishable from one another. There is ample warrant for such a fusion of sensuous and sacred impulses in the devotional manuals of the seventeenth century and in the poetry inspired by the arts of meditation and contemplation.[3] The devotional practice of the Jesuit order in particular calls for an "application of the senses" to the subject of meditation, and Jesuit treatises abound in examples of highly erotic contemplation of the sacred mysteries. The Spanish Jesuit Luis de la Puente advises the Christian who is already adept in the discursive mode of meditation to aspire to the "misticall" vision which may be achieved "by meanes of the five interiour senses": "Seeing, Hearing, Smelling, Tasting, and Touching spiritually."[4] The full erotic possibilities of this procedure are developed in a meditation on the nativity. The "I" of this sequence, the meditating persona, wishes to gather the Christ child into his arms, to "embrace him with greate love." At this point the nativity scene ceases to matter, and an extended simile based on the Song of Songs casts the soul in the role of the bride about to experience the divine bridegroom. "And if I could attaine to the perfection of the spouse that saied: *Let him kisse me with the kisse of his mouth*"; then, the meditating soul continues, "I might aspire to the desier to touch that divine face, and to unite myselfe to his deity, with the union of perfect love, satiating myselfe with only seeing him, and loving him. O what sweetenesse is felt in this spirituall touching! with the which as the same spouse saide, all her bowells were moved, and mollified, desiring to admitte therein her beloved."[5] Mystical contemplation of this kind does not remove the spirit from the world of the flesh; rather, the spiritual urges of the soul are consummated in tactile and erotic sensations.

This overwhelming appeal to the senses in devotional writing no doubt forms the correct background against which to set the fleshly saints and martyrs of baroque religious art. Sypher uses the term "corporeality" to describe the baroque blending of body and soul, the merger of the erotic and the mystical. "For baroque piety and art," he observes, "are able to consolidate and fulfill experience at the level of the flesh, and they do so ardently, triumphantly, unthinkingly."[6] Like the meditating soul, the baroque artist reaches the world of the spirit by appealing to the senses; the transcendent level is "secularized," as the divine illusions of mysticism are embodied, incarnated in human flesh. The baroque emphasis on inner, psychological experience draws the two thematic areas of religious ecstasy and erotic fantasy together: both are, after all, equally mysterious, irrational, and emotionally compelling. Puente's repeated exhortations to experience vicariously the inner sufferings and joys of Christ or Mary Magdalene run parallel to Bernini's artistic presentation of St. Teresa's subjective ecstasy.

It is precisely this blend of erotic and religious feeling that distinguishes Ford's deification of women from the Petrarchan practice of renaissance poets and dramatists. Even in his early and immature colloquy on the subject of Neoplatonic love, *Honor Triumphant*, we may detect the beginnings of a transformation that will lead to a fully baroque treatment of eros. "*Love*," writes Ford, "is the onely band, the alone obligation, that traffiques betwixt earthly creatures and heavenly Angels."[7] The speaker for whom Ford is writing this section of the debate on love is defending the position that "perfect lovers are onely wise," so the tone here is even more rigidly Platonic than elsewhere in the treatise. The speaker contends that love is "not a *blind Cupid*, a sensuall lust," but a principle of unity, "an *entire* [*conjunction*] of soules together." A brief poem interrupts the prose argument at this point, presumably to illustrate the doctrine of love as a unifying principle. It ends with the following lines:

> Love is that harmlesse *prick*, in pleasant brier.
> Which doth most please the [sense], and breed *desire*.[8]

At the very point in the debate that the speaker wishes to exalt love above the sensual world, Ford plants words like "prick," "sense," and "breed." Already there is the suggestion that in matters of love "earthly creatures" are indistinguishable from "heavenly Angels."

But *Honor Triumphant* contains only a dim flicker of a tendency that in Ford's tragedies becomes a radiant incandescence. In *'Tis Pity*, Giovanni consistently sees his sister as a fleshly saint. No matter how overtly religious his worship becomes, it is never a question of leaving the flesh behind; the ritual of adoration is not an expression of distance between the lover and the loved one, but a persuasive argument in favour of the coming together of bodies. As soon as the lovers have become one flesh, Giovanni exults in the warmth of erotic fulfilment:

> Come *Annabella*, no more Sister now,
> But Love; a name more Gracious, doe not blush,
> (Beauties sweete wonder) but be proud, to know
> That yeelding thou hast conquer'd, and inflam'd
> A heart whose tribute is thy brothers life.
>
> (II.i.525–29)

Although he elevates his sister to the "Gracious" level of feminine divinity, Giovanni remains fully aware of, indeed almost obsessed with, her fleshly attractions. The startling and tangible verb "inflam'd" insists on the mood of sexuality. In a wryly ironic way Giovanni makes much the same point by pausing to wonder why women make a fuss about "this pretty toye call'd *Maidenhead*" (II.i.534). Even when he calls love his only "heaven," when he praises his sister as "divine" (II.v.941), or when he offers his tears as a tribute "to *Annabella's* sacred love" (V.v.2367), Giovanni never forgets the sensuality of love, the strong anticipatory pull of erotic desire, the climactic joy of sexual gratification.

Putana, the nurse and go-between of *'Tis Pity*, is the most outspoken advocate of the sexual view of things in Ford's theatre.[9] She has the uncanny ability to turn a religious conceit into a vulgar pun. When Annabella confides that she has "past over" a "Paradise of joy," Putana is quick to retort: "Nay what a Paradise of joy have you past under?" (II.i.568–72). The inversion is almost too graphic to count as a figure of speech. The very experience that rivals and surpasses mystical rapture for the young lovers is no more than a temporary "fitt" from Putana's point of view. She treats Bergetto's suit for Annabella's hand with the same irreverence: Putana accuses Donado, the ambitious uncle, of transforming Bergetto into "a golden calfe"; of thinking that Annabella "wil be a right *Isralite*, and fall downe to him presently" (I.ii.271–72). Again the device is ironic. Putana cites the biblical story of idolatry and sexual licence (Ex. xxxii.1–20) in order to reduce the pretentious symbol of worship to the common denominator of lust. And in a sense she is right, for the play bears out her suspicion that religious eloquence may be an expression of erotic desire.

A failure to appreciate the complexity of Ford's treatment of love has occasionally led critics to a very moralistic view of *'Tis Pity*. S. P. Sherman condemns Giovanni's sacramental language as a form of blasphemy, and holds the dramatist personally responsible. "He crowns their adulterous and incestuous loves with roses," Sherman observes, "and attempts to irradiate their crime with celestial light."[10] Such a description has the disadvantage of taking Putana's reductive statements for the whole truth; it implies a superficiality and hypocrisy which hardly square with the depth and profundity of the play. Ford is not hiding a profane love under a religious umbrella; he is blending the two impulses, artistically, because in Giovanni's experience they have become one. The firm grip of reason would distinguish between the erotic urge and the religious instinct, but Giovanni has passed the limits of reason. "I have...Reason'd against the reasons of my love," he explains to Friar Bonaventura, "But found all bootelesse" (I.iii.382–88). He rejects the Friar's injunction to approach love reasonably just as Sir Thomas Browne rejects the validity of a totally reasonable belief. "As for those wingy mysteries in Divinity, and ayery subtilties in Religion," Browne writes, "me thinkes there be not impossibilities enough in Religion for an active faith."[11] In this respect the baroque dramatist and the baroque philosopher agree with the baroque artist. All are willing to risk the disapproval of reason in their quest for emotional truth.

Love's Sacrifice, as its title suggests, is Ford's most consistent attempt to combine the intensity of erotic passion and the ecstasy of religious pathos. Fernando sees Biancha as his soul's "Good Angell" (I.i.209), as his heart's "goodly shrine" (I.ii.672). Despite his scruples and his bond of friendship to her husband, Fernando makes the most passionate sexual appeals to this erotic deity. When at last she responds, his ambivalent feelings burst out in the form of religious awe:

> heaven forbid that I
> Should by a wanton appetite prophane
> This sacred Temple.
>
> (II.iv.1365–67)

After Biancha's death, Fernando explains that he never "unshrin'd / The Altar of her purity" (V.ii.2623–24). Caraffa, Biancha's unfortunate husband and repentant murderer, worships the "blessed bones" of his dead wife; her "sacred Tombe" has become for him a "shrine / Of fairest purity" (V.iii.2743–46). In most instances it is the lover who uses religious metaphors to express his feeling for the lady, but the process may be reversed. As if to summarize the whole tendency of fleshly sacramentalism, Biancha confesses that Fernando appeared to her "a miracle, compos'd / Of flesh and blood" (V.i.2464–65).

"Of flesh and blood." In this phrase Biancha serves notice that love is not merely an ideal relationship between two souls, but a force that "traffiques" between the miraculous and the sensual. As in *'Tis Pity*, we have a group of characters who see only the sexuality of love. Ferentes, Fiormonda, and D'Avolos modify the tone of *Love's Sacrifice* through repeated references to the strongly sexual quality of amorous relationships. Ferentes actually laments that he lacks the inclination to make love as frequently as opportunities arise (I.ii.434–35). Though Ferentes can make speeches of love that rival Fernando's in courtly deference, experience teaches him to mistrust the rhetoric of worship: Colona, Julia, and Morona become his mistresses very nearly simultaneously. Fiormonda's favourite concepts are honour, reputation, and virtue, but she is quite incapable of repressing her overwhelming erotic desire for Fernando. D'Avolos provides a sexual commentary while Fernando and Biancha exchange trifles over a chessboard: "'tis a *Rooke* to a *Queene*, she heaves a *pawne* to a *Knights place*; by'rlady, if all be truly noted, to a *Dukes place*" (II.iii.1143–44).

At the end of the play Biancha becomes the saint of chastity. Yet, she insists on the beauty of her relationship with Fernando, while maintaining technical fidelity to her husband. In a final attempt to justify her feeling for Fernando she uses the Neoplatonic argument of *Honor Triumphant*: "Can there be sinne in unity?" she asks Fernando (V.i.2356). But Biancha's desire is not purely for the conjunction of souls; like the lovers in *'Tis Pity*, Biancha and Fernando want to become "One soule, one flesh, one love" (I.i.92). The more ardently these lovers strive for an ideal love, the more completely they become absorbed in the attractions of the flesh. Thus, while Biancha is demonstrating the innocence of unity, the dramatic situation never allows us to lose sight of the sensual world; a stage direction calls for the discovery of *"Biancha in her night attire, leaning on a Cushion at a Table, holding Fernando by the hand"* (V.i.2350–52). There are several other occasions in which actual or implied stage directions beg for erotic interpretation. In a very tense scene just after the lovers' first "bed-chamber" encounter, Biancha can scarcely contain her sexual passion for Fernando even in the presence of her suspicious husband and the cautious court. She wipes a stain from Fernando's lip with her handkerchief while the whole court watches; the intimacy of the moment gives her the chance to slip in a telling aside: "Speake, shall I steale a kisse? beleeve me, my Lord, I long" (III.ii.1604–1605). The effect is tantalizing. The prodigious self-control which the lovers exercised a few scenes earlier nearly breaks down under the pressure of sexual desire.[12]

Temples and altars bring into prominence the religious quality of love in *The Broken Heart*. Orgilus longs for the "holy, and chast love" (I.i.121) that once bound his soul to Penthea's. Love is a mysterious force to him, a truth so obscure that even the gods

>are not secure, in searching out
>The secrets of those flames, which hidden wast
>A breast, made tributary to the Lawes
>Of beauty.
>
>(I.iii.411–14)

Since the play is set in ancient Sparta the gods are pagan in this case, but the same ritualistic "flames" are present to cast a glow of religious light into the erotic atmosphere. Penthea's power over her husband, Bassannes, is strong enough to bring about a startling reformation—a conversion remarkably religious in tone. Inspired by Penthea's chastity, Bassanes repents of his former jealousies and learns to see his wife as a "Temple built for adoration onely." The rest of his life will be an attempt to "redeeme a sacrilege so impious" through sacrifices of humility before the "Altars" of love (IV.ii.1835–40). Even Ithocles, the ambitious and unsentimental warrior of *The Broken Heart*, must finally admit that "there is more divinity / In beauty then in Majesty" (IV.i.1737–38).

Just underneath the surface, often repressed as in *Love's Sacrifice*, we can sense the erotic energy that motivates the ballet of love in *The Broken Heart*. Before his conversion, Bassanes argues that sex is a universal impulse; in a set speech on the vices of women he contends that court ladies and country wenches are alike in their lascivious propensities. "On this truth I am bold," he concludes, "No woman but can fall, and doth, or would" (II.i.602–603). At this early stage Bassanes appears to be a stock comic figure—the jealous husband. But gradually he becomes a pathetic lovelorn victim of the very forces he has condemned; he gains in sympathy because he is powerless to prevent the real erotic attraction between his wife and Orgilus. And Penthea herself has at least a double nature. Orgilus first speaks of her as a "shrine of beauty" (I.i.155), as a woman who deserves absolute worship, and when she dies he gathers new strength from her "sacred eyes" (IV.iv. 2253). Yet she is a very erotic angel, and her perfections are of flesh and blood. Orgilus' frenzy is at bottom a desire to taste "the sweets our vowes expected" (I.i.124), and indeed Penthea must admit that tears are for her a means to quench the "hot sighes" of love (III.ii.1185).

In his only history play, *Perkin Warbeck*, Ford transforms Lady Katherine Gordon into a "*blessed Woman*" (V.iii.2678) quite without the warrant of his sources.[13] Perkin's dying tribute to his wife reverberates with piety:

> *Fayre Angell of perfection*; immortalitie
> Shall rayse thy name up to an adoration;
> Court every rich opinion of true merit;
> And Saint it in the *Calender of vertue*.
>   (V.iii.2684–87)

Perkin goes against the grain of history and beyond the limits of reason in a single act of worship. But Ford takes special pains to establish that the relationship between the beatified lady and her lyrical lover is again warmly erotic. Even in this play, where love plays an unusually subordinate role, the ground rules are clearly set out. Huntley, Katherine's father, is worried that the "common servile rage / Of female wantonnesse" (I.ii.430–31) may lead his daughter to choose a man unworthy of her. And in fact his fears are justified, for Katherine is strangely moved when first she sees Perkin, and is willing to suspend her rational judgment about Perkin's family background. The Countess of Crawford, presumably older and wiser in sexual matters than Katherine, guesses at once what has happened. "Madam, yare passionate" (II.i.787), she observes. And Katherine ruminates:

> Beshrew mee, but his words have touchd mee home,
> As if his cause concernd mee; I should pittie him
> If a' should prove another then hee seemes.
>
> (II.i.788–90)

When a woman of Katherine's poise and gentility is speaking to another lady of the court, it is permissible to paraphrase the passion between these lines to read: "Even if he should not turn out to be the man he claims and promises to be, I could not help but love him." Daliell courts Katherine in elegant but uninspired euphuistic jargon; this sort of language cannot appeal to her feelings and Daliell wins only the cool promise that his case will be considered. When Perkin arrives, Katherine feels strange stirrings within her and is ready at once to become his wife. Surely one strand of evidence in the mystery of Perkin Warbeck is his sexual attractiveness to Katherine. The angelic tendency of the last parting of these lovers goes hand in hand with the erotic tendency of their first meeting.

Occasionally Ford manages a similar blend of religious feeling and sexual passion in his tragicomedies, though the result is never so intense as in the tragedies. Auria, the husband in *The Lady's Trial*, argues that a lady's honour should be a "shrine of chastitie and innocence" (III.iii.1439). Spinella is a chaste wife, so Adurni's attempt to seduce her merely proves her angelic qualities. "She is a goodnesse," Adurni concludes, "Above temptation, more to be ador'd / Then sifted" (III.ii.1361–63). Yet, Spinella's sexual desirability is one of the givens of the play; she rouses Adurni to a serious breach of good manners and she unintentionally condemns Malfato to a life of sexual frustration. The miracle of Spinella's chastity assumes importance precisely because of the erotic attraction she induces in the men who surround her. Sexuality runs rampant in *The Fancies Chaste and Noble*, where a whole gallery of secondary characters maintains a persistent rhythm of erotic innuendo. Castamela rises above this environment with a virtue perhaps more fortuitous than miraculous. In the character of Flavia, however, Ford comes very near to creating another erotic deity. Flavia's husband, Fabricio, sells her to the rich nobleman Julio because he assumes she will never remain faithful to him. When he later discovers that Flavia still thinks tenderly of him, that she could have been faithful had he given her a chance, Fabricio is awestruck. "You are an Angell rather to be worshipt,/Then grosly to be talked with," he says in amazement (II.i.626–27b).[14] At the end of the play we learn that Fabricio has taken holy orders and entered a Capuchin monastery to atone for the wrongs of the past. Perhaps his new vows are Fabricio's way of expressing the spiritual inspiration that even a lost and hopeless love can provide.

In *The Queen, or the Excellency of her Sex* the correlation between sexual desire and religious pathos is even more direct than usual.[15] Early in the play Alphonso announces his hatred for the whole female sex and his disbelief in the mythology of feminine divinity. Even after he marries the Queen he feels no erotic attachment to her: he brusquely demands that she refrain from seeing him or speaking to him. Then Muretto plants the fear of cuckoldry in Alphonso's mind, and a remarkable transformation of values sets in. Alphonso imagines the Queen engaged in lovemaking with the courtier Petruchi; the very suggestion arouses his own sexual desire, and simultaneously prompts him to adopt the language of worship. The harder Alphonso fights to maintain his misogyny, the more sexually aroused he becomes, and the more ardently he worships the woman he is determined to hate. The pattern reaches a climax when Alphonso admits the error of his ways and leads the courtiers in a ritual of devotion and confession:

> Lay by your arms, my lords, and joyn with me.
> Let's kneel to this (what shall I call her?) Woman?
> No, she's an Angel. Glory of Creation,   *All kneel.*
> Can you forget my wickedness?
>
> (V.ii.3640–46)

The answer to his question is already implied in the humble trust that Alphonso now places in his wife: "I am I know too vile to be remitted, / But she is merciful" (V.ii.3651–52). Only by thinking of his wife as a whore has Alphonso been able to arrive at the conclusion that she is a goddess. His conversion is the result of Muretto's skilful suggestions that eros and worship may be complementary impulses, that whore and goddess may be one.

The renaissance distinction between love and lust is no longer valid for Ford. In Shakespeare the two are still clearly separated; the poet persona of *The Sonnets* repeatedly praises the Young Man as a paragon of virtue, and vehemently derides the Dark Lady as the nadir of depravity. He summarizes the distinction between love and lust with quite some confidence: "Two loves I have, of comfort and despair."[16] Of course it would be foolish to deny Shakespeare's knowledge of the infinite variety of love, but that is not the issue at stake. Shakespeare's fundamental sympathy with orthodox renaissance values allows and indeed demands that he depict each love relationship as a point on the well-defined scale between ideal love (seeing Cupid) and corrupting lust (blind Cupid). In the drama, Kyd's *Soliman and Perseda* pictures a battle between the "honest love" of Erastus and the "filthie lust" of Soliman in a form almost as schematic as the morality plays.[17] Mannerist playwrights tend to upset the balance by placing all the emphasis on lust at the expense of love. Lust dominates to such a degree in *The Atheist's Tragedy*, in *The Changeling*, and in *Volpone* that the representatives of true love (Bonario and Celia, for example) seem to be helpless cardboard playthings in a whirlwind of diseased and excessive vice. In the baroque phase the distinction between love and lust is superseded altogether. Burton's *Anatomy*, for example, treats the amorous sphere with a psychological sophistication entirely typical of baroque attitudes. His section on "Love-Melancholy" passes over the theological givens and logical distinctions in order to arrive at the core of the matter: specifically human love, its many variations, its psychological causes and effects. The religious tone that often accompanies erotic passion is no longer explained as part of the objective universe, but becomes instead an important quality in the subjective experience of the lover. Ford's approach is also psychological. Stimulated by Burton's ideas,[18] he exploits the rhetoric of religious pathos in order to suggest the diversity, complexity, and ambiguity of human love. Ford's lovers are always aware of the strong erotic motivation that leads them on; at the same time they experience the full grandeur and mystery of love expressed in sacramental terms.

The extent to which this fusion of erotic and mystical feeling qualifies as a typical note of the baroque style may be demonstrated by referring again to the St. Teresa legend and the works of art it inspired. At the climax of her autobiography, St. Teresa describes the seductive and beatific vision which made her the patron saint of baroque art and culture. Her account is astonishing proof of the belief that religious ecstasy can be consummated in the flesh. "I did see in his hand a long darte of gold," she recalls, "and at the end of the yron head it seemed to have a litle fyre, this he seemed to passe thorough my heart sometimes, and that it pierced to my entrayles, which me thoght he drew from mee, when he pulled it out agayne, & he left me wholy enflamed in great love of God, the payne was so great that it made me complayne greevously, & the sweetenesse was so excessive, which this exceeding great payne causeth, that I could not desyre to have it taken away."[19] In this translation by a contemporary of Ford's, no attempt is made to hide the phallic role played by the angel's golden dart. St. Teresa and Giovanni use the very same verb ("enflamed" and "inflam'd") to describe the afterglow of erotic encounter. A comparable spirit is reflected in Puente's description of the soul's desire for the bridegroom, in the sensual images of Crashaw's language, or in the quivering texture of Bernini's marble. Biancha's words about Fernando might aptly describe St. Teresa's feelings about the angel: in both cases the object of love appears as "a miracle, compos'd / Of flesh and blood." Werner Weisbach summarizes this basic baroque tendency by remarking that "a sensualizing process affects the religious material of both visual art and literature."[20] In 'Tis Pity and Love's Sacrifice we find that naturally sensual materials have been given religious shapes. The mystical and the erotic tendencies have become nearly identical; the result is a texture, a tone, a feeling that suggests a fundamental artistic sympathy between Ford and the masters of the baroque style.

The haunting sweetness of death is the one experience in Ford's theatre that rivals the erotic impulse in emotional intensity. Sacramental imagery is especially frequent in Ford's death scenes; words like "martyrdom" and "shrine" and "altar" tend to cluster around the moment of death. Curiously, such religious metaphors do not have the effect of stressing the theological implications of what is happening; rather, they tend to intensify the sheer emotionalism of the death situation. The very characters who most ardently enjoy the pain of death often express a wish to die long before such disaster seems to be inevitable. The desire for death includes a desire for suffering, and indeed it is this masochistic tendency that has left Ford open to charges of morbidity and emotional exploitation.[21] It is neither possible nor desirable to deny the masochistic strain in Ford's tragedy. But it may be helpful to take a fresh look at his sweetly suffering heroes and heroines, and to see their masochism as an expression of the general baroque bias toward delight in emotion for emotion's sake.

Again we find in Ford's non-dramatic writing at least a glimmering hint of the bright glow of death in the tragedies. *The Golden Meane*, a philosophical pamphlet which can be assigned with some confidence to the Ford canon, contains one extended passage on death which foreshadows the sufferings of his erotic martyrs. "*Death* is a happie Haven," Ford tells us in this tentative definition of the subject, "and men shipwrackt in the Sea of this earth cannot but covet it: it is a safe Inne and men poasting in the journeyes of wearinesse cannot but seeke it: It is a path to blessednesse, and such as are good will finde it: It is a banquet of all goodnesse, and such as bee blessed have found it."[22] Ford is not a very original philosopher, and on the whole *The Golden Meane* is little more than a digest of the sort of popular Stoicism embraced by Chapman's heroes.[23] But in Chapman the emphasis falls on the traditional *contemptus mundi* theme, so it is all the more remarkable that Ford should choose to highlight the "blessednesse" of death, that he should go on to describe death as "the greatest humane felicitie." In the tragedies we shall find that death becomes a welcome guest, a trusted friend, and even a passionate lover.

Love's Sacrifice is the play of Ford's most obviously centred on death. Each of the major characters may be considered a martyr, for each is willing to sacrifice life for the sake of love.[24] Biancha provokes her husband into killing her. As soon as she knows that Caraffa suspects a liaison between Fernando and herself, she denies Fernando's guilt in the affair and tries to make a scapegoat of herself. She tells Caraffa that Fernando's vows of friendship made him hesitate, that only through "cunning servile flatteries" did she manage to "procure his love" (V.i.2493–95). Naturally the admission of guilt and the impenitent tone of the confession infuriate the duke; he tells Biancha that she must repent and prepare to die. With a suitably heroic gesture, Biancha bares her breast and says:

> I, doe; and to the point
> Of thy sharpe sword, with open brest I'le runne
> Halfe way thus naked: doe not shrinke, *Caraffa*,
> This dants not me: but in the latter act
> Of thy Revenge, 'tis all the sute I aske
> At my last gaspe, to spare thy noble friend;
> For life to me, without him, were a death.
>
> (V.i.2527–33)

Biancha is willing to sacrifice herself with all the zeal of a Christian martyr. Gesture and word are calculated to call forth the maximum pathos. She submits to the hand of death with joy; she refuses to justify herself; she breathlessly anticipates the agony of her "last gaspe." Biancha's expression of the death-wish recalls both the "resolving sigh" with which Crashaw's St. Teresa wants to "exhale" her soul into heaven, and the triumphant confidence of Christ's radiant face in Rubens' sacred martyrdom (pl. 6).

The duke stabs Biancha, and she dies breathing Fernando's name. Then, in the lover's tribute to the dead mistress, the suggestions of martyrdom become explicit:

> glorious *Biancha*,
> Reigne in the triumph of thy martyrdome,
> Earth was unworthy of thee.
>
> (V.ii.2638–40)

Biancha's death inspires both of the male protagonists with the desire to imitate her example. Caraffa's first reaction is an urge to complete his revenge by slaughtering Fernando; "I'le mix your soules together in your deaths," he threatens (V.ii.2606). But this is exactly what Fernando wants; like Biancha he expresses the death-wish by exposing his "bosome" to the duke's sword (V.ii.2610). Caraffa's belief in the justice of revenge falters; he resolves his doubts through a sublime faith in Biancha's miraculous chastity and prepares to sacrifice the "remnant" of his own life for the sake of love (V.ii.2652). Only Fernando's intervention prevents Caraffa's immediate suicide. The two lovers seem to be competing for a share in the glory of martyrdom.

Love's Sacrifice ends with a climactic scene before Biancha's tomb, where Fernando and Caraffa meet for the last time. Both came here to make their last sacrifices to love, to experience their ecstasies in death. During the funeral ceremony in honour of Biancha, Fernando emerges from her tomb in a *"winding sheet"* and *"drinkes off a Violl of poyson"* (V.iii.2764, 2797–98). The act of total emotional release was not possible for Fernando in life, but he reaches ecstatic fulfilment through death. It is the only way for him to achieve complete identity with Biancha. He describes the effects of the poison in lingering detail:

> It workes, it workes already, bravely, bravely.—
> Now, now I feele it teare each severall joynt:
> O royall poyson! trusty friend! split, split
> Both heart and gall asunder; excellent bane!...
> Swift, nimble venome, torture every veyne.
> I come *Biancha*,—cruell torment feast,
> Feast on, doe; Duke farewell.
>
> (V.iii.2802–2809)

Fernando seems to stretch the moment of death to its maximum length. He does not merely describe the sensation of pain. He uses the imperative mood to invite and demand the mingled agony and ecstasy of dying. In his last apostrophe to Biancha, Fernando expresses the belief that he is somehow sharing in her martyrdom, that he will be mystically united with her.

Caraffa's death follows without delay. He stabs himself and morbidly watches the blood flow from his veins. His response to death is equally masochistic, equally religious in tone:

> sprightfull flood
> Run out in Rivers! oh that these thicke streames
> Could gather head, and make a standing poole,
> That jealous husbands here might bathe in blood.
> So; I grow sweetly empty; all the pipes
> Of life un-vessel life; now heavens wipe out
> The writing of my sinne.
>
> (V.iii.2834–40)

Caraffa's need for pain seems to be linked to his desire for forgiveness. He has after all murdered the chaste Biancha, and he welcomes pain as a form of self-imposed penance. The pool of blood in which jealous husbands will be cured is a submerged reference to the biblical pool of Bethesda in which the physically ill may discover the healing power of water (John v.2–3). If the body can be cured by washing in water, the soul must "bathe in blood." As his veins grow "sweetly empty" Caraffa feels that he is being prepared for heaven. On this view, the more suffering a man can inflict upon himself, the more martyr-like he will become. Ford's heroes rise to the stature of martyrs not because they are particularly noble people, but rather because they suffer so intensely.

In all three of these death scenes, the sweet exhilaration of dying bears a curious resemblance to the warm excitement of erotic passion. We are never allowed to forget that human flesh and blood is being sacrificed for the cause of love. Death ecstasy becomes a substitute for love ecstasy, or better still, the two impulses blend in a final, rapturous moment of emotional triumph. Biancha feels that by inviting death she has given herself to Fernando at last, not only in spirit but in the flesh. Fernando sees death as the only way of becoming one with the woman he loves. And Caraffa rejoins his wife in death, over-coming the estrangement of jealousy in a single impulsive act. Death, like love, is a mysterious voyage into the unknown. In the baroque world, where the highest premium is placed on emotional experience, love and death are the pinnacles from which the human soul may glimpse the promised land beyond reason.

In *The Broken Heart*, the ritual bleeding of Orgilus stands out as the most sensational death scene. Like Caraffa, Orgilus has committed a murder and must die for the offence. Since he is free to choose whatever method of dying he fancies, Orgilus decides that he will bleed to death, and that he will perform the operation himself with minimum assistance from Bassanes. The way the scene is organized, dramatically, stresses the emotions connected with dying: in the total excitement of the moment we almost forget that the suffering lover is also a criminal facing execution. Orgilus grasps a staff in one hand, pierces the vein in his arm, and then invites Bassanes to repeat the bloodletting ceremony on his other arm. Bassanes takes a morbid delight in the proceedings. The blood reminds him of "a lusty wine new broacht" (V.ii.2474); the whole "pastime / Appeares majesticall" (V.ii.2480–81). Instead of making any directly masochistic pronouncement on his own death, Orgilus rather understates the case in his last words:

> So falls the Standard
> Of my prerogative in being a creature:
> A mist hangs o're mine eyes; the Sun's bright splendor
> Is clouded in an everlasting shadow:
> Welcome thou yce, that sit'st about my heart,
> No heat can ever thaw thee.   *dyes.*
>
> (V.ii.2499–2504)

Despite his apparent restraint, Orgilus leaves an impression very similar to that created by Caraffa's last moments. First, the entire scene of preparation for and performance of the bleeding operation is drawn out over what would be a span of at least four or five tense minutes in a theatrical production. Further, Orgilus deliberately chooses a cruel and protracted form of death, so it is fair to assume that he shares with Caraffa the desire for suffering. He wishes to die slowly, so that he can savour each moment of this unique experience as long as possible. The telling word "Welcome" in Orgilus' last sentence indicates that death is for him, too, a moment of consummation that life denied. His action of opening the vein and purposefully waiting for death is the visual counterpart of Caraffa's verbal sentiment: "So; I grow sweetly empty."

Of the tragic lovers in *The Broken Heart*, Penthea alone has no formal death scene; she merely fades out of existence and her maids tell the story of her lingering disappearance. This may appear to be understatement again, unless we remember that Penthea's death scene has been prolonged for the entire period of her marriage to Bassanes. According to Crotolon, Penthea was "buried in a Bride-bed" (II.ii.769). Certainly she spends most of her time on stage anticipating the traumatic experience of dying:

> there's not a haire
> Sticks on my head but like a leaden Plummet
> It sinkes me to the grave: I must creepe thither.
> The journy is not long.
>
> (IV.ii.1883–86)

Speeches of this sort become more and more frequent as her death approaches. It is left to the "Song" that accompanies her offstage death to explain what is already clear—that Penthea is another of love's martyrs:

Love is dead, let lovers eyes,
　　Lock'd in endlesse dreames
　　Th' extremes of all extremes,
Ope no more, for now Love dyes,
　　Now love dyes, implying
Loves Martyrs must be ever, ever dying.

(IV.iii.2181–86)

At this point Ford crowns Penthea's tragic career with a striking *coup de théâtre*: the maids carry Penthea on stage *"in a chaire"* and tell the sad story of her last moments to Orgilus and Ithocles. "She call'd for musicke," Philema explains; "I wept the funerall song" (IV.iv.2199–2202). Like the swan of ancient myth, Penthea can express herself most sweetly through the music of death.

Calantha is usually damned or praised for meeting death like a model Spartan.[25] It is true that the celebrated dance, which she refuses to interrupt when one report of death comes "hudling on another," reflects incredible self-control. But after the dance is over Calantha melts into pathos and says, "Let me dye smiling" (V.iii.2588, 2594). Like the other lovers, she takes an ecstatic delight in suffering, although she sublimates the intensity of her feeling temporarily through the regulated movement of the dance. She is not at all the well-adjusted princess she pretends to be. Her last words express a desire for the poignant song of death:

command the voyces
Which wait at th' Altar, now to sing the song
I fitted for my end.

(V.iii.2597–99)

Since Calantha has gone to the trouble of writing her own funeral hymn, it is fair to assume that she too has been entertaining a silent death-wish. The chorus sings of "Sorrowes mingled with contents" (V.iii.2611), a reminder of the mixture of pain and pleasure in the deaths of Orgilus and Penthea. A further choric line—"Love onely reignes in death" (V.iii.2613)—may contain a crucial ambiguity. "Love, to the exclusion of all other things, is supreme at the moment of death." This is the most usual reading; it is supported by the dramatic situation. Calantha has just been married to the dead body of Ithocles. Even in death (his or hers) her thoughts have been about love. Or, "Only in death, and at no other time, can love find its full expression." On this view, life is a dilemma: perfect love can never be experienced in an imperfect world. The less usual reading receives support from Penthea's paradoxes about virgin wives and married widows.[26] Once again death becomes a consummation which releases the pent-up impulses of a frustrated life.

In 'Tis Pity, all of the masochistic and religious associations that surround death are concentrated in the famous last scenes of cruel melodrama. Giovanni feels that he is doing Annabella a service by killing her. His mood in the stabbing scene is tender; he even begs forgiveness in advance. He kisses Annabella twice, and at the same time implies that she must prepare to die. Annabella responds, as always, with submissive warmth:

> *Anna.* What meanes this?
> *Gio.* To save thy fame and kill thee in a kisse.   *stabs her.*
> (V.v.2399–2400)

By now Giovanni has no patience at all with explanations in the usual sense of the word. He acts on impulse alone, and rejects even the principle of reasoned argument. Any form of rational control might hinder the "glory" of his action (V.v.2408). He can take pride in the deed of murder because from his point of view he has enrolled Annabella's name forever in the register of martyrs.

It is difficult to know whether or not Annabella would share his view of things, but it is certain that she is ready for death, that in fact she longs for it. After her final consultation with the Friar she resolves to leave behind a life that has been a continuing process of dying (V.i.2090–92). To the Friar this means simply that Annabella is willing to renounce a life of sin. But she is really renouncing life itself, for in a sense she too has been buried in her bride-bed. And as soon as the Friar leaves the stage Annabella is free to express her death-wish openly:

> Thanks to the heavens, who have prolong'd my breath
> To this good use: Now I can welcome Death.
> (V.i.2116–17)

When she begins to suspect that Giovanni has come to her bedchamber as a lover-executioner, Annabella offers no resistance. "Then I see your drift," she says; "Yee blessed Angels, guard mee" (V.v.2377–78). This prayer may express a natural wish for protection from Giovanni's dagger, but in view of Annabella's generally yielding disposition, her appeal to the angels is more probably an act of devotion. She seems to expect that her soul will receive a martyr's escort on its flight to heaven. So long as Giovanni kills her tenderly and lovingly, the pain of death will be transmuted by the sweetness of spiritual ecstasy.

Like Biancha and Orgilus, Giovanni consciously invites the death sentence. He flaunts Annabella's heart on his dagger, because for him death is the final triumphant point of unity between his soul and hers. While he bleeds to death, he gives full vent to the masochistic tendency that Annabella had softly understated:

> Oh I bleed fast,
> *Death,* thou art a guest long look't for, I embrace
> Thee and thy wounds; oh my last minute comes.
> Where e're I goe, let me enjoy this grace,
> Freely to view *My Annabella's face.*   *Dyes.*
>
>   (V.vi.2543–47)

Death is personified as a lover who returns Giovanni's "embrace." The word "guest" recalls Annabella's claim that she can "welcome" death, since guests like lovers are treated to the hospitality of a friendly welcome. Again the "wounds" of death echo Christian iconography: metaphorically, Giovanni embraces the wounds of his lover (both Annabella and death), just as the weeping female figures of baroque painting embrace the wounds of Christ's sacred body (see pl. 4). But the religious tone of this comparison does not extend to theological allegory. "Where e're I goe" is a cryptic reference to life beyond the grave, but quite in keeping with Giovanni's skepticism the afterlife is not defined according to theological rules. In fact, we find Giovanni hesitating from time to time between a spiritualized "Heaven" of eternal love, and an idealized pagan "Elyzeum" (V.v.2375; V.iii.2160). What matters is not the correctness of the doctrine, but the psychological propriety of the vision. The afterlife is a world of mutual wish fulfilment which brings the lovers together in a perfect embrace. For this reason death is a welcome guest at the banquet of love.

Even Perkin Warbeck, though he is quite atypical among Ford's heroes, experiences the sweetness of a lover's death. Perkin is never more kinglike than in his moment of death, and in this sense death indeed represents a fulfilment of the frustrated dreams of his life. Long before the reversal of his fortunes, Perkin anticipates his death scene. He tells Katherine not to worry about the dangers of impending war, for:

> if thou hear'st
> A truth of my sad ending by the hand
> Of some *unnaturall subject,* thou withall
> Shalt heare, how I dyed worthie of my right,
> By falling like a KING.
>
> (III.ii.1462–66)

At this stage Perkin represses the unconscious death-wish, but already he senses that he will never be so fully heroic in life as he might be in death. When in fact he is approaching the end, he asks posterity to consider his execution "*A martyrdome of Majestie!*" (V.iii.2628). Regardless of what may happen to him politically, Perkin aspires to the same sacramental wreath that crowns the lovers in Ford's tragedies. As if to answer his wish, Katherine comes forward to kiss him before he is led away. Anticipating the kiss Perkin sighs, "Oh, with that / I wish to breathe my last" (V.iii.2700–2701). The joy of love, like the appeal of royalty, seems intensified to its highest pitch in the face of death. In fact Perkin does not die for love, but Ford manipulates the death scene in order to create the illusion that he too is one of love's martyrs. Again it is fair to observe that in glorifying Perkin's death, Ford is willing to sacrifice the records of Tudor history in order to reach a full emotional climax.[27]

The cumulative evidence of the tragedies in particular aligns Ford's theatrical presentation of death with the baroque tradition. Death scenes in Ford tend to be unusually postured and operatic. His tragic characters derive great pleasure from wishing for death in advance, or from describing the tender agonies of death in loving detail. Such ecstatic treatment of death is the result of an artistic focus quite foreign to the renaissance temperament. In early tragedies, such as *Gorboduc* and *Cambises*, the fact of death is rooted firmly in renaissance moral or political theory. King Cambises himself feels called upon to explain the justice of his death shortly before he dies. This is of course an extreme example, but the same effect may be felt even in much more sophisticated plays like *Edward II or King Lear*. The death of an individual, no matter how important, seems to take its significance from renaissance ideology rather than from the intrinsic pathos of dying. *The Spanish Tragedy*, *The Jew of Malta*, and the many plays of the revenge tradition place much more stress on the cruelty of death. But renaissance characters rebel against their suffering; they do not revel in its sweetness. Barabas describes the unbearable pain of death, but he curses as he dies. A good deal of this negative attitude toward death and suffering carries forward into the mannerist drama. The scenes of slaughter that close *The Revenger's Tragedy* and *Women Beware Women* are propped up by the ideology of revenge, but here cruelty becomes so important that justice is pushed into the background. Punishment, in mannerist tragedy, is quite out of proportion to any conceivable crime. As a result, death is accompanied by the note of disillusionment sounded with such effect by Bosola in *The Duchess of Malfi*. Even *The Maid's Tragedy*, which foreshadows Ford in many important ways, places at least as much stress on the series of cruel accidents that lead up to death as on the suffering that accompanies dying.

George Herbert's poem, "Death," contains a beautiful summary of the transition from mannerist to baroque tragic attitudes. "Death, thou wast once an uncouth hideous thing," says Herbert's speaker in a tone of voice that recalls the skulls and ruined graveyards of mannerist tragedy. But now the martyrdom of Christ has put "some bloud" into death's "face":

> Thou art grown fair and full of grace,
> Much in request, much sought for as a good.[28]

In English drama the sweet face of death first appears in an early and unusual play—Robert Wilmot's *The Tragedie of Tancred and Gismund*—where the heroine finds in death a passport to "the pleasant land of love."[29] But, as a principal character in a recondite and private entertainment, Gismund stands apart from the mainstream of renaissance drama. The beginnings of a baroque longing for death surface again in Cleopatra's fanciful conceit, which compares the "stroke of death" to a "lover's pinch, / Which hurts, and is desired" (V.ii.294–95). In Ford's tragedies of love we encounter death in full baroque magnificence: a death "much sought for," a death "grown fair and full of grace." Ford's uniqueness rests at least partly on his ability to transform the intolerable cruelty of mannerism into the intolerable sweetness of the baroque.

Renaissance humanism is based rather optimistically on the assumption that an appeal to reason will solve political, ethical, and psychological problems. Sir Thomas More's *Utopia* is designed to function to everyone's satisfaction so long as reason is agreed upon as the final arbiter of social disputes, and Sir Thomas Elyot's schemes for educating young noblemen presume an innate rationality that will shine forth more and more clearly after patient exercise and practice. Renaissance psychologists analyze the human soul in terms of a constant struggle between unruly passions and their governor, reason.[30] There is never any doubt about the merit of right reason, or about the subversive quality of the passions. In *The Rape of Lucrece*, Tarquin's reason is conquered temporarily by desire. As a result, "his soul's fair temple is defacèd," and reason, like Lucrece herself, is pictured as "the spotted princess" who under ordinary circumstances ought to rule the citadel (ll. 719–21).[31] The correct state of affairs is developed schematically by Spenser in Book II of *The Faerie Queene*. In his struggle against the five monsters who besiege Alma's castle (the five senses in grotesque shapes), Sir Guyon is very nearly defeated when in amazement his mind exceeds "reasons reach" (II.xi.40.1).[32] But as soon as he recovers reason, the knight of temperance is able to overcome the passions and win the battle. Again it is the influence of reason—in the form of the Palmer—that prompts Sir Guyon to destroy the delicious temptations of the Bower of Bliss.

Mannerism puts these confident assumptions to ironic use. In Tourneur's plays we have plenty of appeals to reason, but they are seldom effective; the struggle between reason and the passions is now terribly unequal, because human reason is but a weak and paltry thing. The baroque style marks a further advance by tipping the scales in another way. Instead of a negative stress on the weakness of reason, we find an overwhelming affirmation of the strength of the passions. Psychology is no longer a matter of balancing opposites to achieve a norm, but a curious enquiry into the infinite reaches of the soul.

In describing the relation of the soul to God, Pascal takes a strategy explicitly opposed to that of renaissance humanism. "All our reasoning must at last bow to emotion," he writes. "Reason presents herself, but she is pliable in every direction....The heart has its reasons, of which reason knows nothing.... It is the heart which feels God, and not reason."[33] A point of view much like Pascal's lies behind Sir Thomas Browne's plea for more unfathomable mysteries in the Christian faith. And Burton's emphasis is always on the side of passion, although he may long for happier days when the appetites were held in check by the rational soul. Passion was "once well agreeing with reason, and there was an excellent consent and harmony betwixt them, but that is now dissolved, they often jar, *reason* is overborne by *passion*: as so many wild horses run away with a chariot, and will not be curbed."[34] Passages such as this one erupt whenever Burton makes an attempt to describe the controlling influence of the rational faculty on the lives of men. "We cannot resist," Burton concludes, when "headstrong passion" takes charge of the soul's chariot. What interests him (and baroque artists in all media) is not the order which reason reputedly builds, but the turbulent emotional storms which the passions undeniably arouse.

As I have already suggested, the uninhibited leap of baroque insight beyond reason and into the world of passion for its own sake is largely responsible for the scenes of erotic martyrdom in Ford's drama. From time to time Ford's characters are reminded that reason is a norm, but they usually feel the effects of the wild, runaway horses far too strongly to pay the norm more than lip-service. The baroque insistence on passing beyond the controls of reason helps to account for the special prominence Ford gives to abnormal psychology.[35] In many cases, melancholy or one of its variations forms the link between sexual rapture and ecstatic death; love leads to madness of one form or another, and madness leads in turn to death. Where madness is generally an evil to be spurned and exorcised in the renaissance, and a symptom of universal evil in mannerism, the baroque dramatist sees mental disorder as a most pitiable human dilemma—as an extreme form of crossing the rational frontier into new emotional depths. Thus, the imbalance of the soul provides Ford with an opportunity for sophisticated psychological enquiry combined with unlimited pathos.

Prince Palador of *The Lover's Melancholy* suffers from the mild but dangerous form of madness that gives the play its title: he is a victim of love-melancholy. Old Meleander lives "distracted and confined to the Castle" (II.i.756–57) on account of melancholy caused by personal loss. Cold, chaste Thamasta tries to seduce Parthenophill in a temporary fit of sexual madness. Rhetias has a good deal of the mental disorder characteristic of the malcontent type, though it is never quite clear how much of this is the stance of the satyr and how much a genuine emotional disturbance. In any case, the play takes shape as an elaborate device for curing the various forms of madness, and thus removing the obstacles that stand in the way of the happy union of various pairs of lovers.

Technically, the business of curing madness is the province of the court physician, Corax, who seems to have been carried away by his recent reading of Burton's *Anatomy*.[36] Corax delights in the assorted forms of madness around him, because each case gives him the chance to observe the new theory in practice. A typical specialist, he is ready and eager to explain his views at the slightest invitation:

> *Melancholy*
> Is not as you conceive. Indisposition
> Of body, but the mindes disease. So Extasie,
> Fantastick Dotage, Madnesse, Phrenzey, Rupture,
> Of meere imagination differ partly
> From *Melancholy*....
>
> (III.i.1250–55)

It is in this spirit of good-natured pedantry that Corax assures his students that the "sundry kinds" of mental disease are "Infinite" (III.i.1261–63), that he designs and supervises the "Masque of Melancholy" in order to exhibit, graphically, at least some of the varieties. Stimulated by the excitement of his new and special knowledge, Corax has quite some disdain for the mere layman's approach to madness. But it does not follow that Corax is the spokesman for Ford's attitude. In fact, characters like Tecnicus in *The Broken Heart* and the Friar in *'Tis Pity* demonstrate that intellectual theories of behaviour are too rigid to grasp the raw data of experience. Corax belongs to a group of characters who will offer to read a lecture in response to a cry for help.

Meleander's recovery near the end of the play seems to be the most striking tribute to Corax's wisdom and skill. But Meleander is not just a patient with a case history; he is a father, too, with a more than natural attachment to his daughters. Cleophila's unflagging devotion to her father during his years of madness has a far more important effect on the old man than anything professional assistance could provide. Meleander tacitly acknowledges this in his words of gratitude just after the cure: his first thanks are to the gods, his second to Cleophila. Further, it is only through the loyalty of Rhetias that Eroclea is kept safe and at last returned to her father unharmed. Behind the mask of discontent, Rhetias wears a heart capable of quiet endurance and deep human sympathy. Corax's doctrinaire method is at best a superficial way of understanding the plight of man's madness. The other form of understanding—the human and intuitive form—is left to less pretentious people like Cleophila and Rhetias.

Palador's cure comes about through a similar combination of questionable science and genuine sympathy. By staging the "Masque of Melancholy," Corax manages to diagnose Palador's malady, but again it is through the kind offices of Rhetias and Menaphon that a cure—Eroclea's restoration—becomes possible. Corax's wisdom turns out to be severely limited. A scholarly reading of Burton is simply inadequate where the problems of mental anxiety and frustration press the human soul to the brink of madness and despair. The real cure is both less technical and more difficult: emotional tensions must be released, and the oppressed spirit must find a way of expressing itself without inhibition. Thus, Meleander's paternal urges rush to the surface again as soon as his love object is within reach, and Palador renews his vigorous youth by embracing the woman he has loved in his dreams. Of course this kind of cure *is* recommended by Burton, as Corax no doubt knows. "The last refuge and surest remedy," for victims of love-melancholy, "is, to let them go together, and enjoy one another."[37] This gem of wisdom can hardly be classified as technical information known only to specialists like Corax, since anyone familiar with *The Knight's Tale* could have spun out a similar maxim. But in his enthusiasm for the machinery of experiment, Corax cannot remember the simplest truths about the human soul. Love-melancholy, like other forms of anxiety, may be treated most effectively in purely human terms. And in this respect the tender care of Cleophila and the judicious plots of Rhetias are far more effective than Corax's scholarship.

Madness is at least a minor theme in *The Lady's Trial*. Auria introduces the subject in a cautionary speech to Aurelio:

> we through madnesse,
> Frame strange conceits, in our discoursing braines,
> And prate of things as we pretend they were.
>
> (III.iii.1538–40)

This is just the sort of madness to which Aurelio's imagination is so susceptible; he sees a case of infidelity in Spinella where there is none. It is also the sort of madness that level-headed Auria guards most strongly against, though in driving the doctrine of reasonable proof to irrational extremes Auria is trusting the "strange conceit" of his own "discoursing brain."

Malfato too is subject to a species of mental disturbance, much like Palador's in *The Lover's Melancholy*. In this case it is Aurelio who prescribes a cure, when he advises Malfato to confide his griefs to a friend: "It is an ease, *Malfato*, to disburthen / Our soules of secret clogges" (I.iii.519–20). This is intuitive psychology, and requires no scientific underpinnings. Finding at last the courage to act on Aurelio's advice, Malfato confesses his grief to Spinella, who of course has been the cause of his frustrated anxiety. Only after she has given his story a patient and sympathetic hearing can Malfato release himself from the madness of unrequited love:

> All is sayd:
> Henceforth shall never syllable proceed,
> From my unpleasant voyce, of amorous folly.
> (IV.i.1760–62)

To express the causes of melancholy without inhibition relieves frustration and resolves emotional tension. Malfato's mental disorder finds a remedy through Aurelio's guidance, and through Spinella's sympathetic willingness to hear out his tale of "amorous folly."

Muretto makes the correct diagnosis and prescribes the cure for Alphonso's madness in *The Queen*. Like Corax, Muretto has read Burton eagerly, and in the long explanation at the dénouement he shows a good deal of the same pedantic attachment to theory that plagued Corax. "Wonder not my Lords," Muretto begins, "but lend mee your attentions, I saw with what violence he pursude his resolutions not more in detestation of the Queen in particular, then of all her sex in generall. That I may not weary your patience: I bent all my Studies to devise, which way I might do service to my country, by reclayming the distraction of his discontents" (V.ii.3583–92). And so on. In brief, Muretto has induced Alphonso's jealous melancholy in order to drive out the madness of misogyny. Now he cures the second madness (jealousy) by denying the cause of Alphonso's suspicions. This works out perfectly in theory, but Alphonso depends as much on the patient good will of the Queen as upon the special knowledge of his psychologist. It is the Queen who continues to love him despite his lack of response, it is she who willingly suffers the humiliation of a cold marriage, it is she who must forgive him and embrace him as her husband in the end. Alphonso fears that his erratic behaviour may have alienated his wife's affections, so at the end of the play he wonders whether she can love him still. "'Tis my part to ask that," the Queen responds; "will you love me?" (V.ii.3660–61). Instead of berating Alphonso for callous neglect and scorn, she is willing, once more, to beg for his love. It is her persistence and her faith, as much as Muretto's ingenuity, that cures the madness of her husband.

In *The Fancies* nearly every character has a favourite obsession which he cherishes to the point of madness. Secco is mad with jealousy, obsessed with the prospect of cuckoldry, and easily convinced that the page boy Nitido has planted his horns. Morosa, Secco's old and lecherous wife, accuses her husband of having the "mad braines" of a "jealous Bedlam" (IV.i.1858–59). Fabricio's similar obsession with cuckoldry prompts him to sell his perfectly charming and entirely faithful wife. Livio, obsessed with the glamour of the court and its preferments, is willing to sell his sister into what he thinks is a harem in exchange for a promotion and a suit of courtier's clothing. In this world of "goodly pandarisme" (I.i.136) and "begging chastity" (I.iii.465) normal human instincts and relationships have little chance for survival. Nitido's comment is choric both in tone and significance: "love, oh love, / What a pure madnesse art thou!" (III.i.1120–21). Octavio, Duke of Siena, presides over this world of sexual madness and leads the dance of obsessions. He surrounds himself with a bower of beautiful ladies, because he enjoys looking at them, fondling them, engaging them in "pretty amorous questions" (II.ii.761). But Octavio is sexually impotent. His "little world of *Fancie*" (II.ii.701) has no firm grounding in reality. Yet, even under these unpromising circumstances, he is by no means the butt of ironic contempt. Partly because of his physiological defect, partly because of his psychological distractions, Octavio becomes a pathetic victim of the very milieu he helps to create.[38] The pattern of obsessions in *The Fancies* is clearly modelled on Jonson's comedy of humours; but in *The Alchemist* and *The Silent Woman* abnormal behaviour generates scorn without sympathy, while in Ford even the most distorted personalities beg for compassion.

In Ford's tragicomedies, the anxieties and frustrations which accompany mental aberration are usually resolved through splendid gestures of trust, reconciliation, and forgiveness. In the tragedies, resolution of mental conflict is possible only through death. Thus in 'Tis Pity Giovanni's overwhelming love for his sister and the distortions it brings to his whole personality must be resolved through the frightful sequence of incest, jealousy, murder, and suicide. When he comes to Annabella for the last time in their closet scene, she reads in his "troubled Countenance" the "Distraction" of his soul (V.v.2355). Later, Giovanni displays the trophy of his murder to the amazed guests at Soranzo's banquet; even Florio must now conclude that his son is wildly insane: "How! alas my Lords, hee's a frantick mad-man!" (V.vi.2472). By suspending the claims of reason, by insisting on the fulfilment of his most passionate urges, Giovanni has become the "foolish mad-man" described by Friar Bonaventura at the beginning of the play (I.i.81). In much the same way, Hippolita's reckless love for Soranzo takes an irresistible grip on her soul, until it turns into an insatiable need for revenge. Soranzo watches the transformation taking place, and calls her a "woman frantick" (II.ii.683). Again jealousy and frustration produce fatal consequences; Hippolita tries to murder the man she loves, but inadvertently drinks her own poison. The Friar would argue that both Giovanni and Hippolita get what they deserve; since both reject reason in order to "converse with Lust and Death" (I.i.116), both must be prepared to suffer the results of sin. But "Lust" is too simple a word to cover the experiences of these lovers, and the norm of reason is too weak and too fraudulent to condemn them. Soranzo is the reasonable lover, and he turns out to be a cunning opportunist; Vasques always keeps his emotions in check, and he is a thoroughgoing villain. Giovanni and Hippolita preserve at least the ability to feel the full impact of anger and love and pain. In the quarrel of lovers it is easier to sympathize with Giovanni than with his respectable rival, and easier to sympathize with Hippolita than with the man she loves and tries to kill.

Caraffa's mental disorders in Love's Sacrifice lead again to resolution through death. As soon as he suspects the possibility of cuckoldry, Caraffa raves. D'Avolos warns him to "temper" his "distractions" (III.iii.1795) in order to plot revenge, and Fiormonda's advice contains the same suggestion: "you will be mad? be rather wise" (IV.i.1985). Caraffa's dream of cuckoldry and disgrace is an index of the troubled state of his mind. After reporting the dream in full detail and trying his best to interpret its meaning, Caraffa must at length admit his emotional condition:

> I am mad.———
>
> Forgive me, good *Biancha*; still me thinkes
> I dreame, and dreame anew.
>
> (IV.ii.2262–64)

From the beginning of the play Caraffa has appeared much "transformed in his mind" (I.i.175). His griefs relax when he finds amusement in the antics of Maurucio, but the release is temporary. Jealousy aggravates his melancholy to the point of madness, and in a final state of pathological frenzy he becomes capable of butchering the very woman he loves to distraction. Caraffa's reaction to the suggestion of cuckoldry differs sharply from Auria's tenaciously sane equanimity in *The Lady's Trial*. Where Auria insists that even reliable testimony must be sifted with great care, Caraffa explodes into jealous rage on the basis of a report from a man he knows he should mistrust. At the same time, Auria's coolness of judgment leaves him emotionally neutral, while Caraffa's blind frenzy invites and demands a sympathetic response.

Fiormonda shares some of her brother's emotional sensitivity and instability. Like Hippolita she courts the man she loves with "extremes / Of violence and passion" (III.ii.1698–99), and when he rejects her, sexual desire takes the perverse form of lust for revenge. None of Fiormonda's actions is admirable, and yet it is impossible to condemn her entirely, because a precarious social position and a fragile mental disposition leave her so emotionally vulnerable. She is a young widow who must suffer both the indignity of Fernando's rebuke and the pressure of constant comparison with a more beautiful though less nobly born rival. She is unreasonable, impulsive, and vindictive, but at least she remains true to the overpowering emotional needs which she cannot repress or deny.

The most pathetic figure of Ford's theatre—Penthea of *The Broken Heart*—is a much less aggressive cousin of Hippolita and Fiormonda. Penthea too is frustrated in love, and in her case frustration produces a madness with more of the obvious external symptoms. She admits that sorrows have "dull'd" her "infected braine" (III.ii.1243), and Ithocles remarks that reason, the "Empresse of her soule," has been toppled from its "proper Throne" (IV.ii.1853–54). Shortly before her death, Penthea's speech takes on a poetic incoherence reminiscent of Ophelia's song of lamentation. Not even Orgilus can comfort her now. Near the end of her long "journy" to the grave, Penthea speaks to

Orgilus in beautifully dislocated language that both hides and reveals her meaning:

> Like whom doe I looke, prethe? nay, no whispering.
> Goodnesse! we had beene happy: too much happinesse
> Will make folke proud they say—but that is he;   ⌠*points at*
> And yet he paid for't home; alas, his heart   ⌡*Ithocles.*
> Is crept into the cabinet of the Princesse;
> We shall have points and bridelaces. Remember
> When we last gather'd Roses in the garden
> I found my wits, but truly you lost yours:
> That's He, and still 'tis He.
>
> (IV.ii.1921–29)

This is madness at the highest pitch of pathos. But even in her most pathetic moments, Penthea is encouraging Orgilus to carry out his plan of revenge; her action of pointing at Ithocles suggests that the "Oracle" (IV.ii.1940) of madness is singling out the guilty person just for the avenger's benefit.[39] Penthea is not so passive as she appears to be; her obsession with love, frustrated by marriage to Bassanes and by her own rigid virtue, turns into an obsession with revenge and a desire for death.

Bassanes feels the impact of a disordered mind almost as fully as any of Ford's characters. Like Caraffa he is married to a much younger woman, so it is hardly surprising that he should feel jealousy. Phulas need only refer to the "horne of plenty" to make Bassanes howl with pain:

> Swormes of confusion huddle in my thoughts
> In rare distemper.
>
> (II.i.629–30)

At this point Bassanes belongs to the family that includes old January in *The Merchant's Tale*, or Heywood's Johan, or Jonson's Corvino; he expresses suspicions quite out of proportion with the evidence, and the law of comic retribution suggests that a real case of cuckoldry would serve him right. But Penthea's attitude toward her husband insists that we form a compassionate estimate of his character, based on the turbulent condition of his soul. It would be so easy for Penthea to argue that Bassanes' "megrims, firks and melancholies" (III.ii.1284) give her the right to exercise her freedom and take Orgilus as her lover. But of course she does no such thing. Even after Bassanes has publicly insulted her in a whirlwind of jealous abuse, Penthea swears that she has been faithful to him and that she intends to remain so. It is a splendid attempt to "purge. . .his griefes" (III.ii.1300), arising from Penthea's sympathy for her husband's troubled condition and from her desire to understand his distorted point of view. Bassanes rises almost to the dignity of the tragic lover, simply because we are invited to see his mental aberration not as a curious affectation, but as a deep emotional disturbance.

Perkin Warbeck suffers from delusions of majesty. The masquers who entertain at his wedding "like to so many Queresters of *Bedlam*" (III.ii.1302) are a choric echo of Perkin's state of mind. After the capture of the pretender and his band, King Henry holds out hope that they may be at last reduced to rationality:

> Time may restore their wits, whom vaine ambition
> Hath many yeares distracted.
>
> (V.ii.2497–98)

But such is not to be the case, for Perkin remains true to his very madness. It is precisely because of his obsession, because of his monomania, that Perkin becomes so much more than a foolish usurper. Lambert Simnel has taken the road of reason, and he is beneath Perkin's contempt. Ford adds the psychology of madness to the inheritance of history in order to claim sympathy for a man who sacrifices himself to a cause that turns out to be another mad pursuit.[40]

The general baroque tendency to embrace emotional experience at all costs finds a particular mode of expression in the special pathos which accompanies madness in Ford's theatre. There is an important shift in style between the fools and madcaps of Shakespeare's underplots and the tortured souls of Ford's dramatic world. Renaissance dramatists tend to use madness as a symbol of disorder, and not as a theme deserving artistic development in its own right. Hieronimo's mad outbursts in *The Spanish Tragedy* are an index of the unstable condition of society; if Hieronimo raves it is because "justice is exiled from the earth."[41] The Ghost and Revenge constantly remind us that the madness of one man must be set against the qualifying background of social and ethical patterns. The norm of reason judges mental aberration, just as the laws of order and stability govern social turbulence. In mannerist drama we find a similar contrast, though the voice of reason and order is much weaker. The rabble of lunatics in *The Duchess of Malfi* and the chorus of imbeciles in *The Changeling* tell us a great deal about the corrupt and arbitrary world in which the Duchess and Beatrice must struggle in vain for stability. Madness is an external force in these mannerist plays—a horrifying disturbance in the environment, a threatening cacophony that relentlessly pursues the characters. In Ford's plays we seldom find madness externalized in this way; instead, we see spiritual anxiety from inside the suffering souls themselves. The distortions of madness are important primarily because they promote a compassionate attitude toward the characters who suffer, and also because they pre-empt facile judgments against characters who fail the test of reason. Ford's drama transforms madness from a yelping chorus of mockery into a sweet and poignant lyric of pathos.

Baroque art delights in illusion at the expense of reality much as Pascal delights in the passions at the expense of reason. Of course we must tread with extreme caution whenever the subject of appearance and reality arises, because in one sense nearly all visual art is based on the principle of illusion, just as almost every dramatist depends on the mask of deception which lends credibility to a theatrical world. Nevertheless, there are crucial theoretical differences between the disguises of the renaissance and the illusions of the baroque. In renaissance visual art, illusionistic techniques are used in order to imitate the visible world as closely as possible; foreshortening makes allowances for the natural delusions of human vision in order to convince us that what we see is an accurate representation of reality. But this sort of illusionism is based on objective laws of perception, such as the rule that light must travel in straight lines. Baroque ceiling frescoes aspire to give us the illusion of movement into infinity (see pl. 15), so the baroque artist must aim at effects which defy the rational mensuration of space. Where renaissance art employs the techniques of visual deception in order to reveal objective reality, baroque art prefers to transform the objects of the visible world in order to suggest the mystery of subjective vision.

In renaissance literature the borderline which separates appearance from reality is firmly drawn or at least clearly implied. *A Midsummer Night's Dream* shows us a confusing sequence of artificial illusions which are gradually and systematically stripped away to expose objective truth at the end. However attractive the dream may be while it lasts, it must end so that waking life may continue. *L'Illusion comique* is a baroque version of similar thematic concerns. In this case, when the first magical vision turns out to be misleading, it is corrected not by appealing to the visible world but by conjuring up another vision. The illusion is not dispelled, but rather remade in another form. The baroque style does not present illusions in purely negative terms—as mere deceptions we would do well to live without. By harnessing the power of subjective insight, the baroque artist and the baroque dramatist transform illusions into visionary truth. The madman and the saint see beyond the visible world, and we are invited to share with them a glimpse of the higher reality beyond reason.

Ford's treatment of illusion and reality might be summarized as a victory of artifice over nature. The well-known episode of the musical contest in *The Lover's Melancholy* introduces the subject of deception and announces the baroque fascination with the power of illusion. As Menaphon tells the story, it is a game of musical skill between Parthenophill and a nightingale. Parthenophill plays the lute; the bird has only her natural instrument. The human contestant is amazed to hear the artless bird rival him, for he has spent many hours in studying music and practising his instrument. The spirit of the game spurs the young man on to surpass himself in skill and subtlety. Menaphon concludes the story as follows:

> *The bird* ordain'd to be
> Musicks first Martyr, strove to imitate
> These severall sounds: which, when her warbling throat
> Fail'd in, for griefe, downe dropt she on his Lute,
> And brake her heart.
>
> (I.i.178–82)

To be sure, Ford did not invent the story; like Crashaw he discovered it in the works of Strada and Marino, and shaped it to his own artistic ends.[42] In Ford's version, the bird dies of a broken heart because natural song can no longer match the delicious rhapsody which artifice contrives. The artist is no longer satisfied with imitating the bird, but feels impelled to create an artificial structure that transforms the values of nature. Parthenophill's ability to outreach the nightingale, like the golden cage which contains the bird in Blake's poem, represents the clear victory of artifice over nature.

As it stands, the musical duel is the closest thing we have to an *ars poetica* from Ford's pen. It is the only extended passage which broaches the art-versus-nature controversy in such a direct fashion. And there is no dogma of mimesis, no mirror of nature theory. To estimate the distance between the theory of art implied in the "music's duel" passage and the standard assumptions of the renaissance, we need only compare it with a description of the beauty contest in Peele's *The Araygnement of Paris*:

> These goddesses, eche placed in her degree,
> Portrayed by Floraes workemanshipe alone,
> Must say that Arte and nature met in one.
> (I.iii.127–29)[43]

For the renaissance artist, the concept of beauty never strays very far from the resources of nature, because ideally the two are perfectly integrated. Even artificial beauty must appear natural, so Peele's goddesses dress themselves in flowers and bask in the perfume of natural scents. Something of the same freedom from artificial aids, and something of the same reliance on floral costuming pervades Botticelli's visual presentations of perfect beauty (see pl. 16). In baroque art, beautiful women have every artificial advantage that costume and jewelry can afford (see pl. 17), just as Herrick's nymphs use artificial perfumes and even aphrodisiacs to heighten their alluring qualities. And in the collision between nature and artifice as Ford pictures it, the bird's heart cracks while the lute remains intact.

The conflict between illusion and reality in *The Fancies* is weighted so decisively in favour of deceptive appearances that many critics have been exasperated and annoyed by the misunderstandings which the play perpetrates. Most of the central characters are easily duped by false suggestions of de-bauchery, and critics admit uneasily that they too have been taken in by the ruse.[44] Castamela is introduced into what appears to be a brothel set up for the pleasure of the lecherous Duke of Siena—or so at least her brother, Livio, believes. There are plenty of hints quite early in the play that Castamela's virginity will not be ravished, but these consolations are very nearly lost in the plethora of suggestive evidence about the licentious tone of the court. Only at the dénouement do we learn that the Bower of Fancies is merely an expensive apparatus for educating Octavio's nieces; until this moment the trick of deception has managed to fool several characters in the play and presumably the spectators as well. In this special sense the play as a whole is an artificial structure, a precarious illusion. The central problem—will Castamela preserve her virginity?—turns out to be a false complication. Castamela's virtue has never been in real danger, since she is not after all the featured attraction of an elegant brothel, and because the one man who has access to her happens to be impotent.

In order to build such a network of deceptions, the dramatist must rely on the suggestive potential of appearances. He must expect his audience, like his characters, to judge by appearances alone, to be taken in by illusion. At no point in the play are we actually told that the Bower of Fancies is a grotto of lust; Troylo-Savelli need only cast the faintest hint in this direction, and the audience, like Livio, is prepared to believe the worst. Troylo points out that a public official at Ligorne secured his post because he led his prince "unto his Wives chaste bed, / And stood himselfe by" (I.i.110–11). With no further evidence than this, Livio draws the analogy and assumes he is being asked to play pander for his sister. Other characters are as easily deceived. Romanello, who has loved Castamela in vain for as long as anyone in the play can remember, suddenly refuses the opportunity to marry her and renounces all claims to her love. He too has judged by appearances alone. Perhaps Ford's irony is more complex than usual in this artificial maze; the Bower of Fancies may be a vehicle for placing gulled characters and deceived spectators on equal footing in order to laugh at both.[45] The spectator who jumps to the conclusion that he is about to see a licentious play must at least admit that he has been as wrong, and as hasty in his judgment, as Livio and Romanello. Debauchery too may be in the eye of the beholder.

Ford develops the potential of this theme of deception more fully in *Perkin Warbeck*. From the moment Perkin steps onto the stage it seems to matter little whether he actually is the Duke of York; what matters is his ability to play the part. He is a master of charm and artifice, and for the people around him at the Scottish court, seeming is everything. After Perkin's noble opening speeches everyone is impressed. King James remarks that no subject could speak in such royal language, and embraces Perkin as "*Cosen of Yorke*" (II.i.777). James fails to understand the implicit pun, because of course he is being "cozen'd" by Perkin's eloquence. Katherine too is easily deceived by appearances; she will soon embrace the impostor as her husband. The Earl of Crawford spells out the effects of Perkin's presence on the Scottish kingdom in terms that stress precisely his deceptive qualities:

> Tis more then strange, my reason cannot answere
> Such argument of fine Imposture, couch
> In witch-craft of perswasion, that it fashions
> Impossibilities, as if appearance
> Could cozen *truth it selfe*; this Duk-ling Mushrome
> Hath doubtlesse charm'd the King.
>
> (II.iii.971–76)

Crawford describes the full course of Perkin's quest when he speaks of rhetoric fashioning impossibilities, and he suggests the full impact of the play when he speaks of appearances capable of cheating truth. Perkin's deception is ever so much more attractive than King Henry's *Realpolitik*, and in this sense the play itself becomes a tribute to the seductive power of appearances.

The English camp holds pretty firmly to the belief that Perkin is a creature of black magic. King Henry, who never misses a chance to condemn the pretender, opens the play with a round accusation:

> Still to be haunted; still to be pursued,
> Still to be frighted with false apparitions
> Of pageant Majestie....
>
> (I.i.167–69)

To the king's loyal servants, old Queen Margaret is the "*Sorceresse* / *Of Burgundie*"; it is through "witchcraft," "Magick," "charmes, and incantations" (I.iii.525–27) that she tries to raise the "ghosts of *Yorke*" (I.i.172) to the English throne. Some of the imagery is borrowed from Bacon's account, to be sure, and the pattern may have been suggested by *Richard III*. Like Richard, Perkin has the record of an unnatural birth, the obsessive desire for a crown that does not belong to him, and the uncanny ability to manipulate people and summon them to his aid. But there are important differences too. Richard is demonic and sinister from the moment he first addresses the audience, and he is certainly evil enough to justify the charges of black magic. But Perkin makes a very favourable impression; whatever he may be in fact, he does not appear to be the prodigy, the monster, described by the English camp throughout the whole first act. From a political point of view this is no excuse for Perkin: it only makes him the proverbial wolf in sheep's clothing, the devil appearing as an angel of light. Although Perkin remains a usurper despite the royal polish, he is all the more seductive because of the attractive magic of his appearance.

The most impressive instance of deception within the play is, of course, Perkin's ability to deceive himself. Near the end of the struggle, when the fortunes of the rebels have begun to decline, Perkin expresses his impatience in rather angry rhetoric. Frion warns his leader to be more moderate, "if you will / Appeare a Prince indeede" (IV.ii.1812–13). Perkin's reaction to the if-clause is almost as violent as Richard III's:

> What a saucie rudenesse
> Prompts this distrust? If, if I will appeare?
> Appeare, a Prince? Death throttle such deceites
> Even in their birth of utterance.
> (IV.ii.1814–17)

In order to preserve his mask of self-deception, Perkin must define all questions posed about it as "deceites" and dismiss them at once as "rudenesse." Even in the final moments of the play, when all of the other characters have been undeceived, Perkin holds firm to his illusion. This in itself is a startling victory for the world of artifice and deception. The real world believes that an impostor will capitulate in the end, but Perkin does not capitulate. Insofar as he remains true to the illusion, then, Perkin is not an impostor. John a Water sums up the matter perfectly: "for my owne part, I beleeve it is true, if I be not deceived, that Kings must be Kings, and Subjects, Subjects. But *which* is *which*; you shall pardon me for that" (V.ii.2484–87). John a Water's qualifying clause— "if I be not deceived"—is of course normal to his pedantic mode of address, but here it is more than a character tag. In a sense it is a necessary qualification, for John a Water lives in a world where people much more intelligent than he are easily deceived. The deception of *Perkin Warbeck* is so compelling that it becomes almost impossible to distinguish appearance from reality.

It is through the power of illusion that Ford's tragic lovers escape reality and seek refuge in the mythology of erotic martyrdom. Indeed, the example of *Love's Sacrifice* clearly shows that baroque illusions are related integrally to the other typical themes of Ford's dramatic world. The action of *Love's Sacrifice* is precipitated by Caraffa's inordinate trust in appearances. He decides to marry Biancha despite her handicap of low birth, because he finds her attractive; he assumes that fleshly beauty implies spiritual purity. Then Caraffa discovers Fernando and Biancha kissing each other, and at once he is convinced that he has been terribly deceived. He promptly allows D'Avolos to deceive him into thinking of Biancha as a "wretched whore" (V.i.2410). Caraffa has thrown away one lens of deception only to accept another. In fact, he never learns the truth about the relationship between Biancha and Fernando. At the end of the play he is willing to accept Fernando's interpretation of the facts, and Biancha for him becomes one of love's chaste martyrs. This is little more than another illusion: Caraffa's last view of the world is still a distortion because he is so willing to deceive himself. Truth for the duke is not the result of patient observation and inference; his nightmare of cuckoldry and his dream of martyrdom are both subjective visions.

The attraction between Biancha and Fernando has its plausible psychological explanation, but both Caraffa and Fiormonda choose to see it in magical terms. The duke oscillates between the belief that Biancha is a female devil, and the view that Fernando is a male witch. At last he lays the blame at Fernando's door:

> yet confesse
> What witch-craft us'd the wretch to charme the art
> Of the once spotlesse temple of thy mind?
> For without witch-craft it could ne're be done.
>
> (V.i.2499–2502)

Fiormonda holds a similar position, but makes Biancha the principal source of evil influence. She believes Fernando would have been virtuous except for Biancha's witchcraft; she warns Fernando that Biancha is a "Sorceresse," that he will be lost unless he learns to "wisely shun that *Circe's* charme" (IV.i.2174–79). These are only gratuitous metaphors, of course, trumped up by people who are jealous of Fernando and Biancha's love, and who badly need an explanation. But like the charges of witchcraft against Perkin, they suggest one level of the truth. Fernando and Biancha are themselves at a loss to explain the powerful force that draws them together. Biancha insists that no man but Fernando could ever have prompted her to break her marriage vows, and for Fernando such love is "Beyond imagination" (II.iv.1324). It is a force that drives the lovers beyond the restrictions of reason and judgement, and in this sense it is a force of magic, if only the psychological magic of eros.

The illusion of magic often lends a quality of mystery to Ford's lovers and their relationships. The most striking instance occurs in the bedchamber scene of *Love's Sacrifice*. Biancha enters Fernando's room "*in her night mantle*" (II.iv.1268), awakens him, and offers him her body and her love. At the same time she reminds Fernando that she has made an oath to be Caraffa's faithful wife. She intends to let him make love to her, but if he does she will kill herself before morning. Fernando is understandably confused. He toys with different interpretations of her threat. Is she serious? Will she laugh at him for being so naïve as to believe that she will commit suicide? This scene follows hard upon Biancha's most strenuous rejection of Fernando's love, so it comes as a shock and a surprise. Like Fernando, critics have been hard pressed to explain Biancha's sudden change of heart and the peculiar vow that accompanies it.[46] Perhaps it is an error in tactics to wish for a foolproof, logical explanation for so irrational and paradoxical an impulse. Biancha is caught in a web of emotional contradictions that bring together the ecstasies of love and death in a single vow. In Robert Davril's words, Ford has "preferred to let this decision rest in all its mystery."[47] There is no simple motive for Biancha's resolution. Ford does not reveal the complete truth where a mystery will more accurately suggest the ambivalence and complexity of his dramatic world.

"Love! thou art full of mystery" (*BH* I.iii.410). The words of Orgilus tell one basic reason why Ford's lovers defy rational explanation, why they seem so remote from ordinary reality, why they can be glorified with the supernatural incense of martyrdom. It is the world of mysterious illusion, not the visible world, that matters for them. Giovanni's arguments are pure sophistry; they fail by every test of logic. But what matters for him is the beautiful and illusory world which he can build around Annabella—a world built up not with steps of logic, but with flourishes of rhetoric. Giovanni's sophistic equation of love, beauty, and virtue is only another way of bolstering this world of beautiful dreams. And despite its shortcomings, this world of illusion is so much more seductive, so much more appealing, than the vulgar reality of Parma. It is easier to accept the illusion that Annabella is a martyr, than the barefaced corruption of the Cardinal. To the very first critic of Ford's drama, the illusion was too alluring, too enticing, for the eye of reason to appreciate: 'Tis Pity, he remarked, "were to be commended, did not the Author paint the incestuous Love between *Giovanni*, and his Sister *Annabella*, in too beautiful Colours."[48]

Langbaine might have lodged a similar complaint against most of Ford's plays. The illusion of kingship represented by Perkin is so much more powerful than the reality of Henry VII's politics; if *Perkin Warbeck* aims at creating truth, it is indeed "A Strange Truth," as the subtitle indicates. The illusion built up around the Bower of Fancies remains much stronger and more suggestive than the tired logic of Octavio's explanation. Alphonso's mirage of misogyny fades into the mirage of woman worship; both are illusions from Muretto's practical point of view, but they are also the most persuasive reality behind *The Queen*.

In general, the major thematic areas in Ford's theatre share an aspiration to transcend reason. Erotic rapture becomes an end in itself, and sexual passion glows with the resplendent flame of the mystical vision. Death ecstasy is a sweet culmination of the irrational impulse—the ultimate negation of reason and all its works. Madness is a pathetic form of unreason, in which the human soul rejects ordinary restraints and affirms the subjective delusion. And illusionism depends on the trick of deceiving the rational eye. Baroque art and baroque theatre glorify the single passionate impulse with reckless abandon, so that we neglect the claims which reason ordinarily makes on us. The real world, in the baroque artistic vision, is not the objectively verifiable plane of experience, but the mountain peak of ecstasy where love's martyrs die eternally.

CHAPTER THREE

TURMOILS PAST LIKE SOME UNQUIET DREAM

An Essay on Dramatic Structure

FOR students of English literature the typical shape of tragic action is derived from the practice of renaissance dramatists. Tragic structure has a binary form, according to Northrop Frye: the tragic hero upsets the balance of nature, and the forces of order retaliate.[1] The hero takes some course of action which is bound to have disastrous consequences, and fate, society, or the gods sacrifice him in order to restore the balance. Thus, Doctor Faustus rejects the normal laws which govern human aspirations, and much of Marlowe's play illustrates the havoc which results when the balance of nature is temporarily upset. But meanwhile the forces of nemesis are gathering in the form of traditional Christian doctrines which Faustus can never quite escape. The death of the hero marks the victory of ordered nature over supernatural aspiration.

Both mannerist tragedy and baroque tragedy deviate from the basic formula. In the mannerist phase we find the clean lines of binary structure undercut by satire.[2] The plot of a mannerist tragedy pictures man in a hopeless struggle against the terrors of a chaotic universe, and the result is pessimistic despair. The typical conclusion of a mannerist tragedy may offer some official restoration of order, but the authority figure in these plays is either too weak to face any further eruption of evil, or else so unredeemably despicable that his rise to power amounts to a dark parody of a genuine return to order. At the end of

The Revenger's Tragedy, for example, though "a nest of dukes"[3] is exterminated during the bloody banquet, we are left with only the weak and selfish figure of Antonio in control. Disorder has not played itself out; whatever balance exists is so fragile and tenuous as to suggest that one tragedy will simply lead to another. This repetitive or cyclical movement is a parody of the natural cycle, just as the shape of satire itself is characteristically a parody of the other literary forms.

The structure of baroque tragedy deviates from the normal pattern too, but in the direction of romance. To borrow Frye's terminology again, romance has a three-stage structure: the long journey, the crucial battle, and the exaltation of the hero are the three pivotal events.[4] Each extant book of *The Faerie Queene* develops the formula. In Book I the Redcrosse Knight sets out "Upon a great adventure" (I.i.3.1) which reaches a climax in the confrontation with the dragon, and ends with the happy citizens of Eden singing hosannas and paving the hero's path with costly garments. If we compare this progression to the binary action of tragedy, it is easy to see that tragedy omits the third stage—the exaltation of the hero. Take the case of *Macbeth*. It is quite plausible to see the Macbeth of Act I as a knight setting out on a perilous journey; like the Redcrosse Knight, he wants to rise to the top of his profession, no matter what the cost. The later acts prepare for the crucial battle between Macbeth and Macduff, which is finally resolved when Birnam Wood comes to Dunsinane. Thus, the binary form of tragedy runs parallel to the first two stages of romance —the journey and the battle. But tragic action does not, in general, include an exaltation of the hero at the close. The best Macbeth can do is die like a man.

Baroque tragic action goes one step beyond the typical pattern, and includes a strong suggestion of heroic apotheosis after the conflict has been resolved. The baroque tragic hero is not content to die as a scapegoat, for he insists on the higher calling of martyrdom. The religious metaphors that accompany death in baroque plays, and the powerful invocations to life after death, tend to carry the psychological or symbolic action beyond the usual frontiers of tragedy and into the realm of romantic wish fulfilment. Ford's Giovanni and Rotrou's Genest see visions of the next world when death approaches, much as Chaucer's Troilus is allowed to see the celestial world after his own catastrophic fall from felicity.

Wölfflin's distinction between closed and open form in the visual arts suggests much the same thing about structural principles in renaissance and baroque styles. The typical binary structure of renaissance tragedy produces a formally closed artifact. The seeds of tragic action are planted in the expository scenes, and the counter-action of nemesis brings the play to a firm conclusion. But in baroque tragedy, where the exaltation of the hero defies the normal boundary of tragic action, we have the illusion of being carried beyond the frame of human events. Soaring visual movement in baroque painting creates open form, and soaring psychological movement in baroque tragedy has a comparable effect.

Since the principles of structure are so fundamentally different in renaissance and baroque phases, we must not expect to find unity of design achieved in quite the same way in each phase. I have already used the word "harmony" to describe the unity of form typical of renaissance art, and the word "fusion" to describe baroque unity. Bellini, Leonardo, Spenser, and Hooker blend the independent parts of a composition into a harmonic whole; Bernini, Rubens, Milton, and Burton fuse the dependent parts of a composition by subordinating them to a dominant theme or motif. Harmony is a matter of carefully balancing similarities and dissimilarities; fusion takes place when the dominant motif is strong enough to weld the various structural elements together into a tense and energetic unity. The formal balance of renaissance style typically strikes a note of rest, calm, and stability; baroque forms excite admiration not for perfect poise, but for dynamic and unbounded movement.

To compare *Romeo and Juliet* with *'Tis Pity She's a Whore* has become almost an obligatory exercise for the critic of Ford's drama,[5] but I shall risk a journey through the chartered streets because the comparison is especially fruitful as an approach to the question of structure in renaissance and baroque tragedy. Superficially the two plays have a great many features in common. Both tell stories of young love that ends in death. Both playwrights provide a garrulous Nurse and a well-meaning Friar as confidants for the young lovers. Both pairs of lovers seem ideally suited to each other; both experience the peak of happiness through love. And both romances are ruined by the meddling of the more traditional older generation.

The important differences between the two plays stand out all the more clearly because of the apparent similarities. First of all, there is a remarkable difference in tone. Romeo and Juliet are well-adjusted members of Veronese society who fit admirably and comfortably into the background of vibrant renaissance Italy. Giovanni and Annabella are outcasts because their desire is anti-social. For Romeo and Juliet, love is one symbol of a universal harmony;

their relationship promises to integrate them with society and with the natural order. For Giovanni and Annabella, love is a force that excludes them from society; by glorifying their act of incest they try to place themselves above the little world of Parma. The overwhelming passion of *'Tis Pity* is strong enough to place all the events of the play onto a subordinate level. In short, the difference between innocent love and incest mirrors the difference between renaissance harmony and baroque fusion.

Romeo and Juliet are equally matched as heir and heiress of "Two households, both alike in dignity" (Prologue, 1). The very first words of the play establish the principle of balance, of agreement between complementary opposites. Romeo's first glimpse of Juliet occurs at the Capulets' party, while she is dancing. At once she becomes the centre of his world. The musical regularity of the dance is in itself a powerful metaphor for suggesting the universal harmony created by love.[6] When the lovers first meet they reinforce the principle of harmony through a gracefully ordered exchange of quatrains and kisses. Then, within a few lines of the lovers' first meeting, Shakespeare manages to slip in the telling surnames Capulet and Montague. Romeo at once realizes his vulnerable position, and Juliet summarizes the state of affairs in an epigram:

> Prodigious birth of love it is to me
> That I must love a loathèd enemy.
>
> (I.v.140–41)

The new level of conflict makes all the difference, because it ties the foreground love-interest firmly to the background of recurrent family feuding. The principle of co-ordination is at work.

The two planes of action will from now on be held in careful contrasting balance. In the foreground stand the lovers, who claim sympathy and excite interest quite apart from their environment. The war between the two noble houses continues in the near background. This plane of action too exists on its own, independent of the lovers. The first two scenes of the play, after all, set up the conflict between the two families with no help at all from Romeo, and without so much as a mention of Juliet. And after the lovers have died, Shakespeare still finds it important and necessary to settle the feud before he can conclude the play. The two planes of action may be described as standing in contrapuntal relation to one another, since there are two independent melodic lines; the points of contrast and similarity between the two produce the structural harmony of the play.

'Tis Pity contains no such careful balancing of opposite claims. One motif dominates—obsessive, abnormal, overpowering love. Dramatic conflict is generated not by forces outside the characters, but by the ambivalent nature of love itself. Giovanni and Annabella are locked in a relationship that is both the most beautiful and the most sordid affair imaginable. We do not need the other events of the play to tell us this. It is not society, or politics, or even religion that destroys love in this case, for here love is self-destructive. In the death scenes, Giovanni himself takes the executioner's part; his last act of love, he explains to his sister, is to "kill thee in a kisse" (V.v.2400).

The subordinate incidents and the minor characters raise the basic question of unity. How, for example, are we to account for Annabella's other suitors? There is Grimaldi, a haughty Roman nobleman who seems to think that Parma's best is his for the taking; there is Soranzo, a family friend who is quite willing to use his influence with Annabella's father and the cunning of his servant Vasques to help him make an attractive match; and there is Bergetto, a rich heir who does not particularly care for Annabella, but who courts her nevertheless at his wealthy uncle's insistence. None of the suitors is attractive because all of them are ready to debase the true currency of love, because all of them come prepared to compromise.

Grimaldi, the first of the three suitors, introduces himself by engaging Vasques in a duel. This outbreak of violence in some ways resembles the street brawl that opens *Romeo and Juliet*. In both plays, early altercations focus the dangers of disorder, but again the differences are more important. Two equally powerful factions are at war in *Romeo and Juliet*. The Prince of Verona enters almost as soon as the fighting begins, to remind the participants of the social dangers posed by violence; for the common good of the social order he cannot tolerate "civil brawls" (I.i.87). Two private individuals fight in 'Tis Pity, and neither is a citizen of Parma; conflict here involves personal grudges, not social issues. Soranzo fears that Grimaldi may be a strong contender for Annabella's hand, so he hires Vasques to provoke Grimaldi into fighting. Grimaldi responds to the challenge, although he feels that the "slave" who confronts him is "no equall match" for a nobleman (I.ii.152, 147). Florio, a private citizen who is naturally biased because the fight concerns his daughter, acts as peacemaker. He attributes the "sudden broyles" to the suitors' "disordered bloods" (I.ii.166–68), and he warns them not to justify crime by invoking love:

> I would not for my wealth, my daughters love
> Should cause the spilling of one drop of blood.
>
> (I.ii.208–209)

Shakespeare's "civil brawls" and Ford's "sudden broyles" might stand as capsule summaries of the way conflict is handled in the two plays. The factions in *Romeo and Juliet* meet in direct opposition; the rivalry is part of a broader social pattern. The contestants in *'Tis Pity* fight along oblique lines. The initial outburst has the form of a love duel, yet neither of the major claimants for Annabella's love is present. Grimaldi is only a weak contender, and Vasques is a mercenary; neither suspects that the real favourite in the struggle is Giovanni. If the factions are openly at war in *Romeo and Juliet*, the lovers in *'Tis Pity* are caught in a labyrinth of espionage and counter-espionage.

Grimaldi's function does not parallel any of the other roles with consistency, so he cannot be drawn into the play's fabric by means of co-ordination and balance. Only the dominant thematic motif—the ambivalent nature of love—can account for his peculiar behaviour. When next he appears, it is to find out whether Richardetto can supply him with a drug that will "move affection" (II.iii.827). Richardetto's advice is to use poison instead, in order to murder Soranzo. Grimaldi consents at once, for the method used to secure his love object does not matter at all to him. The power of love suspends the ordinary laws and restraints that govern noble action, and becomes an excuse for even the coarsest villainy: "in termes of love," Grimaldi argues, "Where Merite cannot sway, Policy must" (III.v.1340–43). When he discovers that he has killed Bergetto by mistake, Grimaldi shrugs off the error and claims the protection of his friend the Cardinal (III.ix.1574–85). The convenient excuse of irresistible passion has relieved him of guilt, just as the Cardinal's intervention relieves him of responsibility.

If Grimaldi were a minor character in a typical renaissance tragedy, his unprincipled approach to love would probably stand out as a foil against which the hero's noble passion could be shown off to best advantage. Just such carefully drawn contrasts distinguish between Mosby and Arden in *Arden of Faversham*, between Balthazar and Horatio in *The Spanish Tragedy*, and indeed between Claudius and Hamlet's father. But Grimaldi and Giovanni cannot act as foils to one another, partly because the action of the play never brings them into direct conflict, and partly because their attitudes and even their crimes are so perilously similar.

It is the second suitor, Soranzo, who eventually marries Annabella, discovers her infidelity, and determines to punish her. Technically Soranzo and Giovanni are rivals for the same woman, but they are never allowed to compete on equal terms. Soranzo may have a legal stranglehold on Annabella, but it is quite clear from her reactions during the courtship scenes that Giovanni is the only man who has any real chance of winning her love. If Soranzo has a counterpart in *Romeo and Juliet*, it must be the County Paris. But this man is in every way a worthy rival for Romeo. He is young, handsome, rich, and in love with Juliet; his principal fault is that he seems a little too conventional. Juliet gives tacit assent to his charm when she engages him in bantering dialogue in Friar Laurence's cell (IV.i). Soranzo, by contrast, is thoroughly repugnant. He has none of the warmth of Giovanni, none of the idealism required of the young bridegroom. The best commendation Putana can give him is a sardonic voucher for his sexual virility. Annabella recognizes the emptiness of his courtship by giving him the most abominable reception. Like Grimaldi, Soranzo is subordinated to the thematic concerns of the play; his schemes, his treacheries, his faithlessness, remind us again and again that love in the world of the play is mixed with baser emotional mettle.

Bergetto is less distasteful than the other two suitors, but equally unprincipled. He too debases love, because he courts Annabella only at the request of his covetous and ambitious uncle, Donado. His courtship, as Poggio reports it, is a mockery of the language of true love: "Forsooth my Maister said, that hee loved her almost as-well as he loved Parmasent, and swore (I'le be sworne for him) that shee wanted but such a Nose as his was, to be as pretty a young woeman, as any was in *Parma*" (I.iv.495–98). Donado's simple response to this report—"Oh grose!"—seems entirely apt. Yet, if this is gross language for a lover, if this is a speech that mocks love, it is only a subordinate form of Giovanni's mockery. The ambivalence of love has been stressed from the moment Giovanni begins to court his sister:

> Such lippes would tempt a Saint; such hands as those
> Would make an *Anchoret* Lascivious.
>
> (I.iii.357–58)

Annabella is understandably confused by Giovanni's tribute. If it is easy to respond correctly to Bergetto's preposterously clumsy rhetoric, Giovanni's language perplexes because it may be either eloquent praise or ironic parody.

The case of Bergetto introduces the wider question of the place of humour in Ford's tragedy. Again the comparison with *Romeo and Juliet* is appropriate and telling. The sexual puns Mercutio delights in and the broad humour of Juliet's Nurse strike us at once as genuinely funny and quite healthy. But Ford's comic characters and passages of witty dialogue are not so universally admired. In fact, it has become a favourite critical game to malign Ford's sense of humour,[7] just as it remains a respectable occupation to praise Shakespeare's. Both points of view have been overstated, perhaps, but they do point to an important principle: comic and serious passages are related through harmony in renaissance structure, and through fusion in baroque structure.

The Nurse's flippant story about Juliet's infancy may be taken to represent the kind of good-natured comic *badinage* characteristic of *Romeo and Juliet*. Like any other child, little Juliet has fallen on her face. She refuses to stop crying until the Nurse's husband comforts her:

> 'Yea,' quoth he, 'dost thou fall upon thy face?
> Thou wilt fall backward when thou hast more wit;
> Wilt thou not, Jule?' and, by my holidam,
> The pretty wretch left crying and said 'Ay.'
>
> (I.iii.39–44)

This little vignette has its own charm, its own meaning, and its own existence quite apart from the rest of the play. Of course it is related to what will happen later on, but that is of secondary importance. Humour may be co-ordinated with serious meaning, but first it is allowed to exist for its own sake. It is precisely because a passage such as this one frees itself from the urgency of the tragic design, that it can be genuinely and enjoyably funny.

The humorous passages of *'Tis Pity* never achieve this kind of independence. Indeed, comic and serious passages are so tightly fused that it becomes difficult to distinguish one from the other. Putana allows herself a form of jesting very similar to that of Juliet's Nurse, but the result is hardly the same. When Annabella describes her first experience of love by reporting that she has "past over" a "Paradise of joy," Putana deflates the comparison without mercy: "Nay what a Paradise of joy have you past under?...and I say still, if a young Wench feele the fitt upon her, let her take any body, Father or Brother, all is one" (II.i.568–74). Putana uses the very same conceit that the Nurse found so attractive: the difference between passing over and passing under equals the difference between falling forward and falling backward. Yet Putana's phrase is hardly funny at all in any accepted sense of that word. Juliet's Nurse laughs heartily at her own joke, and finds the jest compelling enough to warrant three repetitions; Putana's joke, which comes just after we learn that Giovanni and Annabella have consummated their love, could not possibly raise more than a wry and uncomfortable smile. Annabella uses the word "Paradise" to suggest the noble, spiritual qualities of her love. Putana's response is a corrective; it serves notice that heavenly love is only a half-truth, that divinity is at least partly sexuality. The ambivalent nature of love produces a tense fusion of the serious and the comic.

To turn to the central characters of both plays, we find that the principles of harmony and fusion operate at the very core of the tragic structure. Romeo and Juliet are consistently presented as balancing opposites: Montague versus Capulet, the impetuous lover versus the practical woman, and so on. Even after the ceremony of marriage has made them one flesh, the young lovers retain their sharply individual qualities. Love is the bond that draws a line of co-ordination between opposites, and harmony is the result of this pleasing blend of differences.

The same could not be said of Giovanni and Annabella, who share both emotional and biological kinship. In a seemingly harmless conceit, Giovanni observes that nature has given "one beauty to a double soule" (I.iii.400). The phrase is a startling inversion of Neoplatonic doctrine, as expressed for instance in *Tottel's Miscellany*, where "One soull" inhabits "bodies twain."[8] Giovanni's variation has the effect of stressing the fleshly union of bodies at the expense of spiritual union of souls. The device brings the lovers together in a sensual embrace which parallels the erotic fusion of forms in baroque sculpture (see pl. 20). Annabella responds to Giovanni's verbal embrace by admitting that she feels the same overwhelming pressure of desire:

> Live, thou hast wonne
> The field, and never fought; what thou hast urg'd,
> My captive heart had long agoe resolv'd.
>
> (I.iii.407–409)

Both lovers use metaphors of fate and captivity to describe their predicament. For them love is a mysterious force that masters them, subordinates them, and isolates them from all meaningful social participation. They have each other, to the exclusion of all else. When last they meet they are again agreed: both wish for and invite death; both see their final moments together as the apotheosis of love through death. The power of love has fused them into one flesh, one mind, and almost into one soul.

Romeo and Juliet is formally closed. The neat summary of events in the choric Prologue stresses the compact design of the play. The lovers "take their life" and meet their "end." The action unfolds and closes again within "the two hours' traffic of our stage" (6, 11, 12). The first act introduces Romeo, then Juliet, and brings them together for the first time. Both are innocent; both are to some extent naïve. Both admit that love is a new experience for them. Romeo denies that his infatuation with Rosaline had any validity, and insists that he "ne'er saw true beauty till this night" (I.v.53). Juliet feels within herself a "Prodigious birth of love" (I.v.140). She has spent only a few minutes in Romeo's company, yet even before she so much as knows his name, she determines to marry him— that is, if he is not already married. A few moments before the party she had rejected the suggestion of marriage with charming modesty: "It is an honor that I dream not of" (I.iii.66). Juliet's comment about the birth of love might well stand as a caption for this first act. It is a beginning for both lovers. The new experience of love has made the past irrelevant for them. They are taking their life in a new and strange environment; they are just setting out on their most important quest.

The opening scenes of *'Tis Pity* suggest none of this freshness, for although Giovanni and Annabella may well be the same age as Romeo and Juliet, they seem a generation older in the experience of suffering. Giovanni carries the burden of his love with him into the play. *'Tis Pity* opens with Friar Bonaventura warning Giovanni not to pursue the desperate course that can lead only to hell. The form of the argument implies that Giovanni has already taken the decisive first step of his journey. Giovanni rejects his tutor's appeal, because love has already subdued reason. His response to the Friar is purely emotional:

> It were more ease to stop the *Ocean*
> From floates and ebbs, then to disswade my vowes.
>
> (I.i.122–23)

Clearly Giovanni has committed himself to a fatal course of action that no meddling friar could possibly arrest. The vow of love expresses a determination that has grown within him long before the play's beginning.

Annabella is so quickly won because she too has been harbouring a secret desire. As soon as Giovanni has declared his love, she is free to release the emotional energy that has been driving her to the same disastrous precipice. "For every sigh that thou hast spent for me," she admits, "I have sigh'd ten" (I.ii.411–12). The lovers have now reached agreement, so they kneel and exchange oaths that bind them to love or else kill each other. This is the only marriage ceremony permitted to partners in incest. It is not a festive occasion. Love is not linked with birth here, but with death. This type of love is a sort of beginning, but hardly a fresh awakening to a full life. The marriage ceremony itself contains the sombre hint of disaster to follow. The first act of *'Tis Pity* consummates a destructive impulse that is already overpowering when the play begins.

The formal differences are even more striking when we compare the endings of the two plays. The Prince speaks the final cadence of *Romeo and Juliet*:

> For never was a story of more woe
> Than this of Juliet and her Romeo.
> (V.iii.309–10)

Escalus is a representative of order. His controlled language inspires confidence; his gentle tribute demands assent. The binary action of renaissance tragedy reaches a calm conclusion, as complication ends in resolution. In *'Tis Pity*, by contrast, the worldly Cardinal speaks the closing lines after he has made sure that the wealth of the family which has just been destroyed will fall into the tender care of the church:

> Wee shall have time
> To talke at large of all, but never yet
> *Incest* and *Murther* have so strangely met.
> *Of one* so young, so rich in Natures store,
> Who could not say, *'Tis pitty shee's a Whoore?*
> (V.vi.2597–2601)

The Cardinal is a symbol of treachery.[9] His tribute is evasive. His last sentence is a closed couplet, but it is also a question, and a remarkably pointless question at that. He does not put matters to rest; rather, he invites the emotional impact of the play to continue.

Both Romeo and Juliet die without overtly mentioning the afterlife. Romeo is weary of the world. He simply cannot convince himself that life has any validity now that the centre of his universe is gone, so he commits suicide. Convinced that the sight of Juliet in the tomb will be his last, Romeo drinks the poison and says just what the Petrarchan tradition has taught him to say: "Thus with a kiss I die" (V.iii.120). There is a verbal echo of this sentiment in Giovanni's announcement that he intends to "kill" Annabella "in a kisse" (V.v.2400). But the same word, and the same symbolic action, have quite different effects in the two plays. Romeo admits that the kiss will be his last, as he seals his "dateless bargain" with "engrossing death" (V.iii.115). Giovanni is still actively involved, both as a lover and as an angel of death. "Kill" and "kisse" blend into one, with the suggestion that perfect love is possible only through death.

Juliet's death scene is much less spectacular than Romeo's, at least verbally. Only two lines accompany the action of stabbing herself, after which she dies without so much as another word. Perhaps Shakespeare is working within the theatrical limits imposed on him by the boy-actor system, but he is also conforming to the conventions of renaissance tragedy. The restrained understatement of the death scenes in *Romeo and Juliet* makes them seem ever so much more conclusive. The love that sprang up in Act I gave life new meaning, and since love is no longer possible, life cannot be worthwhile. Neither of these lovers has great difficulty parting with life, because the reason for living has been removed. There is no reaching toward the next world, simply because the joys of these two young lovers were rooted so firmly in this one. The lovers meet their death and the play ends. The rest is silence.

Annabella follows Giovanni's injunction to pray, and dies with a half-stifled cry to heaven on her lips. She calls on angels to guide her to heaven, where Giovanni tells her she must go to claim "a Throne / Of Innocence and Sanctity" (V.v.2374-75). By Giovanni's interpretation of events, Annabella's death is a miraculous triumph; he describes the sympathetic reaction of the cosmic order in words borrowed from the crucifixion story:

> The Glory of my Deed
> Darkned the mid-day Sunne, made Noone as Night.
>   (V.vi.2450–51)

And indeed Giovanni hopes to share in the glory of martyrdom; he cries to heaven not for mercy, but for his just reward. The "grace" which he expects to meet in the next world is the lover's privilege: "Freely to view *My Annabella's face*" (V.vi.2546–47). The martyrs of eros in *'Tis Pity* make a dying attempt to take love with them into the afterlife. Here Giovanni pictures a pagan Elysium for lovers—a paradise of pleasure that recalls Antony's vision of a land "Where souls do couch on flowers" (IV.xiv.51).[10] At the same time he clings to the illusion of Annabella as a spotless saint in a Christian heaven. His confusion is not simply bad theology, but an indication of the lengths to which Giovanni will go in order to insist on the transcendence of his fleshly love. In one sense the balance of nature is restored by the deaths of these unnatural lovers. But the conclusion of baroque tragedy moves beyond balance, as hero and heroine are exalted by the power of sacramental language. They have embarked on a perilous journey, they have braved the crucial struggle, and now they triumph in love's apotheosis. Narrative action ends in tragedy, but spiritual action exalts the lovers in the high romantic fashion.

Most tragedy, regardless of style, implies some form of rebirth from the very ashes of death. In renaissance tragedy, Maud Bodkin has shown, "something is present corresponding to the emotional meaning that belonged to ancient rituals undertaken for the renewal of the life of the tribe." The individual is sacrificed so that the larger group may be revitalized, and rebirth typically occurs in terms of the social order: "faith is renewed in the common life with its ideal interests and values which outlive the death of personal selves."[11] In baroque tragic drama, as in baroque art, death is a psychological act rather than a social phenomenon, so it is natural that rebirth should occur in psychological terms. Rubens' paintings of the dying Christ contain the strong suggestion of rebirth through death, but it is not a question of the social group around him being reborn. Triumph over death is expressed through the face and the form of the dying figure himself.

At the very close of *Romeo and Juliet*, Montague and Capulet promise to erect golden statues of the dead lovers, as a pledge of peace between their households. The society of Verona has been cleansed and revitalized, at terrible cost to the hero and heroine of the story. Romeo and Juliet will be reborn as a pair of statues, symbolic of social peace and stability. The physical action of the play was closed by the finality of death; now the symbolic action is closed too, as the order of nature and the peace of society return. In contrast, rebirth has nothing at all to do with society in 'Tis Pity. The lovers project themselves into an afterlife of dynamic, psychological reality, as if to isolate themselves even more irretrievably from the natural and social orders. There is not the slightest hint that their story will have any beneficial effects on the society of Parma, for corruption is still the order of the day when the play ends. But love—even wildly irrational and obsessive love—transcends this narrow little world. Psychological and spiritual rebirth become possible only for individuals who leave society far behind. 'Tis Pity is open in form because the lovers themselves experience triumph through death. The erotic movement which began before the opening scene, and which spills over the closing couplet of the play, propels the lovers psychologically toward a private Elysium.

In their broadest outlines, Ford's tragedies as a whole conform to the patterns implicit in the design of 'Tis Pity. The structural affinity between Love's Sacrifice and 'Tis Pity is particularly close, largely because the thematic values of the two plays are intimately related. In both plays the central pair of lovers seek to isolate themselves from society and the laws it imposes. Subordinate variations of the love theme in both instances add richness, depth, and ambiguity to the central situation. And the action of both plays ends with a Liebestod that celebrates love even when it ends in death. The Broken Heart, although it is less characteristic of Ford's habitual practice, does rely on many of the same structural features. In this play Ford has nearly eliminated the comic scenes, in order to replace them with such ancillary characters as Bassanes and Tecnicus. Still, the principle of subordination is nevertheless required to bring about unity, and the principle of open form once again controls the ending of the play. Though not technically a tragedy, Perkin Warbeck remains closely related to Ford's tragic world in fundamental matters of structural design. The broadly psychological emphasis which Ford gives to historical figures and events brings about a radical change in the shape of the history play. While making every attempt to avoid reducing Ford's individual artistic forms to a common stereotype, I shall argue in some detail that *Love's Sacrifice*, *The Broken Heart*, and *Perkin Warbeck* share at least the essential principles of baroque dramatic structure.

The key to the structure of *Love's Sacrifice* lies in the recurrent use of the word "vow." There are vows of love, vows of marriage, vows of celibacy, vows of friendship, vows of revenge, and vows of banishment. Nearly all of the characters are involved directly in the pattern of affirming or denying the emotional impulses that motivate these oaths. Thus, the struggle to remain true to a vow, the attempt to fulfil a vow, and the desire to break a vow constitute both the physical and the psychological action.

At the centre of the play stand the three members of the love triangle—Caraffa, Biancha, and Fernando. The duke and duchess are bound to one another by the vows of marriage. Biancha cannot forget this bond, though at times she would certainly like to. When Fernando at last gains her sympathetic ear, through persistent courtship, she reminds him of her prior oath: "betwixt my soule and heaven, / I vow'd a vow to live a constant wife" (II.iv.1318–19). She swears her most emphatic oath—the oath of death—"by the faith I owe my Bridall vowes" (II.iv.1362). Near the end of the play she begins to question the validity of her marriage commitment. "What's a vow? a vow?" she asks. Between her and Fernando stand "The Iron lawes of Ceremony" (V.i.2354–55). It is curious that Caraffa, the plaintiff in the case, makes no explicit reference to these vows of wedlock; when he mentions marriage it is with a sense of pride in having won Biancha, or with a sense of horror at being betrayed. Perhaps he does not use the vow formula to summarize the relationship because he is still thoroughly infatuated with the woman he courted so proudly. Yet, his sense of dignity and hauteur, his delight in being a "Monarch of felicitie" (I.i.217), imply a deeply felt allegiance to the conventions and ideals of marriage.

A different set of vows binds Caraffa and Fernando to one another. Biancha explains before she dies that only the "sacred vowes of faith 'twixt friend and friend" (V.i.2492) prevented Fernando from seducing her. Biancha is being unkind to herself, but there is some truth in what she says. In his only soliloquy, Fernando readily disposes of all objections to an affair between Biancha and himself, until he comes to the matter of friendship: "she's bosom'd to my friend: | *There, there*, I am quite lost" (II.ii.866–67). Even if marriage is mere "Ceremony" from the lovers' point of view, friendship remains a binding relationship. The duke tacitly subscribes to the same view in refusing to believe his friend capable of betraying him. Caraffa vigorously represses suspicion, until a troubled dream of cuckoldry calls special attention to Fernando's treachery:

> on my head,
> *Fernando*, like a Traytor to his vowes,
> Clapt, in disgrace, a Coronet of hornes.
>
> (IV.ii.2236–38)

If Biancha is guilty of perjury according to the laws of marriage, Fernando must be condemned by the standards of masculine friendship and loyalty.

Two sides of the love triangle, then, are defined by vows of absolute fidelity before the action begins, and the third side of the triangle, corresponding to the relationship between Fernando and Biancha, is built up by a series of vows as the plot advances. Fernando first approaches the duchess by insisting that he is already her sworn lover; "passion," he says, "and the vowes I owe to you, / Have chang'd me to a leane *Anatomy*" (II.i.815–16). Biancha's immediate response is to denounce Fernando's intentions as "treason" (II.i.829), but at length she must admit that she returns his love. In the bedchamber scene Biancha reminds her lover of the marriage vows she holds dear, and the very fact that she is willing to break these vows acts as proof that she loves him "Beyond imagination" (II.iv.1326). Then comes the most enigmatic oath of all. Biancha desperately wants Fernando to make love to her; she has come to him dressed in only her "*night mantle*" and she begs for the pleasure of sexual embrace. Yet, if he divests her of "this *robe of shame*," Biancha says:

> here I vow agen,
> To thee, to heaven, to the world, to time,
> E're yet the morning shall new christen day,
> I'le kill my selfe.
>
> (II.iv.1335–38)

Biancha is utterly confused by the polarities of her dilemma, and the absolute, one-directional finality of this oath is her way of resolving conflict in a powerful, uninhibited, irreversible plunge. A conviction of loyalty tells her that she must remain true to the duke, but a warmblooded sense of life urges her to take Fernando no matter what the cost. Biancha's oath is a cryptic, shorthand way of expressing and releasing an unbearable charge of emotional energy.

During their last love scene, Biancha and Fernando exchange vows and kisses with a somewhat selfconscious emphasis on the vow formula. In a mood of playful sadness Fernando swears that he will bury himself with Biancha, should she die. He kisses her to seal the oath, and the exchange continues in the same spirit until Fernando concludes with an admission of treachery:

> whiles your lips
> Are made the booke, it is a sport to sweare,
> And glory to forsweare.
>
> (V.i.2375–77)

The metaphor of perjury points out that while the lovers are swearing truth to one another, they are also playing "fast and loose" (V.i.2378) with their oaths of loyalty to the duke. It is on this cue that Caraffa enters and discovers them.

The net effect of all these vows is to bring two conflicting claims to bear on each of the central characters. Fernando cannot fulfil his vows of love without violating his vows of friendship. Biancha's oath of married chastity must break the moment she exchanges an oath of love. Caraffa's vows of marriage and friendship are not contradictory in principle, but in practice they become contraries: through his ardent love and trusting friendship Caraffa places Biancha and Fernando into volatile intimacy.

The punishment for perjury is death. With considerable difficulty, Caraffa manages to punish Biancha according to his view of justice. Then he turns to Fernando, who tells him that Biancha is innocent, that in fact she died without once violating her marriage vows. Caraffa insists that Fernando swear to the truth of this report, so Fernando kisses the duke's extended sword and takes the oath. At once Caraffa is convinced of Biancha's chastity, and his conduct takes a curious turn: he "*Kneeles downe, holds up his hands speakes a little and riseth*" (V.ii.2663–64). This ritualistic action is not explained until the final climactic funeral scene, where Caraffa delivers eulogies to his dead wife and friend, and then changes the tone of his speech abruptly with the phrase, "Now to my vowes" (V.iii.2818). A few moments later he stabs himself. The silent words he uttered in Fernando's presence were in fact Caraffa's final and fatal vow. Like Biancha, the duke can resolve the stresses and conflicts of living only by making a vow that commends him to the grave. Fernando's suicide has a similar motivation. He buries himself alive in his mistress's tomb in fulfilment of his vow never to leave her, even in death. He drinks the vial of poison as though it were a pledge to love.

The vow formula is explicit enough in the main action of the play to demand attention, and in a less obvious way the same pattern pervades subordinate levels of action. The Ferentes episodes, for example, amount to a clear exposition of the results of cynical perjury. Ferentes' very first line is an oath of love to Colona: "Madam, by this light I vow my selfe your servant" (I.ii.359). The oath is conventional enough, but that is part of its significance; Ferentes hides treachery under the cloak of conventional love.[12] Colona leaves the stage savouring the kindness of her lover's oath, but at once Julia enters to expose Ferentes' perjury: "Break vowes on your side, I expect no other" (I.ii.413). It is only a matter of time until the third mistress, Morona, will make the very same accusation: "th'ast robd me of my good name, didst promise to love none but mee, mee, onely mee; swor'st, like an unconscionable villaine, to marry mee the twelfth day of the month, two months since" (III.i.1487–90). The three women form a conspiracy to punish perjury with revenge. Such a pact implies a more sinister kind of oath familiar from a great many dramatic precedents including *Julius Caesar* and *Hamlet*. The women execute Ferentes during a masque at court, and in the explanation that follows the crime, Julia once again stresses the falseness of Ferentes' oaths: "He swore," she says, "And pawn'd his truth to marry each of us" (III.iv.1871–72). In the world of *Love's Sacrifice*, vows are treated with the utmost seriousness because they express the strongest emotional impulses. A lover's oath will prompt either vehement acceptance or violent revulsion in the lady who hears it, and a vow made in bad faith may kill with the shock of recoil.

Fiormonda comes very close to breaking one vow and making another in a single symbolic gesture. She offers Fernando the ring which her dead husband left her, explaining that her husband's claim is "disanull'd, / And cancell'd quite by us that live" (I.ii.527–28). Like Biancha, Fiormonda wishes to prove the infinite strength of her new oath by her willingness to break an old one. Instead of returning a pledge of love, Fernando tells her that he has "vow'd to live a single life" (I.ii.544). In a sense this is true; Fernando is Biancha's sworn lover, and since she remains unattainable his vow of faithfulness to her amounts to an oath of celibacy. Of course Fiormonda cannot see things this way. Fernando's vow of celibacy is a visible source of frustration to her; she recalls it with bitterness when she overhears him courting Biancha. And at the very end of the play Fiormonda falls victim to a similar pledge. She has at last agreed to accept Roseilli as her husband, when he announces that their marriage will not include the "mutuall comforts" of lovemaking. "Learne to new live," Roseilli advises her, "my vowes unmov'd shall stand" (V.iii.2875–76). For the second time Fiormonda must endure an oath of emotional rejection.

Even at the level of broad comedy the lover's vow is an important linguistic unit. Maurucio presents his gift to Fiormonda with the solemnity of a lover, "ever vow'd thy servant" (II.ii.1082). By giving her a living fool as a token of his love, Maurucio is making the perfect statement about his own character. His disembodied and preposterous courtship calls to mind the Sir Fopling Flutters of the Restoration stage, but at the same time undercuts the elaborate code of fashionable Platonic love. Maurucio, unlike any of the serious characters, is capable of leaving the world of the flesh behind as he flutters about the court on the wings of his foppish conceits. "The earnest penny of a love so fervent" (II.ii.1084) buys him a just reward from Fiormonda—a tooth-picker which he may add to his ludicrous equipage and upon which he at once composes another cumbersome couplet. The vow has become a touchstone of the quality of love.

The movement of *Love's Sacrifice* through this substratum of vows coincides with what one would expect of a baroque literary structure, for the motif of the vow holds the various groups of characters together in a tense state of fusion. There are no logical or causal connections between the central action and the Ferentes episodes; yet, through the fusing effect of the vow motif, these two spheres of action are closely bound up with one another. Fernando and Biancha treat marriage with nearly the same disdain as Ferentes does. And like the female furies who murder Ferentes, Caraffa takes justice into his own hands and administers death to the faithbreakers.

Renaissance dramatists tend to make thematic links such as these by a method of calculated contrast. In *Damon and Pithias* the absolute loyalty of the protagonists to one another is set against the absolute treachery of Carisophus and Aristippus; much the same point could be made about the difference between Hamlet's true friend (Horatio) and his hangers-on (Rosencrantz and

Guildenstern). In baroque drama, thematic associations blur the clear distinctions between absolute virtue and absolute vice. As a result, the main plot and the underplot may merge into an atmospheric whole, without the sense that they stand apart from each other as separate alternatives. We are not tempted to say, "Fernando has one way of doing it, and Ferentes another," as if either way of conducting a love relationship were viable. The emphasis is quite the opposite. Both lovers choose a disastrous course; although they do not hold the same views about love, their actions and even their rhetorical outbursts bring them into strangely close proximity.

Another way of saying this is to argue that the main plot subordinates the other episodes thematically. Fernando, Biancha, and Caraffa remain consistently at the core of the play, and peripheral spheres of action become important only insofar as they modify and deepen the tone of the central action. Ferentes and his women sharpen the erotic atmosphere of the play, and in doing so they contribute to the main action without functioning either as foil or as parody.[13] Although Ferentes is technically guilty and Fernando technically innocent, we are left with a dark suspicion that they have a great deal in common; at the same time, the points of similarity between the two plots do not imply any reduction in the quality or value of Fernando's love. When we add to this already complicated picture the oblique relationships of the central group of characters to Fiormonda, D'Avolos, and Maurucio, it becomes clear that no scheme of direct analogies will fit the shape of the play. Only the dominant emotional thrust of the main plot, expressed through the motif of lovers' vows, is strong enough to unify this confusing web of loyalties and betrayals.

Love's Sacrifice has the open form typical of baroque artistic structures. In Act II Fernando courts Biancha for the first time in the play, but she makes a point of saying that this is the third time he has begged for her love. Psychological movement has begun before the play opens, and it will continue after the play ends. Roseilli's vow of married celibacy—the last in a long series of resolutions—makes of him quite literally a "married Bachelour."[14] Hymen will not be triumphant. In other words, the restored order at the end of *Love's Sacrifice* is not a state of affairs that promises to promote happiness and prosperity for those who survive the crisis. Fiormonda's frustration will not end with the dénouement.

The exaltation of the heroine is even more forceful in *Love's Sacrifice* than in *'Tis Pity*, with the result that tragedy moves still further in the direction of romance. Both men, the repentant murderer and the devoted lover, come together for a final act of worship before they too must die. The unusually elaborate stage direction for this scene calls for an ostentatiously religious setting. We are asked to visualize a *"Tombe"* and a procession of religious officials bearing *"Torches"* while *"making shew of Ceremony"* (V.iii.2734–39). All of this to honour a woman who has now become, in the language of both votaries, a blessed saint and a martyr to love. Like Giovanni, Fernando helps to exalt his female deity by expressing the wish and the belief that he will rejoin her through death.

These lovers do not offer themselves for the cleansing and rejuvenation of society. In the act of death they themselves are reborn into a paradise of love which was quite out of reach on earth. As Fernando himself says, when the rumble of death threatens to cut off any possibility of earthly love:

> Let slaves in mind be servile to their feares,
> Our heart is high in-starr'd in brighter Spheres.
> (IV.ii.2338–39)

In aspiring to the hand of his best friend's wife, Fernando disturbs the balance of nature; and in the retaliatory movement of tragic action, both he and Biancha are sacrificed. But in baroque tragedy the hero's aspiration, far from ending with death, reaches out into the infinity beyond death, and beyond the formal conclusion of the tragic design. "The drama's conclusion," observes G. Wilson Knight, "leaves us feeling that what is denied on earth may yet be justified beyond."[15]

In *The Broken Heart* we see even more clearly than usual that the action which precipitates tragedy has upset the balance of nature. The crucial event occurs quite some time before the play begins, when Ithocles interrupts the happy betrothal of his sister, Penthea, and forces her to marry Bassanes instead of Orgilus. In her lucid madness Penthea sees this action for what it is: she calls Ithocles "an unnaturall brother" who has led a "miserable creature" to her "ruine" (III.ii.1178–79). The natural development of each major character is disrupted by this single defiance of the normal erotic urge.[16] Penthea is forced into an unnatural marriage with Bassanes; Orgilus must repress his natural instincts in the interests of social tranquillity; and Ithocles himself is unable to express his natural attraction for Calantha, ostensibly because she is a princess and thus his social superior, but more probably because his feelings of guilt will not permit him to plunge wholeheartedly into just the kind of love affair which he has so callously destroyed.

A frustrating deadlock inhibits love. Each of the characters is far too concerned about honour, far too obsessed with the idea of virtuous conduct, to be able to give vent to the perfectly natural feelings inside him. The ideal of chastity reaches the level of an obsession in Penthea's mind, and in spite of her technically correct behaviour she regards herself a dismal failure. One rape has sufficed to rob her of virginity, happiness, and honour. This over fastidious interpretation of personal honour is bound to arouse guilt feelings, as Penthea herself explains:

> For she that's wife to *Orgilus,* and lives
> In knowne Adultery with *Bassanes,*
> Is at the best a whore.
>
> (III.ii.1200–1202)

Penthea condemns herself in advance on all possible fronts. To forget about Orgilus and make some attempt to adjust to a married life, she regards as a dishonourable betrayal of her betrothal vows. To leave Bassanes for Orgilus would be to add one sin of adultery to another. And even if Bassanes were to die—fortuitously—Penthea sees no way out of the dilemma; she could not possibly disgrace Orgilus by yielding him "No better favours then a second bed" (II.iii.978). With a relentless logic all her own, Penthea goes to perverse extremes to exclude even the bare possibility of happiness. "Honour, / How much we fight with weaknesse to preserve thee," she laments (II.iii.1006–1007). Is honour worth it all, when the human costs are so great? In Penthea we see the tragedy of an "uncommonly good" woman. She sets impossible standards for herself; she upsets the balance of human nature by refusing to allow for even momentary lapses or even the slightest accommodation. Orgilus, deeply affected by Penthea's slavish worship of abstract virtue, fears that her "soft bosome" has "turn'd to marble" (II.iii.938).

This kind of strenuous inhibition, always justified by the catchword "honour," represses the natural instincts of the other young Spartans as well. For Ithocles the inhibiting force is heroic, military honour: he appears to be the sort of man who can sacrifice all personal connections to his professional interests. When he falls in love with Calantha he learns at last how deadening such honour can be; still, a false pride prevents him from approaching Calantha, until Penthea generously intercedes for him. Orgilus finds himself checkmated between two dishonourable alternatives. Not to avenge the "honour of our house" (III.iv. 1435) would be to neglect his duty, but to murder Penthea's brother would be a personal betrayal. Calantha's dignity sets her apart as the model of inherited honour. She is not accustomed to being treated as an equal, and even when she wishes to express love she speaks with the voice of a princess. She accepts Ithocles because "he deserves in all things / To be thought worthy mine" (IV.iii.2109–10).

Again we find oblique and suggestive relationships between major and minor characters, rather than direct comparison and contrast. Hemophil and Groneas, for example, tend to tarnish the concept of military honour represented by Ithocles. They play their biggest scene just after Ithocles has praised them as able soldiers, generously sharing with them the credit for this recent victory in battle. As soon as their leader's back is turned, Hemophil and Groneas try to seduce Christalla and Philema, though without success. "Spirit of valour / Is of a mounting nature," Groneas explains (I.ii.330–31). For these brave captains, the honour won in battle is coin to squander in the bedrooms of the court. This uninhibited behaviour seems utterly different from the dignified restraint of Ithocles; and yet, like his underlings, Ithocles undoubtedly uses military honour as a trump card in the suit to win his lady, Calantha.

Among the minor characters is the familiar figure of the pedant, Tecnicus, who is frequently mistaken for the *raisonneur* by critics who share his views.[17] Tecnicus suspects that something is troubling Orgilus, but instead of listening to the cry of frustration he delivers a long and tedious speech on the various kinds of honour (III.i.1069–89). This is just what Orgilus does not need, for he is already obsessed with the abstract ideal of honour and the duty of revenge. Tecnicus makes a great show of scholarship when it comes to interpreting the oracle (IV.i.1768–71), but he tells us nothing that is not already plain. And in the end this spokesman for "reall Honour" (III.i.1075) leaves for Delphos to avoid being caught in the political turbulence which he sees threatening the fate of Sparta.[18]

The character of Bassanes occupies a strange middle position between the tragic lovers at the centre of the play and the ineffectual buffoons around its fringes. He dwells with masochistic pleasure on the infinite opportunities for cuckoldry, and suspects his wife of incest when she stays too long in private conversation with her brother. "Poore Honour!" he cries, "thou art stab'd, and bleed'st to death" (II.i.598). Bassanes thinks of honour as little more than a technical weapon against cuckoldry. Yet, in his obsession with his honour as a husband he gradually comes to resemble the frustrated lovers with their equally subjective ideals of personal virtue. Like Penthea, Calantha, and Ithocles, Bassanes is bound to fail since he judges himself by the inflexible system of values constructed by his own distorted fantasy.

The thematic unity of *The Broken Heart* depends on this delicate shading of the various interpretations of honour. We do not have the clear polarities of *1 Henry IV*, with its schematic contrast between Hotspur's honour and Falstaff's cowardice, and the compromise in Prince Hal. There is no instance of clearly dishonourable action in *The Broken Heart*, and the examples of decidedly honourable behaviour are at least severely limited if not entirely discredited. Instead of a well-defined scale of values, *The Broken Heart* presents a bewildering variety of different impulses yoked together under the single name of "honour." Unity, under such circumstances, amounts to the atmospheric fusion of various elements by one motif.

At the narrative level, then, Ithocles upsets the balance of nature by worshipping the abstract virtue of honour at the expense of human happiness. Penthea, Orgilus, and Calantha repeat the pattern at the psychological level. But nature begins to assert herself again, and the second stage in the tragic action shows human emotion bursting past the artificial dams of honour and inhibition which the characters have built up within themselves. As Orgilus observes in a frequently quoted epigram, "Griefes will have their vent" (IV.i.1759).

Penthea is the first victim of the psychological retaliation of nature. She has kept her frustrations locked so firmly inside her that they simply must spill out. At last she admits that she really loves Orgilus to distraction, that she resents her troublesome husband, and that she hates her own brother for his unnatural action. Her most natural feelings, paradoxically, pour forth in the disguise of mad ravings. But Orgilus understands that her outbursts are much nearer the truth than they seem: "If this be madnesse, madnesse is an Oracle" (IV.ii.1940). The pressure of emotion and the resistance of inhibition meet in deadly combat, and Penthea becomes the first to die of a broken heart.

Penthea's death triggers off a chain reaction in which nature conquers the inhibitions of each of the remaining lovers. Orgilus succumbs to his natural desire for revenge. Ithocles learns to express his love. And even Calantha, whose dedication to the ideal of restraint lasts longest, pours out her griefs before she dies. She admits that her courageous dance was only a deception—that in fact the death of Ithocles has touched her so deeply that she too will die of grief.

After nature has taken her toll, we feel again that the heroes and heroines of this play are exalted by the language of martyrdom, as the action of baroque tragedy moves into its third phase. Penthea looks forward to the afterlife long before the crisis of death comes. "I must leave the world," she says without regret, "To revell [in] *Elizium*" (III.v.1616–17). The wish recalls Giovanni's vision of pagan happiness. Orgilus repeats the figure just before Penthea's death, as if to insist that the woman he worships will surmount the difficulties of life in triumph (IV.ii.1939). The "Soft sad musicke" (IV.iii.2174) which ushers Penthea's soul into this dream paradise is sacramental in tone. "*Burning Tapers*" (IV.iii.2176) provide a ritualistic glow for the apotheosis of love.

The most spectacular exaltation in death is reserved for Calantha. The final scene is set for ritual, much as it was in *Love's Sacrifice*. There is an "*Altar*" with "*Two lights of Virgin wax*," and the "*musicke of Recorders*" (V.iii.2509–10). Instead of the expected coronation ceremony, the guests are invited to share in the mysterious ritual of life-in-death. Calantha marries the "*livelesse Trunke*" (V.iii.2620) of her lover Ithocles, as if to imply that love will be reborn through death. The reins of state pass into Nearchus' competent hands, but this event seems almost too trivial to deserve notice. Nearchus himself recognizes that the transcendent passion of "these faithfull lovers" (V.iii.2624) has taken them far beyond the world of politics and social obligations. He treats Calantha not as a predecessor, but as a goddess: "Her last will / Shall never be digrest from" (V.iii.2622–23). And indeed Calantha's last will was to rejoin her lover and contracted husband. "Death shall not separate us" (V.iii.2586), she had said as she took his lifeless hand in marriage. This is more than the earthly union of hearts, which only death can untie. Calantha's marriage is living proof of the transcendent aspirations expressed in the words of her marriage hymn: "Love onely reignes in death" (V.iii.2613).

Even the most casual account of the structure of *Perkin Warbeck* would be bound to show that this is no history play of the typical renaissance variety. We are not concerned here with the "mighty monarchies" of English history (*Henry V*, Prologue, 20), but with the romantic quest of one man who believes himself a monarch. If Shakespeare's Henry plays are a practical lesson in kingship, *Perkin Warbeck* is an elaborate game of "let's pretend."

The hero is himself a pretender. Perkin must be either what he claims to be or an actor of consummate skill, so every piece of evidence that detracts from his legitimacy also adds to his stature as an actor. After his capture, when no hope remains for his political ambitions, Perkin does not break down. The English lords try to browbeat him into confessing wickedness and treason, but Perkin refuses to step out of character. Instead of complying he begins to recite his theory of politics, referring in particular to the events of Richard III's reign. Dawbney thinks this is sheer insolence; he wants Perkin silenced. But Henry is more evenhanded. "O let him range," says the king:

> The player's on the stage still, 'tis his part;
> A' does but act.
>
> (V.ii.2438–40)

The English camp finds the play-acting metaphor a useful device for describing Perkin on several other occasions. In his opening speech, for example, Henry calls Perkin a figure "Of pageant Majestie" and complains that the impostor treats him as if he were only "a mockery King" (I.i.169–70). Perkin first won his colours in Ireland, which to English taste is merely the "common stage of Noveltie" (I.i.273). In every case the theatrical metaphor is the English way of insisting that Perkin is a hoax. But there is a shift in tone as the play progresses. The words "pageant" and "common stage" in Henry's initial description recall the disreputable class of jongleurs and mimes of the early renaissance. In the speech from Act V, Henry shows much more respect for the acting profession; Perkin is the player still, but that is no reason to berate him. The actor has won the right to a serious hearing.

Another verbal pattern that helps to define the quality of pretence in this play is the recurrent use of the word "counterfeit." Henry uses the word to rally the political establishment against the impostor, deriding Perkin as "The *Flemish Counterfeit*," and "The Counterfeit King" (III.i.1200; V.i.2370). It is a contagious turn of phrase. Among the members of Henry's camp, Dawbney, Surrey, Clifford, and Lambert Simnel refer to Perkin as a counterfeit; they appear to have taken their cue from Henry's opening reference to Perkin's "new-coynd greatnesse" (I.i.169).

Perkin himself falls into the trap of using the minting metaphor, and although he is careful not to apply the term to his own claims, there is a hint of insecurity in his voice. Before going off into battle, Perkin wishes to assure Katherine that all will be well. "We will live," he says,

> by the lively test
> Of our owne bloud, to let the *Counterfeite*
> Be knowne the worlds contempt.
> (III.ii. 1481–84)

This is very strong language to use against the reigning king, and we can feel Katherine recoil from its ironic undertones. "Pray doe not use / That word," she responds; "it carries fate in't" (III.ii. 1485–86). Bare mention of illegitimacy of any kind arouses doubts even in Perkin's wife, and her distrust is hardly an argument in his favour. Katherine never wavers from the love she feels for Perkin as a man, nor does she delude herself into sharing his vision of majesty.

The next step in the psychological action occurs when similar symptoms of doubt appear in Perkin's own mind. Frion merely asks Perkin to regulate his temper, and an outburst follows:

> Y'ee make me mad, twere best (it seemes)
> That I should turne Imposter to *my selfe*,
> Be mine owne counterfeite.
> (IV.ii. 1818–20)

Perkin's volcano of angry rhetoric sounds only too much like an attempt to convince himself. He voices his own submerged doubts by attributing them to his adviser, and exorcises them by abusing the man as if he were a traitor. This episode contains more than a demonstration of Perkin's inability to accept criticism; it illustrates his insecurity, his oversensitivity, his repressed suspicions about his own claims.

But Perkin is not the only pretender. The unity of the play depends on subtle suggestions of pretence in almost every character. Heron, Astley, Sketon, and John a Water are the most obvious extensions of the pretending theme; they play Perkin's game with him, though not with the master's skill. Sketon, for example, pretends to give grave counsel on matters of state, but his language falls short of the courtly idiom: "he that threeds his needle with the sharpe eyes of industrie, shall in time goe through-stitch, with the new suite of preferment" (II.iii.1092–94). Where Perkin could move the Scottish court with the language of kingship, Sketon's homespun analogies betray the renegade tailor who hides beneath the courtier's pretensions. In fact, all of Perkin's underlings are charlatans rather than revolutionaries; among them, only Frion can play his part with enough sophistication to be a valuable supporting actor.

James's chivalry is another mode of pretending. James is proud of his own compassion, so he welcomes Perkin into his protection with considerable smugness, and seems to imagine that Perkin is a wandering knight who has come to his castle for temporary succour. James offers one of the prime Scottish damsels to the visitor, takes his army out in search of the guest's enemies, and generously ventures his own person in single combat for Perkin's sake. Then he decides that the game has gone quite far enough. So long as Perkin serves the political aspirations of the Scottish camp, James treats him as a fellow gentleman in arms; but once these political goals have been achieved, Perkin finds little sympathy among the Scots. With a great show of knightly friendship and courtesy, James politely dismisses Perkin from his kingdom and from all chances of making good the claim to the English throne.

Even Henry, who fancies himself a realist, can stoop to using pretence where it is needed. The very system of diplomacy he uses to bring about his realistic programs depends on ruses and espionage. Henry relies especially on Durham, because Durham is clever enough to outfox the enemy. He welcomes the arrival of Hialas, because an opportunity to send the Spanish emissary as an undercover agent to the Scottish court excites his sense of diplomacy. Such pretences Henry can understand and condone by calling them "policie" (III.iii.1520). Still more disturbing is Henry's reaction to the news that the Earl of Warwick's life is the only obstacle blocking an advantageous marriage between his son and the Spanish Infanta. Henry ruminates for a moment when this report reaches him, and then calls for a messenger. He gives no direct indication of his plans, but in Act V we learn that Warwick is to be executed, presumably for helping Perkin to escape from prison. Urswick, who explains the case, says noncommittally that Warwick's head "must pay the price" for the attempted prison break (V.ii.2569). Perkin declares that Warwick is innocent, and in the spirit of martyrdom takes all the blame upon himself. There is a lingering suspicion that the charges against Warwick have been trumped up, and hidden under the cloak of Henry's "policie."

At another level of diplomacy, Henry exploits the pretence of the Tudor myth for his own ends.[19] He loses no opportunity to describe the stability of his position on the throne in quasi-mythical terms:

> A guard of Angells, and the holy prayers
> Of loyall Subjects are a sure defence
> Against all force and Counsaile of Intrusion.
>
> (I.i.240–42)

Here is establishment propaganda at its best. Henry knows full well that his guard is made up of powerful nobles and court informers; he does not need Perkin to remind him that he won the crown on Bosworth field. He is capable of barking out a military briefing with precision and firmness, only to add a sentimental postscript: "Heaven is our guard still" (II.ii.967). It is curious that he should use the same terms as his enemy, the counterfeit, does. Perkin claims to have passed through strange lands in safety, "Protected in our Innocence by Heaven" (II.i.727).

Ford's introductory comments in the Epistle Dedicatory and Prologue to *Perkin Warbeck* indicate that he set out, quite consciously, to revive the history play as the renaissance knew it. But his artistic principles were so different from Marlowe's or Shakespeare's that he created instead a baroque history play. He abandoned the renaissance principle of co-ordinating opposites, and instead subordinated his matter to one dominant motif. In *Richard II*, a renaissance play about kingship, the claims of the reigning monarch and the claims of the aspirant are held in careful, contrasting balance. Richard's emblem of fortune's buckets, one rising while the other falls (IV.i.184–89), stands for the structure of the play itself: rival claims are weighed in the balance of poetic action. In *Perkin Warbeck* the dice are loaded from the start in Henry's favour, and there is no real discussion about rival claims. Perkin does not betray his pretence, but he certainly does not establish his authenticity either. The emphasis here is not on balanced conflict between protagonist and antagonist, between York and Lancaster; rather, it is on the powerful suggestive possibilities of the pretence itself. Perkin's pretence is so complete and so absorbing that he subordinates the minor pretenders to himself. The play becomes a demonstration of the miracle of deception, rather than a study in the givens of history. Facing death, the impostor can cry out in victory because the moment of martyrdom gives him a majesty denied to Henry and James. These earthbound kings are interesting only as minor actors on the stage through which Perkin has "ranged."

Politically, the action of *Perkin Warbeck* is inconclusive. We do not learn whether or not Henry manages to cement his cherished alliance with Spain. We do not see the repercussions of Warwick's execution. There is no assurance that Henry will no longer be "haunted" or "pursued" by problems and challenges to authority (I.i.167). Yet in *Richard III*—the very play that presents the accession of Henry VII and the birth of the Tudor dynasty—we do feel a major chord cadence. Henry sounds it himself, as he promises to unite "the White Rose and the Red," as he predicts the end of "civil wounds" (V.v.19, 40). The Elizabethan audience could endorse a view of history that promised order after chaos; for them Henry VII was the father of a prosperous royal line. But for a Caroline audience, much less convinced of the stability of kingship, Henry VII's place in history was open to reassessment.

Henry Richmond's closing speech in *Richard III* sets political matters to rest, and at the same time creates the impression that the play is formally closed. A much older Henry Richmond fails to close either political cases or artistic form at the end of *Perkin Warbeck*. He ends the play with a platitude about purging the body politic of "corrupted bloud" (V.iii.2784). It is not an entirely convincing simile in this context, for Perkin has not discredited himself. Katherine still loves him, and acknowledges him in spite of disgrace as her husband. Even Henry must admit Perkin's bravery. Death is a victory of personal insight, even deluded personal insight, over establishment propaganda. The psychological movement begun by Perkin will not end arbitrarily. In a history play, of all places, one expects a social rebirth at the end of the action, and this indeed is what occurs in the typically closed form of the renaissance history play.[20] But in *Perkin Warbeck*, martyrdom is an event with no political or social significance; like so many of Ford's lovers, Perkin and Katherine isolate themselves from society as they are remarried symbolically at the edge of the tomb. It is Perkin's unbroken spirit, and not the general good, that is reborn through suffering and death.

Ford's tendency to reshape the conventions of renaissance tragedy and history in the direction of romance can be clearly observed in plays like *Love's Sacrifice* and *Perkin Warbeck*. Surprisingly, it is more difficult to demonstrate a similar structural transformation in the group of plays variously called comedies or tragicomedies. *The Lover's Melancholy*, *The Lady's Trial*, and *The Queen* are certainly "romantic" plays in many respects, but so are a great many English comedies from Peele to Shirley. *The Old Wives' Tale* and the love plot of *Friar Bacon and Friar Bungay* advertise their indebtedness to the legends and folk romances of medieval tradition;[21] the plays of Shakespeare's last phase, especially *The Tempest* and *The Winter's Tale*, achieve a far more mature blend of comedy and romance. In addition, the tragicomic pattern of Beaumont and Fletcher is derived in large measure from the labyrinthine dilemmas of love in popular prose romances.[22] As a result of this pervasive influence of romance on comic form, it would appear that Ford is much less innovative in the tragi-comedies than in tragic and historical drama. Yet, there are important differences between the playful delicacy of renaissance comedy and the nostalgic illusions of Ford's tragicomic world.

One of the most popular of all renaissance plays, *A Most Pleasant Comedie of Mucedorus*,[23] seems almost to have been written with the express purpose of illustrating the typical action of renaissance comedy. The formula is particularly clear because there is so little else. The plot is a boy-meets-girl story. Mucedorus, the young prince of Valencia, disguises himself as a shepherd in order to court Amadine, the princess of nearby Aragon. But the King of Aragon has already decided that his daughter must marry one of his nobles, Segasto. To prevent this unwanted match, Amadine hides out in the forest with Mucedorus. Segasto pursues them, discovers the lovers' hideout, and returns them to the court of Aragon. At the crucial moment, Mucedorus reveals that he is not a mere shepherd, but a neighbouring prince in disguise. This is enough to change the King's mind; he gives his daughter to Mucedorus, and even Segasto applauds the match.

The popularity of *Mucedorus* may have been due in part to the prestige of its source—Sir Philip Sidney's *Arcadia*—but more probably its appeal rested on the bold and barefaced use of all the standard conventions of renaissance comedy. It should come as no surprise, then, to discover that Frye's outline of the typical structure of renaissance comedy reads almost like a scenario for *Mucedorus*. "The normal action," Frye writes, "is the effort of a young man to get possession of a young woman who is kept from him by various social barriers: her low birth, his minority or shortage of funds, parental opposition, the prior claims of a rival."24 Segasto's claim to Amadine's hand, and the King of Aragon's opposition, stand in the way of a marriage between Mucedorus and Amadine. So far we are on familiar ground. The impediments to love are "circumvented," Frye continues, and betrothal or marriage at the end of the play, accompanied by a festive atmosphere of banquet and dance, stands for the birth of a new society. In *Mucedorus* the lovers escape the harsh laws of Aragon by hiding in the forest, and circumvent punishment by announcing at the end that Mucedorus is really a prince, who thus has the comic right to abduct princesses so long as everything turns out properly in the end. The action closes with the King inviting everyone to a marriage celebration. Frye adds that the blocking characters of the old society—the very people who stand in the way of the love match—usually experience a "change of heart." Again, as if following Frye's recipe, the author of *Mucedorus* ensures that both the parental King and the rival Segasto are reconciled to the marriage. Segasto goes so far as to volunteer his services to prepare the wedding entertainments. Since Mucedorus and Amadine are prince and princess of Valencia and Aragon respectively, their marriage becomes a variation on the union of two noble houses theme which, for Elizabethan audiences, would naturally suggest the birth of a new society.25

The normal action of renaissance comedy, if Frye's description and the *Mucedorus* paradigm can be taken as evidence, produces closed artistic form. The first scene brings the lovers into contact for the first time, and the last scene brings them together permanently in marriage, while conveniently disposing of the obstacles that stood in their way. The same may not be said of Ford's tragicomedies, where the normal action produces open form. In *The Lover's Melancholy*, the action that precipitated the frustration of the three pairs of lovers occurred some two years before the play formally begins. It is no longer external circumstances, but psychological factors in the characters themselves that prevent the birth of the new society of love. And although the play ends with an invitation to a "generall Feast" (V.i.2724), one suspects that the marriage celebrations are only the first step toward resolving the continuing problems of the psychology of love.

The representative of the old society in *The Lover's Melancholy* is Agenor, the now deceased Prince of Famagosta in Cyprus. Sophronos indicates at the beginning of Act II that the present political ills of Cyprus stem from Agenor's attempt to abduct Eroclea, and of course the very same action has produced the maze of misunderstandings in which the lovers of Famagosta are currently lost. Palador and Eroclea were contracted lovers, so Agenor's designs had the added stigma of the cruel parental decree. Meleander and Rhetias have circumvented the plot by disguising Eroclea as a boy and sending her to Corinth. Only her safe return can restore the natural balance required before all of the couples can be paired-off to satisfaction.

By the principles of renaissance construction, Eroclea's return would be the automatic signal for the festive dénouement, but for Ford it is only the beginning. It would have been possible, of course, to begin the play with a scene contrasting Palador's love and Agenor's lust, to move on to the attempted rape and the flight to Greece, and to conclude with reconciliation and a change of heart on Agenor's part. Such a play would have followed the young love, parental opposition, and circumvention formula of renaissance comedy. But Ford gives us the normal renaissance comic action only through exposition; he opens the form of his play by beginning with an emotional movement that is already well under way.

This shift in structural strategy means that the emphasis will fall on psychological rather than external conflict. The social barriers preventing love have already been removed by the death of Agenor and the accession of Palador; the obstacles that now stand in the way of happiness are the various forms of delusion and imbalance in the lovers themselves. Palador is obsessed with his own melancholy, as the counsellors of state repeatedly warn. Sophoronos thinks his prince is "too indulgent" to the whims of his "owne affections" (II.i.660–61). According to Aretus, the young prince does not even hope for a change of fortune, because his melancholy is "so wrapt up in selfe-love" (II.i.668). Corax argues that Palador should be a man, but is "In manners and effect indeed a childe" (II.i.674). The "Masque of Melancholy" is designed ostensibly to show the prince how foolish and self-indulgent his obsession with melancholy is, but instead it caters to his weakness by reminding him of Eroclea. There is no usurping tyrant, no favoured rival, no recalcitrant father to prevent erotic fulfilment in this play; instead, as Corax observes, "Love is the Tyrant of the heart" (III.ii.1686).

The other lovers show similar symptoms. Cleophila's obsessive preoccupation with her father's illness prevents her from taking an independent position as woman and wife. Like a child, she waits on Meleander hand and foot; she asserts no will of her own. From this immature point of view there is "more content" in misery than in the prospect of happiness (II.ii.958–61). Near the end of the play Cleophila begins to suspect that she has been misled by a "mistaken duty" to her father (V.i.2258), and at this point she has grown up sufficiently to assume her true role as wife to Amethus. Menaphon thinks that his love for Thamasta is blocked on social grounds; he suspects his mistress of class snobbery because of his comparatively low birth. Actually, Thamasta is another victim of self-delusion. Parthenophill brings out her romantic desire for the handsome youth who will carry her off into an idyllic pastoral world, and only sexual reality forces her to recognize the mistake. Again in Thamasta's case it is a psychological block (and not a blocking character) that must be dealt with before reconciliation and marriage may occur.

The emphasis on psychology throws a slightly skeptical shadow over the play's artificially neat ending. Prince Palador hastily distributes the hands of the lovers in the accepted fashion, and announces that "Sorrowes are chang'd to Bride-songs" (V.i.2726). Given the postulates of renaissance structure, this alone would be enough to close the case once and for all. We do not worry about what will happen to Segasto and the King of Aragon after *Mucedorus* ends, because we have not been invited to consider them in psychological terms. There is no nagging suspicion that they will change their minds and send anonymous threatening letters to the newly wedded lovers. In *The Lover's Melancholy* we have been asked to look at the problems of love in psychological terms; we have seen a process of maturing, but not a sudden leap to perfection. The blocking characters of renaissance comedy are deceived or converted instantaneously by a clever sleight of hand, but the tyrant of the heart may be won over only "by degrees" (IV.iii.2182). Melander lives on at the end of the play, as sad and self-pitying as ever; marriage will be a test of Cleophila's ability to play the role of woman instead of regressing to the role of child. Palador himself suggests in his closing speech that only part of the problem has reached solution, that the lovers must simply "Leave the rest to time" (V.i.2719). The formal conclusion of the play is ruthlessly arbitrary when considered from a psychological point of view. Palador's closing comment might stand as a reminder of the open form typical of the baroque style.

The structural problem of unity remains much the same in comedy, since again it is a matter of drawing relationships between multiple plots or spheres of action. *Mucedorus*, for example, contains a subplot which features a highwayman-ogre called Bremo. This character lurks in the forest, waiting for opportunities to ravish virgins and murder young princes. Amadine and Mucedorus are of course ideal prey for him, but by using their wits and Bremo's own weapon, the lovers manage to kill their assailant. Bremo is the *idiotes* of the play.[26] Like Malvolio or Jaques he stands opposed to the spirit of festivity. He is a structural device rather than a character, for his function is to act as the focus of the anticomic mood. Again the transparent use of conventions in *Mucedorus* makes the point particularly clear. The Induction which opens the play pictures a debate between the rival spirits of Comedy and Envy; each of them contends that he is going to control the action. Envy says he will do his very worst to spoil matters, but Comedy assures us that the festive mood will prevail. In the Epilogue the argument is resumed, and Envy is forced to concede at least a temporary setback. The two moods of comedy and anticomedy are brought into a co-ordinate relationship with one another; the festive world and the sullen world are allowed to compete on equal terms.

In *The Lover's Melancholy* it is once again the young lovers who stand at the centre of the action, although in this case there are three couples. The other characters and episodes are subordinated to the main action, as we should by now expect. There is Cuculus, for example, the fop who intends to start a new fashion by advertising his "female" page, Grilla, as the newest thing in the courtier's list of necessary appendages. Cuculus stands in oblique relationship to the lovers of the main plot. He is outside the romantic world in one sense, for he is not really serious about any of the supposed mistresses he courts (III.i. 1136–1200). He is far too busy with his own foppish image to be an effective lover. On the other hand, Cuculus becomes a great deal like the central characters insofar as he too allows love to delude him. Like Thamasta, he makes a fool of himself by courting a disguised member of his own sex. Since Cuculus is not an independently exciting character, his fopperies become important only as subordinate versions of the theme of love's folly.

The "Masque of Melancholy" stands in a similar subordinate relationship to the main action. Critics have often pointed out that Corax does not really need this slightly pedantic device to discover what is wrong with Prince Palador.[27] Indeed, the masque need not be taken too seriously as psychological dogma, for it is a structural mechanism rather than a scientific treatise. Various forms of melancholy are impersonated, such as the "strange fury" called wanton melancholy (III.ii.1666) which may provoke women into a frenzied three-day dance.

Love-melancholy is not represented in the masque, Corax explains, because art lacks the powers "To personate the shadow of that Fancy" (III.ii.1676). Two forms of love, the most animalistic and the most rarefied, have been brought together under the single heading of melancholy. The two types are in fact fused in *The Lover's Melancholy*, for in practice they become virtually indistinguishable. In a renaissance comedy they would have been carefully separated as primitive lust (Bremo's view) and civilized love (Mucedorus' view). In addition to this thematic fusion, there is an important structural fusion which merges the play itself and the masque under one governing motif. Both the play and the masque within the play are about the "rare delusions" (IV.iii.2069) which melancholy lovers must suffer. The figure of wanton melancholy in the masque is a partial explanation for the illusion of love, supplemented by Corax's discursive presentation of love-melancholy. In the same way, the main action combines the sexuality of the mating impulse with the aspirations of noble and refined love. When the two opposite poles merge, the love relationship becomes potentially a "Heaven on earth" (V.i.2338). And although Corax must admit that he lacks the literary gifts required to dramatize love-melancholy in its highest form, the play as a whole demonstrates that Ford has succeeded where Corax fails.

In almost every case, the titles of Ford's plays act as master keys to the riddles of structural design. Frequently the full significance of these titles is obscured by modern conventions of spelling and punctuation. *The Lovers Melancholy*, for example, is the form of the title used for this play in its first edition; for no obvious reason this has been consistently modernized as *The Lover's Melancholy*, although *The Lovers' Melancholy* is equally probable. The plural form has the advantage of suggesting a motif that extends to all of the lovers in the play. A similar case may be made for *The Ladies' Trial* as an alternative to the usual modern form, *The Lady's Trial*. The vagaries of seventeenth-century printing and typography would allow for either rendering of the original title, *The Ladies Triall*. The singular form puts all the emphasis on the main plot—the controversy surrounding Spinella's reputation. The plural form extends the testing motif to the other ladies of the play—especially Levidolche and Amoretta.

The issue at stake in all three spheres of action is the virtue of feminine chastity in its broadest definition. Any suspicion of unchaste behaviour acts as a blocking feature; that is, it prevents the happy union of lovers toward which the action of comedy moves. *The Lady's Trial* offers a way of circumventing such suspicions in order to arrive again at a moderately festive conclusion.

Auria is not a jealousy-prone madman; his dramatic ancestors are not Corvino and Bassanes, but Othello and Caraffa. Auria is simply a good husband who is a little too credulous. He places too much faith in the testimony of his best friend, Aurelio, and like the characters in *The Broken Heart*, he puts too much stress on the social virtue of reputation. Auria returns to Genoa after a short absence, only to find his wife missing and his honour as a husband in question. His natural instincts tell him to trust Spinella and be patient, but his sense of social propriety—catalyzed by Aurelio's strident voice—convinces him that Spinella's virtue must be put on trial. He arranges what amounts to an inquest into the death of his honour; with forced calm he listens to Aurelio's version of the story, then to Adurni's.

When Spinella begins to speak the courtroom analogy breaks down, for Spinella does not cite a single fact in her own defence. She begins by addressing her husband directly and passionately: "my Lord, my Lord" (V.ii.2489). Since he is determined to be suspicious, she argues, since he will count only legally verifiable fact as evidence, reconciliation is impossible. She invites Auria either to avenge his presumed wrong or to abandon her. Then comes the greatest stroke of eloquence Spinella can muster. She faints. Where legalistic trifling could not succeed, psychological warfare does: "Thou hast conquerd," Auria admits (V.ii.2498). He has learned that chastity is not a quantity to be discovered in legal debate, but a quality of character that must be taken on trust.

Benatzi and Levidolche learn a similar lesson about the nature of chastity. Like Auria, Benatzi has left his wife and home because of economic necessities; like Spinella, Levidolche has been courted while her husband is away; in both cases, the man who sues for the love of the married woman is Adurni. While Spinella remains firmly chaste, Levidolche gives in. Thus far we appear to be in the domain of renaissance comedy, where balanced parallelism between comic and anticomic moods is the usual procedure. But in fact there is no neat antithesis between the Spinella plot and the Levidolche plot. On the one hand, Levidolche's story is not allowed to develop into a fully independent action. We hear various rumours about Levidolche's wantonness, particularly from her enraged uncle Martino, but the rest of her story must be pieced together from scattered and cryptic references throughout the play, and from the scene of reconciliation between herself and Benatzi. In the development of the theme of forgiveness lies the second indication of the peculiar status of this subplot. Levidolche and Benatzi are reconciled and enter a new marriage, just as Auria and Spinella do. Benatzi must go even further than Auria in learning to take matters on trust: he must accept Levidolche's confession, forgive her sins of the past, and take her promise of future fidelity on faith. Both comic and anticomic tendencies are present in the Auria-Spinella story, just as both tendencies are equally present in the Benatzi-Levidolche story. *The Lady's Trial* is not a collision between two different worlds, but a fusion of two similar worlds that blend into one motif.

The play concludes with the usual call to festivity in celebration of the multiple marriages, but the tone in which Auria makes the invitation is unusual:

> Command doth limit us short time for revells,
> Wee must be thrifty in them.
>
> (V.ii.2645–46)

Such frugality would have been thought ridiculous in a renaissance setting, especially if spoken by a hero who had just made his fortune in the Moorish wars. Any self-respecting renaissance entertainer under these circumstances would promise to outdo all his predecessors where revels are concerned, in keeping with the principles of closed comic form. The new society that is born at the end of a renaissance comedy is not subject to the restrictions of the old society, and as a result virtues like thrift become irrelevant. Old complications are forgotten in symbolic and idealized festivity.

Auria has a much more difficult problem on his hands. He must rejoice in the four marriages that end *The Lady's Trial*, while at the same time suggesting that the problems posed by married life are likely to continue. The first of these marriages is his own. He has been emotionally estranged from his wife, and reconciliation occurs through symbolic remarriage. His first marriage to Spinella was a reckless commitment of passion prompted by Spinella's superficial attractiveness, if we may credit Aurelio's description of the match (I.i.295–306). Auria's problems, like Caraffa's in *Love's Sacrifice*, have been the result of too chivalric a view of marriage. His new marriage must place less emphasis on external symbols and more on emotional needs, if Auria is to avoid further eruptions of jealousy and mistrust. Benatzi and Levidolche have been literally estranged, so their remarriage is a second cause for celebration. Levidolche has already affirmed that forgiveness and penance are not simple actions of the moment, but attitudes that must be carried through life if the new marriage is to be a fruitful one.

Then there are the first-time marriages to round out the celebrations. Auria gives the hand of Castanna, Spinella's sister, to Adurni—the very man who tried to seduce Spinella. Both partners agree to the match, though as Spinella remarks, "The courtship's somewhat quick" (V.ii.2518). Adurni observed earlier that Spinella's shining virtue taught him what he never knew before about the beauty of chastity; no doubt he will have further lessons to learn from the second of this "paire of sisters faire and matchlesse" (V.ii.2481). Amoretta, who has spent her scenes in the play flirting pretentiously with various fops whom she supposes to be dukes or grandees, will marry the witty servant Futelli. Even this lisping maid has learned something about the nature of chastity. Futelli's pranks have shown her how foolish her pretensions to grandeur were, and she is now willing to settle her loyalties on one man whom she values for his merits rather than his titles. This last relationship will not bear very penetrating psychological analysis, perhaps, but it does fit the broader pattern suggested by the other couples. Marriage, even for Amoretta and Futelli, will be a continuing process of learning.

The baroque quality of this dénouement may be further explained by comparison with the ending of Shakespeare's most conventional comedy in the renaissance style, *The Two Gentlemen of Verona*. This play closes with a series of marvellous theatrical surprises, none of which undermines the spirit of celebration. Valentine resigns his claim to Silvia, only to have Julia outwit him and restore Silvia to his embrace. Proteus renounces his "one error" (V.iv.112) of inconstancy, and accepts Julia's love at last. Thurio very sensibly admits that his attempts at courtship have been misguided, and the Duke distributes a general pardon that includes even the outlaws. The festive events announced at the close will celebrate a new world which corresponds to the lovers' desires. "I have my wish for ever," Proteus can declare with confidence. Julia's response is simply affirmative: "And I mine" (V.iv.119–20). Impediments to love are a thing of the past at the close of *The Two Gentlemen*. But in the open form of baroque tragicomedy, the psychological movement set up by the action of the play lives on. A new world has been created at the end of *The Lady's*

Trial, but it is new only in so far as the characters have learned from the experiences of the old one. It is a psychological extension of the action, and not an idealized *volte-face*. Auria will be the governor of Corsica in this new world. This is surely an advance on the near bankruptcy of his earlier position, but it is still a situation that carries responsibilities. Auria must learn to govern wisely, just as Adurni, Amoretta, and the other lovers must learn to live well. If renaissance comedy closes when happiness has become actual, baroque tragicomedy ends with happiness as, at most, a potentiality.

The full title of *The Queen, or the Excellency of her Sex* again furnishes a leading clue to the structure of the play. The subtitle may be read simply as a modifying tag: the Queen is the paragon of feminine excellence. Or it may be a statement of theme: this play is about the Queen, and also about the excellent nature of the sex to which she belongs. The second way of reading the subtitle adds a level of irony, because one chief concern of the play is to question renaissance assumptions about the excellency of the female sex. Unlike the figureheads of Petrarchan poetry, the Queen is not a static creature around whom the lover's world must endlessly revolve. Rather, she is a woman dynamically involved in the battle of the sexes.[28]

Alphonso's barefaced misogyny puts the battle into motion. He rejects the Queen's love not out of personal antipathy, but simply because she is a woman. He hates her sex "in general" (I.i.386). The obstacle that prevents erotic fulfilment is once again presented in psychological terms; something within Alphonso's own personality stirs up his hatred for the female sex, and banishes the Queen from his bed even after he has consented to marry her. Muretto further complicates matters by inducing sexual jealousy in his master's mind, until Alphonso fears that he has been cuckolded before he has consummated his marriage. Such humiliation is intolerable, so Alphonso determines to humiliate in turn the woman who has made him suffer. His tactics in this sexual war are rather crude: he publicly accuses his wife of infidelity, and prepares a scaffold with every intention of executing her. The Queen remains calm despite the threats to her reputation and her person, but she does fight back. "Y'are men," she says to her advisers, "and men (O me) are all unkinde" (II.ii.1273–74). Following Alphonso's lead, she draws the lines of battle along the great sexual divide. Men fight with weapons of cruelty; she will respond with submissive humility. The stance of submission is of course genuine, but it is also an extremely effective way of fighting. The Queen's tactics amount to something like passive resistance; by rendering good for evil she will heap coals of fire upon her enemy's head.

The relationship between Velasco and Salassa also follows the battle of the sexes pattern. Velasco offers his love to Salassa in the true chivalric spirit, while she returns his love with crucial reservations. She is "jealous" of his masculine spirit of valour and of his opportunities to perform heroic actions (II.iii.1474–76). Since Velasco is a warrior and a general, both his character and his occupation symbolize male domination. Salassa is a widow, so presumably she has already learned what it means to be dominated by a man, and she is not eager to take on the submissive female role again. She orders Velasco to give up fighting, even in self-defence, for a period of two years. The conditions are odious to him, but he accepts them because they outline the only way for him to prove his love to Salassa's satisfaction. Through the device of the love trial, Salassa has cleverly reversed the sexual roles. For once she finds herself in the dominant position; Velasco must submit his will to hers, just as he must submit his strength to the abuse of every choleric groom who cares to pick a quarrel with him. Only by divesting himself of the very qualities that define his masculinity—courage, authority, and strength—can Velasco become a worthy lover.

The method by which Ford integrates the two spheres of action is again an instance of baroque fusion. In both principal plots, the ambivalent emotions of the major characters produce a merger of comic and anticomic moods. From the Queen's point of view, Alphonso is both the desired love object and the source of frustration. His love is the only road to happiness, and his stubborn rejection of her is the only threat to happiness. From Alphonso's point of view it is the Queen who blends comedy and anticomedy into an ambiguous combination. She is desirable, and yet she is tainted; she holds forth the promise of happiness in love, only to clap him with the cuckold's horns. Velasco finds himself in a similar dilemma, for just when his lady begins to respond to love, she promptly jettisons him into military and social disgrace. And Salassa feels the opposite emotional charges of love and jealousy active within her whenever she encounters Velasco.

In renaissance comedy the impulse toward fulfilled love and the destructive impulse that blocks love are usually embodied in distinct and separate characters or symbols. Matthew Merrygreek crystallizes the festive mood, and Ralph Roister Doister is the anticomic *idiotes* who has to be defeated before Custance and Gawin Goodluck are united. In Gascoigne's *Supposes*, a hero called Erostrato takes on the role of festive entertainer himself, every time he disguises himself as the clever slave Dulippo; meanwhile a respectable and wealthy suitor, Cleander, focuses the anticomic mood. In Ford's tragicomedy, through a process of psychological blending, these opposed tendencies are fused within the hearts of the lovers themselves. Comedy and envy are no longer prologue puppets who compete for mastery over the play; they have become warring factions within the minds and souls of those who struggle with the complex emotion of love. Alphonso's misogyny is the strongest anticomic tendency in *The Queen*, and yet it is he who invites everyone to join in "*Hymen's Feasts*" (V.ii.3784–85). The romantic lead and the blocking character are fused, in order to show how similar the opposite impulses of love and hatred may be. Almada, a neutral attendant who has the right to be a commentator, notices the ambiguity of Alphonso's attitude toward the Queen. "'Tis strange my Lord," observes Almada, "Your love should seem so mighty in your hatred" (V.ii.3389–91).

The inconclusive ending of *The Queen* indicates again Ford's predilection for open artistic form. Alphonso's harsh treatment of his servants, for example, interrupts the festive atmosphere with a peculiar note of discord. Bufo and Pynto noisily enter for the last time, and insistently tell their own ludicrous stories of frustrated love. Bufo complains that he was almost tricked into marrying Mopas, disguised as a woman. Pynto is angry because Shaparoon, whom he took to be a lady of the court, has turned out to be nothing but an "ugly bawde" (V.ii.3762). Both men demand justice. Alphonso responds by banishing them forever from his sight: he divests them of the courtly clothing they have recently acquired, and then turns them out of doors. This harsh judgment seems not to be justified by anything Bufo and Pynto have done earlier; indeed, it tells us more about Alphonso's character than about his foolish servants. To Alphonso, Bufo and Pynto are reminders of his own rash attempts to dethrone the female tyrant. Pynto's complaint against the "ugly bawde" in particular recalls the ease with which Alphonso could once rail at women. The new king recognizes that his struggle to be a wise monarch and a good husband will be no easy task. He banishes Bufo and Pynto because they are symbols of his own follies, because they stand for the chaotic scheme of values against which he must continually fight.

Lodovico and Herophil will be a minor couple in the feast of Hymen that is to follow the play. Ordinarily marriage is a symbol of new order, and marriage partners frequently state this view in one way or another. Lodovico is not so sure. "If in the end we make long work," he says, "and beget a race of mad-caps, we shall but do as our fathers and mothers did" (V.ii.3750–52). Lodo-vico's view holds open the possibility that marriage will merely produce another generation of chaos; at best it will be only a way of keeping the madness of sexual jealousy under control. Above all, the very concept of the relationship between the sexes as a battle is a dynamic view of things—a view which resists definition in static terms. The principal lovers in *The Queen* do not look forward into vistas of unchanging bliss, for they define the future, on the basis of past experience, as a struggle. "I hope," says Velasco, "Our faults shall be redeem'd" (V.ii.3856–57). And Alphonso uses the same tentative term as he closes the play:

> Thus after storms a calm
> Is ever welcomest: Now we have past
> The worst, and all I hope is well at last.
>
> (V.ii.3872–75)

In general, the action of Ford's tragicomedy may be described as a movement toward reconciliation. At the beginning of each play we have a state of happiness already achieved, represented by marriage in *The Lady's Trial* and *The Queen*, by betrothal in *The Lover's Melancholy*. But some form of madness or emotional imbalance threatens to destroy happiness. The threat is real enough to lead to symbolic death in each case: Spinella swoons away into a lifeless state, Eroclea is thought to be dead by those who love her, and both the Queen and Salassa are rescued from the scaffold at the last possible instant. The process of rebirth thus carries the suggestion of symbolic resurrection. The new life which emerges in each case is the result of the characters' confrontation with the nightmare of death and deprivation. In renaissance comedy the usual conflict between youth and age leads to the creation of a world where youth triumphs and desire is fulfilled. In Ford's tragicomedy the lovers appear older and wiser as they struggle with the complexities and ambiguities of love itself. His romantic couples lack the freshness and spontaneity of renaissance lovers, because they move through a progress of estrangement which leads to the edge of death, and at length to reconciliation and remarriage.

In one crucial respect, at least, the pattern of action typical of Ford's tragicomedies marks a shift which brings comedy closer to the conventions of romance. The clue may be found in Denis de Rougemont's description of the archetypal romance, the story of Tristan and Iseult. The obstructions that keep these lovers apart are, says de Rougemont, "in one sense arbitrary." Tristan and Iseult are in love with being in love, so the absence of the love object acts as a stimulus to the kind of passion they value most. "*Thus*," de Rougemont concludes, "*the partings of the lovers are dictated by their passion itself*."[29] The action of renaissance comedy ensures that impediments to love are real by anchoring them in the vested interests of the old society. The satiric world of mannerist comedy, best represented by Jonson and Marston, magnifies these obstacles to gigantic proportions, until it becomes difficult to believe that love will achieve any genuine triumph over the rampantly evil society. In Beaumont and Fletcher's tragicomedies, where "satire and romance exist side by side," the "bad dream" of evil may be dispelled by a triumphantly romantic ending.[30] With Ford, the obstacles to erotic fulfilment are removed entirely from the objective world and transplanted into the subjective experience of the lovers; the separations between the protagonists in *The Lover's Melancholy*, *The Lady's Trial*, and *The Queen* depend respectively on the delusions of melancholy, jealousy, and misogyny. This shift toward internal conflict has the effect of throwing special emphasis on the turbulent emotional states that love induces, just as the arbitrary separations between Tristan and Iseult promote endless discussion and examination of romantic passion. In this important though restricted sense, the renewed psychological emphasis of the baroque style again motivates a structural transformation in the direction of romance.

The Fancies Chaste and Noble stands apart from Ford's other tragicomedies, because it includes a much stronger satiric flavour and thereby closely resembles many of the Beaumont and Fletcher plays. Unity in *The Fancies* is largely a matter of atmosphere, for the regular design of renaissance comedy has disappeared entirely, or at least it is so cleverly disguised that even the audience is deceived. Romantic love in this play is not so much an end in itself, as a means to an end. To put it crudely, love has become a commodity that is bought and sold; the world of *The Fancies* resembles a house of prostitution.

Troylo-Savelli opens the play with a frank though ironic statement of the bawdyhouse view of life. People who succeed, he tells Livio, are people who can put a price on love. Then he lists several examples from his experience of men who acted as bawds for their own wives or relatives, and thus advanced to positions of authority and responsibility.[31] Livio recognizes this sort of activity for what it is: "at best 'tis but a goodly pandarisme" (I.i.136). Yet he cannot resist the prospect of promotion, and he merrily accepts the position of "chiefe provisor" of the duke's horse (I.i.182)—the very employment which Bosola undertakes in *The Duchess of Malfi*. With his new rank Livio also takes on the responsibility for compromising his sister's chastity as Troylo shall direct him. Later he wavers, threatens to resign the post in disgust when he suspects his sister has been violated, and then accepts a new assignment on Troylo's reassurances. But Livio's fickle nature does not alter the apparent facts about the world in which he lives: Siena remains to all appearances a bawdyhouse writ large.

Among the examples of "pandarisme" cited by Troylo to convince Livio is the case of a merchant called Fabricio who sold his wife Flavia to a nobleman called Julio. These characters appear later in one of the subplots, and tell the story from their own point of view. Fabricio maintains that he loved his wife all the while, but feared that because of his financial misfortunes she would never retain her loyalty against challenges by more attractive men. He was merely anticipating the inevitable when he sold Flavia to the highest bidder. The proceeds of the sale could be turned to advantage as a refuge against bankruptcy. But Fabricio's only appearances in the play are surreptitious visits to Flavia during which he collects additional money. The procedure borders on blackmail—a technique which implies that Fabricio too has found a way of cashing in on the earnings of the bawdyhouse.

In another subplot Secco, a barber of eighteen, marries Morosa, a lady-in-waiting of some threescore years at least. Such an uneven match invites suspicion and ridicule. Morosa's motives for marriage are purely sexual, if we may judge from her verbal preoccupations. But Secco's consent has been procured by some influential member of the court, and in this society we can assume that influence is extended through the power of the purse. Troylo explains that the match between Morosa and Secco has been engineered by court policy, "to prevent / Suspicion" (II.ii.801–802). This explanation is not entirely satisfactory, since Troylo is notorious for withholding facts; yet it does serve as another illustration of love being put to base or at least questionable uses.

Secco lives in constant fear of cuckoldry, and consumes most of his energy trying to get even with his tormenters. One of these is Spadone, a pretended eunuch, who insinuates that Secco has been cuckolded by the page boy Nitido. Secco does not know whether to believe Spadone, until he forces a confession from his enemy at razor's edge. "I am no Eunuch, you finicall asse," Spadone admits, "I am no Eunuch; but at all points as well provided, as any he in *Italy*, and that thy Wife could have told thee" (V.ii.2480–83). Evidently it is not Nitido who has cuckolded Secco, but Spadone himself. To complicate matters still further, we learn in the last few lines of the play that Spadone—this grotesque and sinister figure of dark comedy—is a faithful and trusted member of Octavio's household. At first glance this belated fragment of exposition seems to add nothing at all to the play, but there may be one way of making it fit. Spadone, it would appear, has been carrying on an affair with Morosa. This relationship comes to an end through the collusion of the ruling family— including the duke and the heir apparent. Thus, Secco is simply the unfortunate gull on whom Morosa may be conveniently discarded. The debauched courtiers of Siena think nothing of demanding such a price in order to have the whole matter hushed up and the family's reputation salvaged. As Troylo has intimated, Secco and Morosa have been brought together by "policy" of state. Once again love has been figuratively bought and sold.

The official ruler of this equivocal dramatic world is Octavio, Duke of Siena. He contributes to the bawdyhouse atmosphere by keeping a harem known as the Bower of Fancies. In fact he does not ravish the women in the harem, for with the exception of Castamela they are his nieces; but he fondles them and engages them in dalliance in order to please certain "outward sences" (II.ii.743; III.iii.1578). Recently, critics of this play have argued that the Bower of Fancies is not nearly so shocking as it appears to uninitiated characters like Livio and Romanello, and as it must appear to the audience. Perhaps the most ingenious hypothesis is Juliet McMaster's suggestion that the Bower is an academy for the practice of fashionable Platonic love.[32] It is certainly true that Octavio welcomes Castamela to the circle of Fancies with the language of courtly Platonism. "Love *deare Maid*," he begins in what amounts to a restatement of the Platonic argument in *Honor Triumphant*, "Is but desire of beauty" (III.iii.1563–64). But the representative of Platonic love is impotent, and by implication the code which he subscribes to is barren. Indeed, even though Octavio cannot participate in physical lovemaking, he fosters a public image of himself as "a mighty man / For th' game" (II.ii.804–805). The whole apparatus of the Bower is an extension of the duke's deluded and unnatural sexual fantasy. Like his subjects, Octavio is incapable of living at peace with his erotic urges, so he constructs the illusion of prostitution even where the real commodity is lacking. The "Fancies" are aptly named, for their whole purpose is to lend support to a "phantasticall" erotic delusion (III.i.1084).

Since the titular head of Siena is impotent, real power falls into the hands of Troylo, who acts as *metteur en scène* for this pageant of illusions. It is Troylo who manipulates Livio, Castamela, Secco, Morosa, and Romanello into compromising situations. At the end of the play he protests that his motives have been above reproach, and Octavio explains that Troylo contrived the confusions of the plot only to test Castamela's love. He wanted to find sincere love in his prospective wife, not merely a formal profession forced on her by Livio's ambition (V.iii.2634–39). Of course Octavio is whitewashing his brother's motives, for Troylo is by no means immune to the debauchery of Siena. He has used every insidious means to play upon the stops of the other characters, to capitalize on their romantic aspirations and dreams in order to secure his own position. In a broad sense Troylo is the pander *par excellence*. He has done what he can to buy Castamela's love; he has established her brother in a comfortable position at court; he has given Castamela herself access to all the luxuries she could wish for. The dramatic world of *The Fancies* puts a price even on the sort of love that pretends to be most noble.

It would be difficult to conceive of a form more open than this one. Again the comic resolution takes the usual turn toward marriage, as Troylo lays claim to Castamela's hand and Livio is assigned quite arbitrarily to be Clarella's husband. A dance follows to celebrate the nuptials. Yet one can hardly imagine that all the problems of this corrupt society have been solved, or that a new and ideal society is about to be born. Octavio will continue as Duke of Siena, and since sexual adjustment is impossible for him, presumably the various mercenaries and bawds who have risen to power under his régime will continue in their positions also. There is no salvation for society, although there may be hope for individuals. For the characters who marry at the end of *The Fancies* there is at least one favourable precedent. Julio and Flavia came together as the result of a corrupt business transaction, but Flavia has managed to make the best of a bad state of affairs and the relationship between these two people is now warmly affectionate. Theirs is the nearest approach to unselfish love that the play offers. Accordingly, the lovers who are to be married may at least hope that love born of corruption will still turn out to be love. In *The Fancies* love exists despite society, not because of it. If the dance is a symbol of rebirth, it is a symbol that applies only to individual psychological regeneration.

Marriage and festivities at the close of the play, then, do not lead automatically to the stability of an ordered world where man has come to terms with his sexual nature. Too many questions are left unresolved, and too many crucial characters are cavalierly dismissed.[33] Fabricio quite unexpectedly decides to take monastic vows; Romanello gives up his claim to Castamela's hand and determines to live a single life; Livio and Clarella will be married at once although they know next to nothing about each other. Octavio makes the generous promise of large dowries for the other Fancies—Floria and Silvia—but they will have to wait for offers of marriage. It is significant, perhaps, that Ford provides no convenient visiting courtiers to take the hands of these newly revealed princesses. Even lovelorn Romanello does not take the opportunity to step forward and seize his happiness. Perhaps most important of all, Secco and Morosa will have to live on together in awkward bondage even though Spadone's sexual guilt has been exposed. Matches are easily made in this world of panderism, but the consequences of mercenary love are not so easily shaken off.

Thus, the final scenes of *The Fancies* confirm what we have come to expect of baroque dramatic form. Action is not neatly rounded off or confidently closed; the bawdyhouse atmosphere may be mere illusion, but it is a powerful one. Nobody is convinced that all will be well in Siena as soon as Troylo and Castamela join hands. In the Epilogue, Clarella asks the audience to overlook and applaud the "harmlesse pleasures" of the play (2681). This is no trivial request. Clarella tries to dismiss the disturbing effect of the bawdyhouse motif by arguing that it was merely a fanciful trick of *trompe-l'œil*. Her rhetoric is similar to Henry's in *Perkin Warbeck*. The uprising has not changed matters, the king argues:

> turmoyles past
> Like some unquiet dreame, have rather busied
> Our fansie, then affrighted rest of State.
> (V.ii.2376–78)

From a political point of view, Henry may be right. But in artistic terms, the unquiet dream created by baroque art and baroque theatre is the very quality that lives on.

In order to draw together a few general conclusions about the structure of Ford's plays, it may be helpful to stand back for a moment and scan the spectrum of his dramatic works for indications of recurrent structural features. We may begin with the figure of the pedant, who appears most obviously as Corax and recurs in metamorphoses such as Tecnicus, Friar Bonaventura, or Muretto. Aptly defined by Meleander as "A kind of learned foole" (*LM* IV.ii.1934), the pedant can be recognized invariably by his ridiculous mode of address and by his gratuitous offers to deliver an oration even under the least appropriate circumstances. The Friar in *'Tis Pity*, for example, is overjoyed to see Annabella weep for her sins, and urges her to "weepe faster yet, / Whiles I doe read a Lecture" (III.vi.1401–1402). Each of Ford's schoolmen has a pet theory which he rigorously applies to the action of the play in question; in every case the theory fails not because it lacks intellectual sophistication, but because it is too inflexible to deal with complex emotion. The pedantic theorist always relinquishes his authority in moments of crisis, either by leaving the scene of the action entirely, or by allowing a more practical and humane wisdom to supplant his technical knowledge. Thus, Tecnicus and the Friar abandon their tutorial posts when disaster threatens, and Corax steps aside at the crucial stage to watch Rhetias take over the cure of melancholy. Frion in *Perkin Warbeck* and Octavio in *The Fancies* are further modifications of the theoretical genius. Frion persuades Perkin to make a last assault through Cornwall according to plan, even though the dream of kingship is no longer a real possibility, and Octavio supplements the frustrations of impotence with the academic scheme of the Bower. The precise content of the various theories ranges from scholastic morality to Burtonian psychology to Platonic doctrine. None of these systems can count as the norm of Ford's dramatic universe, because in the pedant's hands each theory becomes too rigid to give more than a superficial account of the ambivalent human emotions it purports to explain.

Ford's consistent central focus on the relationship between one or more pairs of lovers is a self-evident structural feature, but still an important one. The nominal exceptions are *Perkin Warbeck*, where the love story is augmented considerably beyond the demands of the sources, and *The Fancies*, where Troylo and Castamela disguise their attachment until the dénouement. In the other plays the world of love subordinates everything else, so that even the traditional themes of ambition, revenge, or justice seem almost peripheral. In none of the plays does a single character rule the stage in splendid isolation, in the manner of Doctor Faustus or Bussy D'Ambois. Again, Ford's primary interest in the varieties of emotional experience seems to require that his heroes and heroines be involved in human relationships—above all in erotic relationships.

All of the plays contain more than one plot, and although Ford's practice varies, his most characteristic strategy is to construct three spheres of action for each play. Richard Levin notices this tendency and includes Ford among the exemplars of the pattern he calls "three-level hierarchies."[34] This classification is accurate so long as we remember that secondary and tertiary plots are never fully independent actions with an interest of their own, that the causal connections between the various levels are often extremely tenuous, and that the technique for creating a unified whole is thematic subordination.

Perhaps the most interesting recurrent structural device in Ford's drama as a whole is the frequent use he makes of the masque within the play. The only plays that do not include a masque are *The Lady's Trial*, in which Auria invites the assembled lovers to attend the "revells" that will follow the play, and *The Queen*, in which the frustrated Queen of Aragon momentarily contemplates visiting her husband in "some rich mask / Of rare device" (III.iii.1904–1905). *The Fancies* provides for two masques: one to celebrate the marriage of Secco and Morosa, and one to confer a blessing on the match between Troylo and Castamela. The first of these is not described in any detail, but we may assume that an entertainment at Morosa's wedding would follow the tradition of the anti-masque with its thinly disguised bawdry and its release of animal spirits. The second masque concludes the play, and is designed to show "how love oreswayes / All men of severall conditions" (V.iii.2667–68). Its governing idea, no doubt, was a variation of Corax's "plot" for the "Masque of Melancholy."

Ford uses the masque within the play to best effect in the tragedies, where the inserted masque becomes a vehicle for suggesting and confirming the peculiar blend of love and death which so often characterizes the primary tragic action. In *'Tis Pity* the female masquers appear in "*white Roabes*" (IV.i.1650) to dance at the wedding of Soranzo and Annabella, but within minutes the white marriage garment becomes a shroud for Hippolita. In itself the event is an ill omen, for it bathes the joy of the "bride-banquet" in the "blood" of revenge (IV.i.1734). Furthermore, it recalls the unofficial marriage of Giovanni and Annabella, with its mingled vows of love and death. The masque in *Love's Sacrifice* shows Ferentes' three mistresses dancing with him, accosting him "*in divers complementall offers of Courtship*" (III.iv.1852–53), and then suddenly stabbing him until the music stops. Once again death has entered the play disguised as a masque of love. The ritual will be repeated during the funeral ceremony at the end of the play, in which Biancha and Fernando are married symbolically in the tomb.

The most elaborate of all the masques is the series of dances and revels which forms the framework for the last two scenes of *The Broken Heart*. The penultimate scene begins as a vigorous dance to grace the wedding of Prophilus and Euphranea. But the messengers of death intrude three times, and the final scene transforms the masque into a ritual fulfilment of the oracle's prophecy:

> *When youth is ripe, and Age from time doth part,*
> *The livelesse Trunke shall wed the Broken Heart.*
> (IV.i.1777–78)

Calantha appears in the "*white robe*" (V.i.2513) which again stands for both marriage and death. The funeral song is a climax of affirmation in the belief that has grown out of the whole tragic design: supreme love becomes possible only through the ultimate release of death.

Only once in his career did Ford try his hand at a regular court masque. He collaborated with Dekker on *The Sun's Darling*, and this production betrays very little evidence of the skill and imagination with which Ford designed the revels in his tragedies.[35] The value of this collaborative experience is to be found, perhaps, in the suggestive use of dance, music, and spectacle which Ford carries into the masques within the plays. In other respects, Ford's masques in miniature rise far above the achievement of *The Sun's Darling*, precisely because they redevelop the themes of tragedy through the opulent masque machinery. In a sense the entertainments in Ford's tragedies anticipate the design of Shirley's masque of *Cupid and Death*. In this allegorical fantasia Death gains apparent victory by devising a slaughter of lovers, but Cupid recovers when the last scene is "*changed into Elysium*" where lovers may enjoy "eternal spring."[36]

Ford's use of the masque to mingle love with death is a radical departure from renaissance tradition, where masquers enter the stage to announce the victory of natural forces over the threat of desolation. Again Ford's artistic practice resembles more closely the world of continental baroque drama. In *Catharina von Georgien*, a play of Christian martyrdom by Andreas Gryphius,

Ford's most characteristic themes reappear in a dramatic form that remarkably parallels *The Broken Heart*. Shortly before the death of the heroine, the action stops to accommodate a masque-like procession of personified virtues. The most prominent of these figures are Love and Death. They engage in a dialogue of love-in-death which recaptures the mood of Calantha's requiem:

> Death: In death alone does true love stand reveal'd.
> Love: And love can quell the pow'r of death to part.
> Death: He who loves in death, loves without reproof.
> Love: He who dies in love, dies with tranquil heart.
>
> (IV.523–26)[37]

For Catharina the joys of Christian martyrdom create a fusion of the death-wish and the erotic impulse. As a result, her last words include a typically baroque resonance: "Welcome sweet death!"[38] In Ford's tragedies the aesthetic result is comparable; all of his martyrs transcend the unquiet dream of reality through their belief in the brighter vision of love.

1 /
Gianlorenzo Bernini. *The Ecstasy of St. Teresa.* 1645–52.
Cornaro Chapel, Santa Maria della Vittoria, Rome
(Foto del Gabinetto Fotografico Nazionale, Rome)

2 /
Giovanni Bellini. *St. Francis in Ecstasy*. c. 1485 (Copyright the Frick Collection, New York)

3 /
Raphael (Raffaello Sanzio). *The Descent from the Cross.*
1507. Borghese Museum, Rome (Foto del Gabinetto
Fotografico Nazionale, Rome)

4 /
Peter Paul Rubens. *The Descent from the Cross.* 1603.
Borghese Museum, Rome (Foto del Gabinetto Foto-
grafico Nazionale, Rome)

Peter Paul Rubens. *The Raising of the Cross*. 1609–10. Antwerp Cathedral (Courtesy of Roger–Viollet, Paris)

5 /

Donato Bramante. *The Tempietto*. 1502. San Pietro in Montorio, Rome (Foto del Gabinetto Fotografico Nazionale, Rome)

7 /
Pietro da Cortona. *Santa Maria in Via Lata*. 1658–62.
Rome (Foto del Gabinetto Fotografico Nazionale,
Rome)

8 /
Rosso Fiorentino. *The Descent from the Cross.* 1521.
Pinacoteca, Volterra (Courtesy of Alinari/Scala)

Tintoretto (Jacopo Robusti). *The Last Supper*. 1592–94.
San Giorgio Maggiore, Venice (Courtesy of Alinari/
Scala)

9 /
El Greco (Domenicos Theotocopoulos). *The Vision of
St. John the Divine*. 1610–14 (The Metropolitan
Museum of Art, Rogers Fund, 1956)

11 /
Peter Paul Rubens. *The Rape of the Sabines*. c. 1635
(Reproduced by courtesy of the Trustees, The
National Gallery, London)

12 /
Nicolas Poussin. *The Rape of the Sabines*. c. 1636–37.
The Louvre, Paris (Courtesy of Roger–Viollet, Paris)

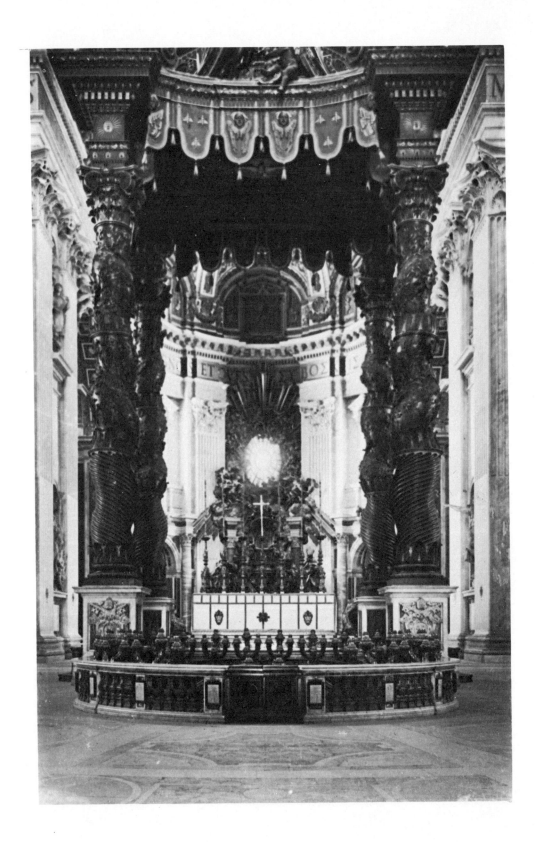

14 /
Jacques Verberckt. *Le Cabinet de la Pendule.* 1738.
Versailles (Cliché Musées Nationaux, Paris)

13 /
Gianlorenzo Bernini. *Baldacchino.* 1624–33. St. Peter's,
Rome (Foto del Gabinetto Fotografico Nazionale,
Rome)

15 /
Pietro da Cortona. *The Triumph of Divine Providence.*
1633–39. Gran Salone, Palazzo Barberini, Rome
(Foto del Gabinetto Fotografico Nazionale, Rome)

16 /
Sandro Botticelli. *The Birth of Venus*. c. 1480. Uffizi
Gallery, Florence (Courtesy of Alinari/Scala)

17 /
Peter Paul Rubens. *Marie de Médicis Landing i*
Marseilles. 1622–25. The Louvre, Paris (Courtesy
Roger–Viollet, Paris)

18 /
Hans Holbein the Younger. *Henry VIII*. 1540. Palazzo
Barberini, Rome (Foto del Gabinetto Fotografico
Nazionale, Rome)

19 /
Anthony Van Dyck. *King Charles on Horseback*. c. 1638
(Reproduced by courtesy of the Trustees, The
National Gallery, London)

20 /
Gianlorenzo Bernini. *The Rape of Persephone.* 1622.
Borghese Museum, Rome (Foto del Gabinetto Foto-
grafico Nazionale, Rome)

CHAPTER FOUR

LANGUAGE SUITED TO A DIVIDED MIND

An Essay on Verbal Style

A DECIDED shift in graphic technique occurs in visual art as we pass from the renaissance to the baroque phase. Renaissance artists rely on the clarity of linear design to reflect the logical structure of the universe; shapes must be precisely limited and defined so that they will fit neatly into the ordered framework described by the laws of perspective. In the mannerist phase linear values are sharply questioned, shapes are frequently distorted, and perspective is flagrantly violated. The mannerists continue to use linear technique, if only to produce ironic effects by transgressing its inner logic. In the baroque phase, painters and sculptors abandon strict linear design in favour of painterly techniques. The baroque artist suggests shape not by stressing outlines, which he sees as slightly hazy rather than absolutely clear, but by relying on large splashes of colour and massive swirls of marble. In short, the logical system of the renaissance gives way to a psychological method of treating shape. The baroque artist sees in masses rather than in outlines, because sweeping emotional gestures are more important to him than strictly logical coherence.[1]

The distinction between linear and painterly technique is a well documented concept in art history, and nearly any renaissance and baroque paintings would illustrate it to a greater or lesser degree. Botticelli's fastidious and precise draughtsmanship depends on a linear interpretation of shape; minute inspection of the human form in his paintings reveals an artificial outline which traces the contour of each delicate finger and toe (see pl. 16). Similarly, in Raphael's *The School of Athens* the whole world of renaissance philosophy is contained by the most regular, Euclidian framework. Rubens' work best illustrates the painterly style. His series of twenty-four monumental canvases in honour of Marie de Médicis shows elements of history, biography, and mythology blending imperceptibly into one another. In stylistic terms, shape blends imperceptibly with shape and colour with colour. The painting called *Marie de Médicis Landing in Marseilles* (pl. 17) shows Neptune and a group of mermaids rising from the sea to greet the royal barge. It is impossible to draw a precise boundary between flesh and water; the nymph-like legs of the mermaids and the foamy surface of the water merge mysteriously into one.

The same distinction cannot be illustrated easily from native English painting, but the shift in graphic technique must certainly have been evident to any seventeenth-century Englishman of reasonably cultured tastes. Holbein's *Henry VIII* (pl. 18) is a showcase of renaissance technique in portraiture, just as Van Dyck's numerous portraits of Charles I (see pl. 19) are paradigm cases of baroque technique. Holbein sees his subject in strictly linear terms. The imposing grandeur of the original *Henry VIII* fresco is hardly muted at all in the preliminary cartoon in the National Portrait Gallery, where colour is entirely absent and linear values must carry the artistic burden alone.[2] Each line is drawn with precision and confidence, as if to outline a view of kingship according to the definite principles of renaissance law and ideology. Van Dyck's Charles is no longer the figurehead in an ordered political system. He is a man distinguished from other men only by the intensity and subtlety of his psychological bearing. A linear cartoon of Van Dyck's portrait would amount to caricature. It would not suggest the almost mystical forlornness that characterizes this king's face, for it could not do justice to the subtle shadings of light and colour that mark the painterly style. It would not see Charles, as Van Dyck certainly did, in psychological terms.

If we read the change from linear to painterly technique as nothing more than a matter of brush strokes or chiselling tools, then of course it cannot be extended to the non-visual arts. But if we concede that graphic technique may be a symptom, as Wölfflin has argued, of the way artists see their world, then it may have important consequences for our understanding of technique in the verbal arts. The shift from a logically based technique to a psychologically based technique, in particular, is not limited on *a priori* grounds to any one medium. The history of musical styles, for example, provides ample reason for broadening this distinction to include other forms of creative activity.

Renaissance musicians, like painters and poets, see their artistic practice as a sweet and harmonious imitation of nature.[3] Musical theorists may depend in part on their medieval heritage, but they tend to emphasize the sense of new discovery which they share with renaissance contemporaries in other fields. Like visual artists, the musicians of the renaissance use precise, mathematical language to describe the more technical aspects of their craft. Where the painter depends on the laws of perspective and proportion to integrate his way of seeing with the objective realities of the natural order, the musician can point to the equally precise and equally mathematical laws of harmony and counterpoint. He can identify the intuitively satisfying mathematical ratios between the vibration frequencies of two strings tuned in octaves; he can demonstrate, by means of ratios, why certain combinations of tones produce concord, and why others are dissonant. For renaissance musicians, like Ockeghem or Josquin des Prez, composition is a way of reflecting in sound the logical order of the universe.

Although music historians have not yet on the whole accepted mannerism as a legitimate stylistic phase, they do speak of a period of experiment that coincides with the late renaissance or the early baroque and includes such figures as de Rore, Willaert, and the brothers Gabrielli.[4] In this experimental stage, composers begin to use dissonance much more freely for special effects, and the regulated counterpoint of the renaissance begins to break down. Whether or not one chooses to call this musical development "mannerism," it does in fact run parallel to the nervous, anti-logical visual orientation in painters like Rosso and Parmigianino. Musicians in this period of transition still depend on the ordered system of renaissance sound values, but at the same time they develop techniques that undercut or violate the logical framework.

Baroque musicians break away entirely from the conventions of modality, still standard in renaissance music, and replace the old modes with a more flexible system of tonality. Musical theorists and practitioners begin to emphasize the dramatic character of music rather than its abstract form. The doctrine of the passions, or affections, becomes a principal point of departure for the baroque musician.[5] This theory is an adaptation of the ancient doctrine of the humours, which offers what now seem to be crude physiological explanations for man's various psychological states. The accuracy of the theory is not at stake here; regardless of its present reputation among psychologists, the doctrine of the affections did provide baroque music with a significant psychological base, just as Burtonian theorizing became a crucial imaginative stimulus for writers like Ford. Where renaissance musicians take pride in the pleasing sweetness of their compositions, baroque composers tend to give precedence to the more violent affections, or unruly states of mind.[6] The distinction between renaissance and baroque music in this respect is decisive, though far from absolute. The expressive qualities of the renaissance madrigal, for example, look forward to the grand rhetoric of baroque opera. But the general tendency remains: harmoniously balanced emotion in renaissance music gives way to ecstatic and overwhelming emotion in the baroque.

This change in emphasis from a logically-based to a psychologically-based musical technique has important and obvious consequences for the development of religious music. Such works as Ockeghem's *Missa "Mi-Mi"* or Josquin's *Missa Pange Lingua* may stand for the polyphonic style of renaissance religious music. In Josquin's mass the counterpoint is particularly elaborate, and the various sections of the liturgical service are held together by a complex interweaving of the main theme. The liturgical Latin of these renaissance masses does not lend itself naturally to emotional treatment, and in any case the composers do not write music that would enhance verbal expressiveness. Instead, they build an abstract structure of sound that complements and runs parallel to the equally abstract and equally formal structure of the text. Music, in the renaissance, is not so much a vehicle for expressing the emotional content of worship, as an edifice of sound that is pleasing to God because of its own inner logic.

With Claudio Monteverdi's motets from *Selva morale e spirituale* and Heinrich Schütz's *Johannes-Passion* we are in quite another world. The music of worship has become a matter of passionate involvement. In Monteverdi's *Salve Regina*, a duet for two tenors, we find the sensuous expressiveness of the new operatic style used in the context of religious worship. Generally speaking, the words of the text assume primary value in baroque vocal music, and the composer does his utmost to give prominence and colouring to the emotive content of the operatic aria or the religious service. In the *Johannes-Passion* Schütz carries the affective tendency of baroque church music to its maximum potential. The text for worship is no longer the traditional mass, but a narrative sequence from the vernacular Bible (Luther's translation). Christ, Pilate, Peter, and a few supporting characters participate in a dramatic exchange in which music is used to reflect emotional states, to build and resolve psychological tension. Polyphonic part-writing intrudes now and again, but only in the mob scenes of the Easter story. The style that was once the standard of Christian worship is now put to specifically dramatic use: it expresses the mood of an angry and hostile crowd. The sung dialogue of the *Johannes-Passion* blends the affective possibilities of sound with the rhetoric of religious language.

In renaissance verbal practice, as critics and historians are fond of observing, logic and rhetoric go hand in hand.[7] Both disciplines are thought of as arts of communication, and both depend upon reason. Renaissance theorists assume that skill in rhetoric requires some proficiency in logic, and frequently the same scholar will write a treatise on each of these two sister arts. *The Arte of Rhetorique* by Thomas Wilson confirms the connection and gives it the status of textbook orthodoxy for several generations. "Rhetorique is an art to set furthe by utteraunce of wordes," says Wilson by way of definition, "or rather an artificiall declaracion of the mynde, in the handelyng of any cause, called in contencion, that maie through reason largely be discussed."[8] The significant word is "reason." For the renaissance rhetorician ordered speech is a way of reflecting, artificially, the patterns of an ordered mind in an ordered universe. To guarantee that students of rhetoric will not miss his point, Wilson again and again urges them to consult the "places of Logique"[9] for clarification of one matter or another, presumably referring them to his own textbook on logic, *The Rule of Reason*. In more practical terms, the logical basis of renaissance rhetoric clearly accounts for the precision in argument characteristic of Sidney's *Defence of Poetry*, or indeed of Shakespeare's sonnets, where key introductory words like "if," "then," "thus," "since," and "but" act as logical signposts.

The controversy surrounding Peter Ramus and his disciples in England and elsewhere is to a large extent a dispute about the provinces to which logic and rhetoric properly belong.[10] The spirit of Ramism marks the beginning of the mannerist phase in rhetoric. Connections between the arts of thought and expression are now questioned, and a less confident system of rhetoric is put forward. In fact, the basic principles of Ramism insist that a clear distinction be drawn between logic and rhetoric. Dudley Fenner's *The Artes of Logike and Rethorike*, the first complete English version of the Ramistic system, demonstrates a radical mistrust of Wilson's Ciceronian assumptions. The most noteworthy feature of Fenner's treatise on rhetoric is an appendix on "the rules of Sophistrie." Here we have a formal acknowledgement that language, even the most structured and apparently logical language, can be deceptive. Fenner gives the following example to illustrate a trick of sophistry he calls "Doubtfulnes by a Trope":

> That which Christ saith is true:
> Christ saeith that bread is his body.
> Therefore it is true.[11]

This trick will not work, says the Puritan Fenner, because the word "body" is used in the figurative sense by the speaker (Christ), and interpreted in the literal sense by the audience (the Roman Catholic Church). Yet it is precisely this kind of equivocation between concrete and abstract that Donne will shortly put to artistic use in the *Holy Sonnets*. Ramism prepares the ground for mannerism in poetry by pointing, though negatively, to the possibility of a doubtful, suspect logic behind the flowers of rhetoric. The logical consistency that expresses the confident assumptions of renaissance style becomes a vehicle for ironic contrast in the mannerist phase.

It is more difficult to document a baroque phase in rhetorical theory, partly because theory simply fails to keep pace with rhetorical practice. There is at least one rhetorical manual, however, which takes a baroque view of the subject. This is a book by John Smith of Montague Close, entitled significantly *The Mysterie of Rhetorique Unvail'd*. Rhetoric, says Smith, "is a faculty by which we understand what will serve our turn concerning any subject to win belief in the hearer: hereby likewise the end of the discourse is set forward, to wit, the affecting of the heart with the sense of the matter in hand."[12] The psychological bias of this definition is apparent at once. None of Smith's predecessors speaks of affecting the "heart" while proposing views about the function of rhetoric; certainly none is so fond as Smith of the adjective "vehement" used to describe the effect of a rhetorical figure on the speaker's audience.[13] Smith pays no attention at all to the logical organization of discourse. His emphasis falls instead on the figures of pathos, such as *erotesis* or *ecphonesis*. As if to confirm his psychological bias against any possible suspicion, Smith saves the last two pages of his treatise for a description of *pathopoeia*, "a form of speech whereby the Speaker moves the mind of his hearers to some vehemency of affection." This figure occurs whenever the speaker himself is deeply moved by "love, hatred, gladness, sorrow," or any other "vehement" emotion, and "doth by evident demonstration, passionate pronunciation and suitable gestures make a lively expression thereof."[14] This, then, is the taste for rhetoric which Smith wishes his reader to savour after closing the book. It is a major departure from renaissance principles, which permitted pathos but scanty treatment. In England at least, Smith appears to be the first rhetorical theorist to search for a psychological basis to the art of verbal discourse.

Smith's theoretical observations, of course, have plenty of firm links with baroque developments in rhetorical practice. Sir Thomas Browne's prose frequently reads like an application of *The Mysterie of Rhetorique Unvail'd*. He begins *Urne Buriall*, for example, not with an abstract statement of his theme, but with a series of highly charged rhetorical questions: "But who knows the fate of his bones, or how often he is to be buried? who hath the Oracle of his ashes, or whether they are to be scattered?"[15] Browne demands an emotional attitude from his reader; not content to speculate about the logical problems of theology, he plants at each crucial stage in his argument a rhetorical device that will ensure an emotional response. As he reaches the climax of *Religio Medici*, Browne makes a last attempt to guide the reader's sympathies into agreement with his own: "*He that giveth to the poore lendeth to the Lord*; there is more Rhetorick in that one sentence than in a Library of Sermons, and indeed if those sentences were understood by the Reader, with the same Emphasis as they are delivered by the Author, wee needed not those Volumes of instructions, but might bee honest by an Epitome."[16] Despite the implied disclaimer, Browne would undoubtedly have been able to identify his own rhetorical device as *ecphonesis*, defined by Smith as "a pathetical figure, whereby as the Orator or speaker expresses the vehement affection and passion of his own mind, so he also excites and stirs up the minds and affections of those to whom he speaks."[17] Browne has not abandoned the rules of rhetoric, but he has shifted the emphasis so that his style looks much less like a logical demonstration and much more like an emotional plea.

Generally speaking the language of drama tries to "win belief" by appealing to the heart at least as much as to the reason. But in Ford's plays the appeal to the heart is unusually vehement—more so than in renaissance drama. The rhetoric of baroque drama gains in pathos, often at the expense of logic, until even such a figure as paradox, which we tend to associate with writers who lavish particular attention on logical patterning, becomes primarily a vehicle for expressing subtleties of emotion.

Of all Ford's characters, Penthea uses paradox with greatest effect, especially in her cryptic explanations of the debauched state of marriage:

> There is no peace left for a ravish'd wife
> Widdow'd by lawlesse marriage.
> (*BH* IV.ii.1953–54)

In itself this description embodies at least two contradictions: (1) marriage by definition is the legal and social sanction of a love relationship, so the phrase "lawlesse marriage" is a technical absurdity, and (2) "widdow'd by...marriage" is also absurd, since again by definition, death is the only possible cause of widowhood. And with reference to the events of the play, a third contradiction emerges. Bassanes is the only man who has made love to Penthea, and since he is her legal husband it is technically impossible to describe her as a "ravish'd wife."

But a paradox is not a simple contradiction. It is an apparent contradiction, and it is just this that makes the figure so poetically useful. A true paradox is capable of resolution, and the grounds on which such resolution can be made distinguish one sort of paradox from another. In Penthea's case, contraries of speech are resolved on psychological grounds, for if one understands Penthea's state of mind, if one investigates her complex feelings about marriage, then her paradoxical statements begin to sound much less like "madnesse" and much more like an "Oracle" (IV.ii.1940). In spirit Penthea is married to her first love, Orgilus. From her point of view, the vows that she and Orgilus exchanged have the validity of marriage vows, so her relationship with Bassanes must be adulterous. The explanation is simple enough if one understands that Penthea's paradoxes are the result of the way she feels about the traumatic events of her life, that is, if one interprets them in broadly psychological terms.

Even Penthea's more confusing figures will bear similar interpretation. The will scene, for instance, contains a series of paradoxical assertions which depend again on ambivalent emotional responses. Penthea leaves her youth "To Virgin wives, such as abuse not wedlocke / By freedome of desires" (III.v.1573–74). On the surface this line looks like smug self-congratulation for remaining faithful to Bassanes, and "Virgin" seems to have its weakest meaning, "chaste." But we already know that Penthea is haunted by the idea that her formal marriage is a guilty, adulterous relationship. The paradoxical state of virgin-wife is Penthea's view of her own life as the betrothed mistress of Orgilus, before she was married to Bassanes; it is an idealized way of looking at the betrothal period. For Penthea the relationship to Orgilus had all the advantages of marriage without any of the frustrations. The same clause of the will applies to "married maids," or those who prefer virtue to "delights by marriage" (III.v.1577–79). Again Penthea recalls her betrothal period with nostalgic longing. The description "virgin wife" stressed the condition of virginity which Penthea could retain even during her marriage-betrothal; the phrase "married maid" now stresses the fact of spiritual marriage (to Orgilus) which Penthea claims to have experienced while remaining physically virginal. "May those be ever young," she concludes (III.v.1580). The idealized, youthful state of betrothal is so attractive to Penthea that she wishes to preserve it indefinitely; the gift of youth to virgin wives is her paradoxical way of expressing a desire to return to the life of innocence which experience has taken from her.

A similar paradox occurs when Penthea and Orgilus meet for the last time. Orgilus gives her hand a parting kiss, and Penthea notices the coldness of his lips, the paleness of his face. Then she says:

> every drop
> Of blood is turn'd to an Amethist,
> Which married Bachelours hang in their eares.
> (IV.ii.1936–38)

The married bachelor is Orgilus. He is married by virtue of the betrothal contract, and he is a bachelor still because he lives in solitude, because his love for Penthea has never been consummated. In other words, Orgilus is still in that ideal phase of betrothal for which Penthea longs. His development has been arrested; his love has been frozen, petrified, just as the vitality of his blood has hardened, metaphorically, into the purple mineral substance called amethyst. Again the paradox reflects Penthea's complex and ambiguous feelings about her love and her marriage. Virginity and marriage have equal attractions for her, and as a result she remains suspended between two contradictory urges. Orgilus is both the spiritual husband of the betrothal period, and the chaste lover who must not be looked on in sexual terms. By idealizing the happiness of the past, Penthea crystallizes her love into a form that cannot grow or develop. The price of ideal love is metamorphosis into a hard, inanimate gem.

So in a sense Penthea's development has been arrested, too. "Indeed," she says to introduce another paradox, "I've slept / With mine eyes open a great while" (IV.ii.1881–82). Marriage to Bassanes, Penthea seems to be suggesting, has been both the beginning of a perpetual sleep, and a rude awakening from a pleasant dream. She has been asleep ever since she married Bassanes, if one takes sleep as a metaphor for spiritual death. Thus, even while physically awake, she has been asleep in spirit, just as she has been spiritually ravished by the man who is physically her husband. And in a second sense, she is now awake to those cruel realities of an unhappy marriage which form no part of the betrothal fantasy. Although her eyes are now open, although she has a new awareness of life's brutality, she still dreams of the lost world which she knew before her awakening. The sleeping-waking figure, like the marriage paradoxes, is a poetic way of suggesting the tensions and contradictory impulses within Penthea's personality.

A modern psychologist might say all this much more bluntly. Penthea clearly has an approach-avoidance complex where sex is concerned. She likes the idea of marriage, but she cannot throw off her inhibitions about the physical act of lovemaking. She can see Bassanes only as a sexual savage, because he has made love to her. And by the same token she can see Orgilus only as the enchanting young lover, because he has not. Her obsession with virginity indicates a tendency toward sexual frigidity. Fortunately, poetic language is not so brutal. In the figures of paradox Ford has found a much more sensitive vehicle for exploring emotional conflict and crisis than outright statement. Penthea speaks best in paradoxes, in "language suited / To a divided minde" (I.iii.444–45).

Penthea's characteristic figures of expression are not incidental decoration, for they give concrete shape to Ford's basic thematic tendencies and they develop in miniature the structural pattern of *The Broken Heart*. For a Christian audience the paradox of virgin-wife or married-maid would intensify the religious quality of Penthea's love, by association with the Virgin Mary. Milton's ode *On the Morning of Christ's Nativity* opens with an invocation to the divine Son of a "Virgin Mother" or a "wedded Maid" (l. 3); this double use of sacred paradox may well have influenced Penthea's rhetoric of virginity. The sleeping-waking figure contains an implicit death-wish, and springs from the theme of death as a welcome, long-awaited guest. The very vehicle of paradox combines the strenuous inhibitions and the irresistible impulses which motivate Ford's characters. The result is a pattern of verbal conflict that parallels the structure of the play. Each paradox contains at one polar extreme a suggestion of the frustrating manacles of honour, and at the other extreme a desire for ultimate resolution of frustration through irreversible action. Paradox allows us to look into Penthea's mind to discover in her private emotional dilemma another variation of the shape of *The Broken Heart*.

The emotional complexity of the baroque paradox can best be appreciated by comparison with the logically-based paradoxes typical of renaissance style. Barabas, in Marlowe's *The Jew of Malta*, expresses even his most obvious desires in the form of paradox. His ideal is to "enclose / Infinite riches in a little room" (I.i.36–37). This statement embodies a logical contradiction, since an infinite quantity of anything cannot be contained in any finite space, let alone a little room. But here paradox is capable of logical resolution. "Riches" may be understood in an abstract sense, as the power which accompanies wealth, let us say, and then it becomes logically possible for an infinite amount of power to inhabit a tiny space. We know that Barabas despises the outward show of wealth. His own insistence on the rare essence of wealth (control) as a higher good than the material stuff (gold) helps to resolve the paradox in a logical way. The events of the play demonstrate that what is logically possible is not in practice attainable, but this is another matter. The important point, in linguistic terms, is the thoroughly logical character of Barabas's statement. Of course this paradox does tell us something about the speaker's character, but it tells us something relatively simple, and it does not act as a vehicle for creating psychological depth. Barabas reveals a simple, one-directional acquisitive urge through the monetary paradox; the figure may hint at the complexity of capitalist economy, or at the complexity of Christian theology, but it does not suggest psychological complexity in the speaker himself.

The sort of paradox typical of renaissance style finds more frequent expression in comedy, where the logical implications of language act as a framework for *badinage*, or function as rules for the game of wit. In *Love's Labour's Lost*, Berowne praises Rosaline's beauty by coining a paradoxical maxim: "No face is fair that is not full so black" (IV.iii.248). As if to demonstrate the logical character of his remark, Berowne goes on to explain it at some length to the baffled King. Rosaline is not fair in the sense of "pale-complexioned," but she is fair in the sense of "beautiful." Her dark complexion, in fact, changes the values of the fashionable world, so that dark skin becomes the standard of beauty and the word "fair" naturally applies to it. "And therefore is she born to make black fair" (IV.iii.256), Berowne concludes, insisting on the logical nature of his demonstration by repeating the key word "therefore" three lines later. A scene of verbal fencing follows in which the bachelors twist Berowne's paradox this way and that for the sheer joy of it. The verbal world can be turned upside down in sport, because the well-defined logic of discourse will set matters straight again in the end.

Ford's paradoxes do not show such rigour, for in the baroque literary phase verbal technique is a matter of psychological rhythm, not of logical precision. Penthea's figures of speech are no doubt the best examples of Ford's emotionally subtle use of paradox, but there are plenty of other cases. In *Perkin Warbeck* for example, the impostor betrays a divided mind beneath the façade of self-assurance. "Princes are but men," he says, "Distinguisht in the finenesse of their frailtie" (IV.v.2242–43). "Frailtie" is not a quality that the renaissance would use to praise its princes, and it scarcely counts as a mark of distinction in plays like *Edward II* or *Richard II*. There is no way of justifying Perkin's view by reference to renaissance writings on kingship, where the order of society falls into a logical pattern in the manner of Hooker's universal hierarchy. The "finenesse of...frailtie" makes sense only in terms of the psychological values of the play. Perkin becomes a kinglike creature not because he convinces us with logical arguments, but because he impresses us with his sensitive temperament, with his innate nobility of character. In fact, Perkin's claims to kingship seem to be precisely the same as Charles I's, to accept for a moment Van Dyck's interpretation of the matter (see pl. 19). Perkin's most regal moment is also his most vulnerable, his most pathetic, because it is the moment in which he most nearly approaches martyrdom. Thus, he can use the term "frailtie" to distinguish princes from other men, partly because he knows that this quality will underscore his status as a martyr, but also because he already recognizes how precarious are the grounds on which his claim to the throne rests and on which his life depends. In this case, paradox shows us a mind divided between princely self-assurance and all-too-human fear. Again verbal paradox becomes Ford's vehicle for suggesting the central paradox of the play itself—the paradox of the worthy impostor.

In her speeches of shame and repentance, Annabella uses paradox to express the turbulence of her spiritual condition:

> here I sadly vow
> Repentance, and a leaving of that life
> I long have dyed in.
>
> *(TP V.i.2090–92)*

The implicit sexual meaning of the verb "to die" gives Annabella's mournful speech an initial ambiguity. But there are deeper paradoxical forces at work. Death and life are connected in a way perfectly compatible with Christian sentiment, but quite incompatible with the rules of logical discourse. We recall the wisdom of Christ: "He that findeth his life shall lose it: and he that loseth his life for my sake shall find it" (Mat. x.39), and the impassioned outcry of St. Paul: "I die daily" (1 Cor. xv.31). But Annabella's religion is not the sort that takes great stock by scriptural citation; religion, like love and like death, is primarily an emotional experience for her. The life-in-death paradox is a psychological truth rather than a theological mystery or a logical puzzle. Life has been death for her because she has taken a course of action that violates the most basic principles of her own moral outlook. She has been persuaded, first by Giovanni and then by Soranzo, to commit the unforgivable sin of blasphemy against herself. Mortification of the flesh is a mild penance for the soul already mortified by spiritual pain. And at the same time, life with Soranzo has been another form of death, where not only her moral convictions but also her erotic instincts have been mortified. Physical death, when at last it comes, is a triumphant, unambiguous release from the contradictions of a suffering existence.

Annabella's final speech supplies a further illustration of paradox used in a sensitive and evocative way. Her last lines imply the mingling of love and death so characteristic of Ford's tragic world:

Forgive him Heaven—and me my sinnes, farwell.
Brother unkind, unkind—mercy great Heaven——oh——oh.   *Dyes.*

(V.v.2409–10)

The vibrant effect of these lines depends in part on a special combination of paradox and repetition. "Brother unkind" is paradoxical by seventeenth-century standards, since "kind" still carries its secondary connotation, "natural, or related by nature." Moreover, this repetition of the word "unkind" is the one instance in the whole of '*Tis Pity* in which Annabella ventures even a tentative criticism of her brother. To use the mild reproof of "unkind" so late in the day is an outrageous understatement. Once again Annabella is trying to reconcile two contrary impulses—her constant devotion to Giovanni even in death, and her conviction that he has led her into a life of sin. She uses the word "unkind" (in the sense of "unnatural") to protest against Giovanni's actions, and (in its normal sense) to ensure that her protest will sound as gentle as possible.[18] Just as Giovanni combines the roles of lover and killer, so Annabella's paradox brings together the conflicting responses of desire and pain. Even the most technical figures of speech gain vitality and richness from the baroque blending of love and death.

Anticipating I. A. Richards and Cleanth Brooks, Aristotle gives pride of place among the devices of figurative language to metaphor. Renaissance rhetoricians agree with Aristotle, no doubt partly because much renaissance poetry illustrates and supports his judgment. Thus, Thomas Wilson argues that any oration can be "wonderfullye enriched" and made more convincing through the use of metaphor. The logical bias is again at work, as Wilson's definition indicates: "A Metaphore is an alteration of a woorde from the proper and naturall meanynge, to that whiche is not proper, and yet agreeth thereunto, by some lykenes that appeareth to be in it."[19] What Wilson means by "not proper" may be gleaned from the classified list of examples which follows the definition. His first category deals with translation of "a worde from that which is in the minde, to that which is in the bodye." He is speaking about metaphors like

Friar Laurence's warning to Romeo, "They stumble that run fast" (II.iii.94). The actions of running and stumbling (verbs "proper" to the body) are used to figure forth corresponding activities of the mind. In typical renaissance metaphors the precise logical relationship between tenor and vehicle is of utmost importance; for the renaissance poet metaphor has almost the same status as analogy has for the logician.

George Puttenham's *The Arte of English Poesie* is in many ways a conservative document which confirms the Ciceronian assumptions of renaissance rhetoric, but some of the technical remarks show poetic theory already moving toward the mannerist phase. Puttenham's discussion of metaphor, or the figure of *transport*, revises Wilson's definition in certain basic respects. "There is a kinde of wresting of a single word from his owne right signification, to another not so naturall, but yet of some affinitie or conveniencie with it."[20] This account of metaphor, especially the important word "wresting," comes much closer to Samuel Johnson's famous dictum on the language of the metaphysical poets. "The most heterogeneous ideas are yoked by violence together," writes Johnson in what amounts to his description of the mannerist style; metaphysical wit delights in "a combination of dissimilar images, or discovery of occult resemblances in things apparently unlike."[21]

In mannerist poetry, metaphor is still felt to be under the control of logic, at least insofar as conscious violation of the logic of analogy is one of the chief functions of metaphor. In Donne's short seduction poem, "The Flea," an impeccably structured argument is played off against the glaring fallacy of the central metaphor. Lovers are in fact not like insects. The following lines from *The Revenger's Tragedy*, in which Gratiana repents of her earlier attempt to sell Castiza's body, illustrate the curious relationship between metaphor and logic in mannerist drama:

> O you heavens,
> Take this infectious spot out of my soul,
> I'll rinse it in seven waters of mine eyes!
> Make my tears salt enough to taste of grace!
> (IV.iv.50–53)

As in the example from *Romeo and Juliet* we have an implied comparison between a physical action (crying and washing) which serves as the vehicle of the metaphor, and a mental process (repentance) which functions as the tenor. The metaphor seems conventional enough in view of the many reminders in *Macbeth* about the symbolic value of water as a cleansing agent. Yet the choice of the word "rinse" tends to arouse uncomfortable suspicions about the passage. If washing is like repentance, then rinsing is certainly not like the strong form of repentance to which Gratiana lays claim. "Rinse" is a mild, half-hearted form of "wash"—a form that involves no detergent, no scrubbing, and no pain. Thus Gratiana fails to convince us of the logical relationship between vehicle and tenor precisely because a much more closely argued comparison would clearly be possible.

We have the same uneasy feeling about "salt" in the following line. Salt has the proverbial quality of making wounds smart, and Gratiana's overt meaning seems to be: "I'll intensify the act of repentance by weeping real, salt tears." But the verb "taste" follows, and forces salt back into its usual household role as a seasoning agent. The logic of analogy in this line insists on two levels of comparison, and the second more trivial level acts as an ironic reduction of the initial lofty comparison. We suspect Gratiana's sincerity for the same reason that we suspect the sincerity of the speaker in "The Flea." Both are undercut by the reductive tendencies of their own logic.

The baroque metaphor is best introduced by example. In *'Tis Pity*, even before the lovers have confessed their secret to each other, Giovanni offers his dagger to Annabella and invites death with a splendid rhetorical appeal:

> And here's my breast, strick home.
> Rip up my bosome, there thou shalt behold
> A heart, in which is writ the truth I speake.
>
> (I.iii.366–68)

Once again a physical action, here a sinister and grotesque physical action, represents a mental activity. Ripping up the bosom is the vehicle which stands for discovering the truth about Giovanni's intentions; the metaphorical process draws an implicit analogy between the two activities.

What are the grounds for making this comparison? Surely they are not primarily logical. We do not have here the naturally convincing analogy of the renaissance, where running and being mentally agitated or stumbling and making a mistake are so closely parallel that it is hardly necessary to analyze the metaphor once its terms have been spelled out. Nor are we in the mannerist world, where logic suggests an ironic relationship between vehicle and tenor. The only convincing grounds for drawing any comparison at all between ripping up the bosom and discovering a secret are, it appears, psychological grounds.

What defeats logical expectations in this case is the enormous disparity between tenor and vehicle. Discovering somebody's thoughts is, under any normal circumstances, so unlike ripping up his bosom that it is both logically questionable and linguistically audacious to suggest the comparison. The key to the ground of the metaphor, then, lies in the fact that Giovanni is not speaking under normal circumstances. He is under great mental duress, and his metaphor seems so strained because it reflects a complementary emotional strain. The glaring theatricality of his gesture, the grand overstatement of his metaphor, are ways in which he is able to release frustrated energy and emotional tension. Giovanni is about to confess a willingness and a consuming desire to commit incest. It is not this action itself but the powerful and ambiguous motivations that lie behind the act which demand expression in baroque metaphor. In general, renaissance metaphors are built up out of the stuff of experience; they condense, reclassify, and enrich the actual world in which the characters live and breathe. Baroque metaphors are made of psychological material. The world of illusion and fantasy which the characters themselves have created is also the world from which their language springs.

This particular metaphor of Giovanni's is part of a very important linguistic pattern in 'Tis Pity and indeed in Ford's plays as a whole. Tearing of the flesh, especially where it will expose vital organs, invariably suggests the discovery of some kind of truth, and usually psychological truth of a mysterious kind. Soranzo, for instance, uses the metaphor in a fit of mental agitation following the discovery that Annabella is pregnant. When she refuses to identify the father of her unborn child, Soranzo cannot contain his fury:

> Not know it, Strumpet, I'le ripp up thy heart,
> And finde it there.
>
> (IV.iii.1832–33)

Soranzo is bothered not simply by the evident fact of cuckoldry, but by the brazen way in which his wife flaunts the beauty of her sin. It is not physical truth only that he is after; his attack aims at the heart, the seat of the emotions, the source of spiritual truth. The subtlety of Soranzo's threat is all the more apparent when compared with the straightforward punishment he has in mind for the unknown man who has cuckolded him. Soranzo intends to "Teare the prodigious leacher joynt by joynt" with his "teeth" (IV.iii.1835–36). The furiously jealous husband will destroy Annabella in order to find out the mysterious inner motivations which elude his understanding; he will destroy her lover out of sheer anger and frustration. Soranzo has come to the brink of madness, where tearing human flesh seems the only release from a turbulent inner world.

The flesh-ripping metaphor adds psychological colouring to the letter incident in 'Tis Pity. In her second repentance scene, Annabella asks the Friar to deliver to her brother a "paper double lin'd with teares and blood" (V.i.2089). The reluctant Friar delivers the letter as requested, and addresses Giovanni with this ominous invitation:

> Unrip the seales and see:
> The blood's yet seething hot, that will anon
> Be frozen harder then congeal'd Corrall.
>
> (V.iii.2169–71)

Again the ripping process is a way of getting at the truth. The meaning intended by the Friar may be innocent enough, because the prosaic point of view sees only the literal truth contained in the letter and only the physical action of ripping open the seal. Despite his professional qualifications, the Friar is blind to the mysteries of a deeper and darker world.

The letter contains the news that the lovers' sin of incest has been discovered. If this is borne in mind, the Friar's metaphor gains an ironic level of considerable interest. Giovanni ruptures the seal of the letter to discover truth, just as Soranzo had threatened to rip open Annabella's body to discover the origins of her sin. The heat of blood is a traditional reference to the seething rage of sexual passion; both Annabella and Giovanni are still caught up in the tempest of desire, although the very blood that boils with sexual energy will soon congeal in death. Ripping the flesh invariably leads to frozen blood, just as ripping the seal hardens Annabella's handwriting.

The completion of this metaphoric pattern occurs in Giovanni's momentary scene of bloody triumph. He enters the banquet hall with Annabella's heart on his dagger. As he explains his action to the astonished guests, Giovanni falls back again and again on the flesh-ripping metaphor. His "Daggers poynt plow'd up / Her fruitefull wombe," he says; he "dig'd for food" in the mine of her bosom; he acted out a *"Rape of Life and Beauty"* (V.vi.2460–61, 2453, 2447). Finally he swears by the love he bore Annabella that what he claims is true: *"These hands* have from her bosome ript *this heart"* (V.vi.2493).

The dagger scene is traditionally studied under the heading of gratuitous sensationalism.[22] Gratuitous it may be, and sensational it certainly is. Yet, if one takes into account the linguistic pattern that leads up to it, and if one accepts a psychological interpretation of this final metaphor, then the scene becomes an organically functional climax to the play. Giovanni is making one last grotesque attempt to unlock the truth as he sees it. He performs the executioner's part in order to vindicate, against all odds, his belief that incestuous love can be ennobling, self-sacrificing, beautiful. He carves a martyr's heart out of the breast of a sinner.

Of course Giovanni's version of the truth is a delusion, but baroque martyrs are quite willing to act on the evidence of their private visions. Giovanni's flagrant piece of melodrama is the psychologically natural result of living in a world dominated by illusion. He believes that Annabella is holy; he believes that his incestuous love is more pure and beautiful than any experience the rational world could provide; he believes that Annabella is willing to die to preserve the purity of this passion against the debauchery of marriage to Soranzo. And when he brings her heart into the banquet hall, he believes he has proved beyond doubt that his deluded view of the world is the right one. At last he has evidence to show that his baroque metaphors do correspond to some kind of reality—a poetic reality created by his own imagination.

The word has become flesh. The poetic metaphor has become a transcendental symbol, and psychological truth blends imperceptibly with religious truth. Against his will and his better judgment, Friar Bonaventura has become the high priest who initiates a sacrifice of flesh and blood. Annabella's heart is torn from her body in order to confirm Giovanni's belief in her purity, just as the entrails of the sacrificial lamb are torn and scattered to confirm the Hebrew belief in a pure Messiah. Annabella's perfect body has become the unblemished sacrifice. Yet, her flesh is torn not to atone for the evils of her society or to appease the wrath of an angry God, but simply to breathe the life of martyrdom into a private and chimerical mythology of love.

The flesh-ripping pattern is by no means unique to Ford, though his way of using the metaphor is genuinely distinctive. A few instances of similar phrases in other plays will again set off those qualities that help to define Ford's verbal technique. Marlowe's Tamburlaine curses a contemptible villain called Almeda by urging him either to jump from a precipice or to devise some other way of extinguishing himself. Then, as if to suggest the soaring magnitude of his disdain, Tamburlaine piles one form of torture upon another: "Or rip thy bowels and rend out thy heart" (2 *Tamburlaine* III.v.121). Hyperbolic thunderings of this sort underscore the aspiring hero's conception of himself as the scourge of God. The pattern recurs in Massinger's *The Unnatural Combat*, where it takes a form much closer to Ford's usual practice. In this play, Malefort Senior admits to the governors of Marseilles that his son is a traitor and a pirate, but insists on his own "integritie and truth"; if his deeds alone do not justify him, the judge may "Rip up this bosome, and plucke out the heart / That hath beene ever loyall" (I.i.339–41).[23] Here ripping the flesh does represent discovery of inner truth—the simple truth of unalloyed fidelity. Like Marlowe, Massinger uses the expression as hyperbole, for the very idea of taking Malefort literally is out of the question. In *'Tis Pity* Ford appears to be revitalizing an old metaphor, partly by augmenting the emotional complexity of the tenor, partly by consummating the gruesome suggestions of the vehicle through physical action.

A slightly modified form of the torn flesh metaphor pervades the verbal texture of *Love's Sacrifice*—the play which comes closest to *'Tis Pity* in tone and style. In a courageous act of self-restraint after the extremely provocative chess game with Biancha, Fernando promises never to speak to her of love again. Still, he vows eternal constancy in terms that recall Giovanni's confession:

> if, when I am dead you rip
> This Coffin of my heart, *there shall you read*
> *With constant eyes, what now my tongue defines,*
> *Biancha's name carv'd out in bloody lines.*
> (II.iii.1234–37)

Since Fernando's lips are now sealed, it is only through a rape on the flesh of his bosom that Biancha may discover the depth and permanence of his love.

The implied action of carving has already set the process of mutilation into motion, for the suffering caused by love is an internal affliction inscribed on the core of Fernando's being—his heart.

In much the same way, Caraffa feels that by tearing human flesh to expose vital organs he may find out the secret that the lovers withhold from him. When Fiormonda catalyzes the suspicion of cuckoldry which is growing in his mind, Caraffa warns her to speak only truth, or he will "unrip / That wombe of bloody mischiefe" with his "nayles" (IV.i.1978–79). Mental uncertainty is so unbearable for him that he threatens his wife with the same macabre fate. If she refuses to confess her secret, he will:

> Rip up the Cradle of thy cursed wombe,
> In which the mixture of that Traytors lust
> Impostumes for a birth of Bastardy.
> (V.i.2424–26)

When at last he puts his threat into action, when he does sever Biancha's flesh with the point of his dagger, Caraffa finds out the truth about her even though it is an ironic discovery. Tearing the flesh was his desperate method for confirming his worst suspicions; now the torn flesh of his virtuous wife becomes the spiritual clothing of a martyred saint. He approaches the altar of death in the last scene to worship the woman he has killed, and offers a sacrifice of tears as a "tribute to those wounds / Which I digg'd up" (V.iii.2755–56). Of course this version of the truth is no more satisfying, objectively, than the distortions of Caraffa's jealousy were before; but to the duke's tortured mind objectivity is not a positive value. Like Giovanni, Caraffa creates a truth of his own by acting out the suggestions of his imagination.

The ripping metaphor in *Love's Sacrifice* tends to centre on the womb, and in *'Tis Pity* Giovanni uses the word "rape" to describe the action of tearing Annabella's body. Indeed, intimations of rape are surprisingly frequent throughout Ford's dramatic works. In *Perkin Warbeck*, Durham describes the pretender as a "Viper...which gnawes" at the "entrayles" of Scotland (III.iv. 1614); in *The Broken Heart*, Ithocles speaks of ambition as a serpent which "knawes / A passage through the wombe that gave it motion" (II.ii.731–32). These examples of verbal rape are coupled with savage animal imagery that makes the implied action repugnant. But usually in Ford, metaphorical rape unites the sexual impulse and the death impulse in just the sweetly ecstatic combination for which his tragic lovers long. Giovanni begs Annabella to tear his flesh, and she does not resist his dagger; Fernando opens his bosom for Biancha, and she bares her breast for Caraffa. The violence of the death wound and the violence of erotic climax come together once again in the rape metaphor. In a sense this fusion of sex and death anticipates Marvell's famous lines in "To his Coy Mistress":

> And tear our Pleasures with rough strife,
> Thorough the Iron gates of Life.[24]

But Marvell's metaphor of rape and violent death has a harshness which looks back to the mannerists and a solidity which looks forward to classicism. In Ford it is the laws of ceremony which are made of iron, while by contrast the gates of life are sensuous and soft. Though ripping the flesh is still painful, the pain becomes overwhelmingly sweet because it melts together in one physical sensation both of the ecstatic impulses which baroque lovers welcome with such relish.

Around the altars where Ford's heroes make their sacrifices to love, we find a rich cluster of sensory images including blood, sweat, tears, flames, and wounds—the characteristic material substances of baroque poetry. The epigraph which Crashaw prefixes to "The Weeper" is a key to the imagery of the poem, and indeed a key to the imagery of the baroque style:

> Loe where a WOUNDED HEART with Bleeding EYES conspire.
> Is she a FLAMING Fountain, or a Weeping fire![25]

This fluid combination of images is a special contribution of the meditative tradition to the language of poetry. The story of Mary Magdalene and the scene in Gethsemane become such fruitful *topoi* for the meditative writers, because they allow for maximum development of baroque imagery. Puente advises the Christian to imitate the example of the Magdalene, who "watered, and bedewed" Christ's feet "with her brinish teares" in order to express "an amorous internall sorrow." In much the same way, the Saviour's agony in the garden stirs up "a lively apprehension of dolerous paynes" through the power of "imagination." Jesus could not wait for the real, physical agonies of death, Puente writes, "but he chose rather that his owne imagination and holy zeale, should serve him for executioners, by soe lively a representation of those cruell torments, which he was shortly to suffer in every part of his body: so that, that alone suffised to make him sweat bloud from his head, his face, his shoulders, his brest, and from the rest of his body."[26] Of course Puente goes on to spell out the doctrinal significance of both episodes, but not until he has fully exploited the power of imagery to call forth the internal sorrow of suffering. Again the mythology of meditation inspires parallel developments in visual art and literature. We need only recall the special importance of Mary Magdalene in baroque painting, or the poignancy of baroque crucifixion scenes, to recognize that patterns of baroque iconography and clusters of baroque imagery spring from the same mythological source.[27]

In this connection Ford's relationship to the baroque tradition is more than a matter of speculation. His first specimen of fully baroque writing—*Christes Bloodie Sweat, or the Sonne of God in his Agonie*—develops the same sensuous and mystical images that we find in Puente's meditation "Of the Bloudy Sweat of Jesus Christ." At the beginning of Ford's poem, the speaker finds himself "ravish't" with the heat of a "sacred flame." A divine voice instructs him not to write about the vanities of the world, but to sing of spiritual sorrow instead:

> Set then the tenour of thy dolefull song,
> To the deepe accentes of my bloudy sweate!
> Sweete straines of Musicke, sweetly mixt among,
> The discord of my paines, the pleasure great.
>
> · · · · · · · · · ·
>
> Here then unclaspe the burthen of my woes,
> My woes distil'd into a streame of teares,
> My teares, begetting sighes, which sighes disclose
> A rocke of torment, which affliction beares.[28]

The language of this poem lives up to the expectations created by the title. Blood, sweat, and tears are present on nearly every page, and wounds are almost as frequent if one counts references such as "torment" and "affliction" in the passage just quoted. Like Puente's meditating soul, Ford's speaker enlists the sensuous materials of the imagined scene in order to recreate the ecstasy of suffering. Of course the images stand for more than Christ's psychological condition, because there are unavoidable symbolic meanings at work. The speaker frequently urges the wandering soul to bathe in the pool of Christ's bloody sweat and have his sins purged. Sinners may be excluded from heaven, "al because they were too slacke in teares,"

> Which are the ready tokens *Christ* hath lent,
> His bloody sweate on earth to represent.
>
> .   .   .   .
>
> This is a rule in text for certaine given,
> An eye still drie doth seldome come to heaven.[29]

In the context of Christian meditation, these baroque images participate in a symbolic process that describes the relationship between Christ and the soul. Christ's sweat in the Garden of Gethsemane and his blood on the cross are complementary symbols of his suffering for mankind, and of his power to regenerate man's soul. Human tears stand for the honest repentance which leads to new life. Flames, as in the Pentecost story, represent the coming of the Holy Spirit to guide the soul through life. But this is by no means a theological system of unusual complexity; in fact, it is hardly a theological system at all, for the emphasis is not on argument or dogma but rather on the direct religious experience of the human soul.

In its moments of greatest power and greatest emotional suggestiveness, Ford's dramatic verse reverberates with these typically baroque images. Caraffa's speech at Biancha's tomb is the purest example of this image cluster at work. The duke offers up his "bleeding teares" to anoint the "wounds" of Biancha's blessed body (V.iii.2749–55). This act of worship reformulates the imagery of the duke's earlier speeches on similar subjects. In his initial response to the thought of cuckoldry, for example, Caraffa feels his "frozen blood... kindled" like "flames of burning sulphure" (III.iii.1777–79). The tomb speech contains repeated references to Caraffa's rage, choler, and fury, and thus recalls the powerful flame imagery of this first angry outburst. And the language of repentance in the tomb speech brings to mind the words in which Caraffa has urged his wife to repent. "Weepe in teares of blood," he advises her (V.i.2509). Biancha's guilt appears so monstrous to Caraffa that "were the sluces of thine eyes let up, / Teares cannot wash it off" (V.i.2512–13). Now he must cleanse his own soul in a metaphorical pool of blood, while weeping tears of repentance and adoration. And in his final reference to Biancha's wounds, Caraffa consolidates the imagery of the passage by introducing the flesh-ripping metaphor again. What makes this linguistic pattern particularly effective is not any single instance of "blood" or "tears" or "flames," but the cumulative effect of these images in combination. By the time Caraffa makes his climactic funeral speech, the various images in the cluster are already established linguistic elements and have become part of the fabric of the play. Thus, he can draw on the associations that have been built up in previous scenes in order to bathe the funeral passage in a mysterious, sacramental glow. The tear-blood-wound configuration dresses the duke in rhetorical robes of penitence. Like Crashaw's Mary Magdalene, Caraffa speaks the language of "The Weeper."

Before tracing this pattern through some of Ford's other plays, we may step back once again in order to look at the relative function of imagery in renaissance, mannerist, and baroque stylistic phases. No one could deny the importance of imagery to the texture of a renaissance play like *Doctor Faustus*. Indeed, in Caraffa's penitence we have something like a remote echo of Faustus' memorable lines:

> See, see, where Christ's blood streams in the firmament!
> One drop would save my soul, half a drop! Ah, my Christ!
>
> (V.ii.143–44)

But here the powerful appeal to blood does not have the direct sensory quality which we usually associate with imagery, and which seems to be particularly strong in baroque imagery. The reference to blood is a theological allusion rather than an image in its own right. And the other atmospheric components of the baroque image cluster—wounds, tears, flames, and sweat—are entirely absent from Faustus' final speech, even though the subject is repentance, death, and hell. Instead we have references to Pythagoras, to

Lucifer, and to "Adders and serpents" (V.ii.185). Facing death, Faustus is still arguing back and forth about the theological matters that plagued his mind throughout life. He cannot loosen his intellectual grip; he cannot plunge wholeheartedly into the experience of death, as the baroque martyrs and saints do.

The distinction between linear and painterly technique in the visual arts is particularly helpful as a key to the differences between renaissance and baroque imagery. In Faustus' death speech, despite the emotional stress of the moment, the lines of argument are still in firm control. Images are used to illustrate particular theological points, to define Faustus' reactions in precise terms, or to create a clear picture of the eternal torment for which he is bound. The speech has a calculated unity—a unity of strict design. Each image stands by itself, independently suggesting a certain sensory quality or a definite thematic idea. The unity of the speech is a matter of drawing links of correlation between these separate images until a coherent design emerges. The images of Caraffa's tomb speech do not function in this regulated linear fashion. In the baroque image cluster, one sensory impression merges with another and the images produce a vision that is slightly hazy rather than precise. In Crashaw's poetry tears change imperceptibly into sweat, and sweat into blood. In the same way, Caraffa's sacrifice of "bleeding tears" blends two liquid images into one, and blurs the border between two sensory impressions. In general, the renaissance image presents a clear picture of reality, while the baroque image cluster disguises reality in atmospheric mystery.

Mannerist verse makes ironic use of renaissance imagery. In Webster the terrors of hell are still part of the language of tragedy, but something peculiar has happened to the standard images of destruction. It has become difficult to believe in eternal damnation, as Flamineo's "death scene" in *The White Devil* shows. Vittoria thinks she has murdered her brother, yet she is not penitent or even deeply stirred. Bitterly she tells him that his sins will "fetch fire from hell" to guide him on his way (V.vi.140–41). Flamineo's response lacks theological conviction:

> O I smell soot,
> Most stinking soot, the chimney is a-fire,—
> My liver's parboil'd like Scotch holy bread;
> There's a plumber, laying pipes in my guts,—it scalds.
>
> (V.vi.141–44)[30]

The fire of hell is brought down from its traditional level of eternal importance by the prosaic chimney image. Even the verb "fetch" seems more appropriate to a chimney-sweep than to the messenger of death, and the plumbing conceit reduces the pain of death to the level of mechanical gadgetry. Of course Flamineo feels he can afford to be frivolous because he is only pretending to die, but then the very fact that he can treat the prospect of death with such irreverence is in itself an indication of the mannerist style.

Just as the sure vision of the renaissance requires precise images, so the doubts of mannerism express themselves in images of distortion, reduction, and ironic inversion. The lines that define and clarify in renaissance style become jagged, contorted, negative in value. In the baroque phase, images are no longer primarily words that define, either in the positive sense of renaissance style or in the negative fashion of mannerism. Baroque images are so suggestive precisely because they refuse to define, to outline, to limit.

The baroque image cluster shared by Crashaw's "The Weeper" and Ford's *Love's Sacrifice* is more than happy coincidence, as a few further references will demonstrate. In *The Broken Heart* many of the more emotional speeches are tinged with imagery of the "weeper" variety. Ithocles seems to be the one character who avoids such emotive language, since by his standards the rhetoric of war and ambition is more meaningful. But when he sees Penthea in extreme suffering he is at last drawn to confess his own love for Calantha, and in this state of vulnerability he suddenly adopts the baroque idiom. In an attempt to comfort Penthea he says:

> Trouble not
> The fountaines of mine eyes with thine owne story,
> I sweat in blood for't.

(III.ii.1236–38)

Even this Spartan warrior can mingle tears, sweat, and blood until they become indistinguishable from each other. In a moment of psychological penance Ithocles stands in as much need of these mystery-laden liquids as any of the softer characters.

Bassanes varies the pattern slightly in his most passionate reaction to Penthea's madness:

> Fall on me, if there be a burning *Etna*,
> And bury me in flames; sweats hot as sulphure,

Boyle through my pores: affliction hath in store
No torture like to this.

(IV.ii.1902–1905)

This image cluster is even more violent than the usual baroque configuration. The elements present are flames, wounds, and sweat; the languid influence of tears is absent. A specific image of the volcanic mountain with its eruption of molten lava adds not only heat and intensity, but also malleability. The melting action of the volcano could stand as an emblem for the process by which baroque images blend and merge under the heat and pressure of passion.

Bergetto's death in *'Tis Pity* is a perplexing event, and here the typical baroque images have an ambiguous function. Nowhere in the play is Bergetto a fully sympathetic figure; he lacks both the intense emotions of the tragic lovers and the pragmatic virtues of Putana and the Friar. Yet, in his moment of death the baroque images surround Bergetto and almost canonize him as one of love's martyrs. Richardetto reports the details of the accident: "what's here? all blood! O sirs, / *Signior Donado's* Nephew now is slaine." Then he instructs Philotis to use her linen "to stop his wounds" (III.vii.1490–96). Bergetto's own words break the solemnity: "Oh my belly seeths like a Porridge-pot, some cold water I shall boyle over else; my whole body is in a sweat, that you may wring my shirt....Is all this mine owne blood? nay then good-night with me, *Poggio*" (III.vii.1485–99). Bergetto has only this one grand moment, and the supporting characters do their utmost to invest the scene with the rhetoric of pathos. But the blood, sweat, and flames of this passage emerge from the "belly" and the "Porridge-pot" of the ironic mode. Bergetto himself is either too foolish or not foolhardy enough to sustain the illusion of martyrdom.

In a broader sense the entire action of *'Tis Pity* may be outlined as a series of modulations on the baroque image cluster. At the beginning of the play Giovanni's "hidden flames" of desire and Annabella's secret "teares" are the dominant sensory images (I.iii.382, 434). Friar Bonaventura transmutes the quality of Giovanni's fiery passion as he warns Annabella to shun the "flaming horrour" of hell (III.vi.1409). In an aphorism worthy of the Friar, Vasques calls Hippolita a "Fire-brand, that hath kindled others and burnt thy selfe" (IV.i. 1694); Hippolita's career of evil must end in the "cruell flames" of death (IV.i.1714). At length the sin of incest is discovered, so Annabella writes her last message to Giovanni in a "paper double lin'd with teares and blood"

(V.i.2089). Discovery leads to catastrophe. When Giovanni approaches Annabella in the closet scene he is weeping "funerall teares" (V.v.2359), for he knows he must kill her in an act that combines love with worship. "How overglorious art thou in thy wounds," he will say to her (V.v.2420). The rhetoric of martyrdom is now complete. Annabella's "reeking blood" will inspire Giovanni to face his own death in the spirit of glorious triumph (V.vi.2437).

Analysis of individual figures of speech is by necessity an artificial undertaking which runs the risk of implying that poetic technique is a layer of decoration. In Ford's case nothing could be further from the truth. To correct any misapprehensions, I have selected for particular attention a representative passage from *Love's Sacrifice* in which all of the primary themes of the play are adroitly suggested through characteristic verbal patterns. Caraffa is reporting a troubled dream of cuckoldry to his wife:

> me thought
> (Marke what I say) as I in glorious pompe
> Was sitting on my Throne, whiles I had hemm'd
> My best belov'd *Biancha* in mine armes,
> She reacht my cap of State, and cast it downe
> Beneath her foot, and spurn'd it in the dust;
> Whiles I (oh 'twas a dreame too full of fate)
> Was stooping downe to reach it; on my head,
> *Fernando*, like a Traytor to his vowes,
> Clapt, in disgrace, a Coronet of hornes:
> But by the honour of anoynted kings,
> Were both of you hid in a rocke of fire,
> Guarded by ministers of flaming hell,
> I have a sword ('tis here) should make my way
> Through fire, through darknesse, death, and all
> To hew your lust ingendred flesh to shreds,

Pound you to morter, cut your throats, and mince
Your flesh to mites; I will,—start not,—I will.

(IV.ii.2229–46)

At the surface, technical schemes and devices of metre support the psychological movement of the speech. The duke's anxieties have aroused a whirlwind
of confused emotions within him, so the lines are restless with enjambments
and hesitations. Frequent parentheses (to the actor these constitute pauses, to the
rhetorician *aposiopesis*) indicate that Caraffa finds it impossible to proceed in a
step-by-step progression. He interrupts his train of thought first to be sure of
Biancha's attention, then to interject a complaint about the cruelty of fate, and
next to threaten Biancha with his sword. In the last line he pauses again to insert
a belligerent command.

At the beginning of the speech Caraffa pretends to be calm, but his nerve is
shaken by the spectre of jealousy which his imagination creates. By the end of
the passage he is in a frenzy. The menacing verbs "hew," "pound," "cut," and
"mince" form an emotional crescendo that builds to a sudden climax, and then
explodes in the final, broken assertion: "I will,—start not,—I will." Caraffa's
threats, like his thoughts, refuse to follow a logical order: it would be impossible for him to cut the lovers' throats after he had already pounded them to
mortar. Thus, the fantasy conjured up by jealousy prompts a tirade in which
threat follows threat regardless of logical consequences. Even the tiniest
stylistic devices are pressed into service in order to suggest impulsive and uneven
movement of psychic energy.

The figurative language in this dream sequence is extremely rich in variety
and suggestiveness, and it springs organically from the structure of the play as a
whole. First, there is the pattern of monarchial imagery, or what we may call
the language of grandeur. The duke pictures himself, in this dream world
where wish fulfilment is the criterion of plausibility, as a king who sits in
"glorious pompe" on a "Throne." At once we are alerted to the disparity in rank
between this mighty potentate of dreamland and the real duke of a petty Italian
city-state called *Pavy*. In Caraffa's very first speech we have seen a hint of this
aggrandized self-image. Embracing his wife in one arm and his best friend in the
other, he pronounces himself "a Monarch of felicitie" (I.i.217). He defines
domestic happiness in royal terms, assuming always that he holds the top rank
in the hierarchy.

We seldom see the duke engaged in governmental activity, and the few references to his political decisions hardly inspire confidence. As if to point out how far domestic matters outrank affairs of state in his scheme of values, Caraffa prides himself on having acted against the conservative advice of the senate in selecting Biancha for his wife. After the public murder of Ferentes, the duke first announces that he intends to administer swift justice, and then capitulates for personal reasons, without so much as a cursory glance at the evidence. The symbolic trappings and the prestige of his office are what matter to the duke. The delusion of royalty is much more real to him than the actual events in his little kingdom.

To return to the dream sequence, we find Biancha throwing her husband's "cap of State" (the emblem of royal felicity) into the dust. D'Avolos has aroused Caraffa's suspicions, and the duke now fears that Biancha will humiliate him and destroy his fictional monarchy. The dreaming duke stoops down (the posture is decidedly servile) to retrieve his crown, but Fernando substitutes instead a "Coronet of hornes." The coronet is of course a small crown, worn by lesser nobility, which varies in size according to rank. Caraffa's best friend has deprived him of the regal grandeur of the dream world, in order to define the duke's new rank with the cuckold's emblem. This inverted use of the imagery of kingship adds point and ironic thrust to D'Avolos's remarks: princes are grander than peasants, D'Avolos believes, only insofar as their horns are "mounted some two inches higher" (II.iii.1250). In much the same spirit, D'Avolos provides knowing commentary for the chess game between Fernando and Biancha; a pawn usurps the place of a knight (or duke), and a few moments later the queen is captured (II.iii.1143–61). Biancha herself picks up the rhetoric of grandeur when she admits that Fernando has supplanted Caraffa in her affections: "You have beene onely King," she confesses to her lover at last (II.iv.1297). The duke's pretended rank now seems trivial beside the monarchy of love, just as his professed power becomes impotence when compared to love's "tyranny" (II.iv.1299). In the end Caraffa's make-believe kingdom is just as fragile and just as unpredictable as the play-world of the chessboard.

The dream now turns into a nightmare. The humiliated duke accuses Fernando of acting "like a Traytor to his vowes." This apparently innocent formula alludes again to the system of interlocking vows which forms the structural core of the play. Caraffa explicitly invokes the bond of friendship between himself and Fernando, and implicitly calls attention to the corresponding bond of marriage between himself and Biancha. What he does not realize, of course, is that Biancha and Fernando have already exchanged a set of vows which elevates their own relationship beyond the level of earthly felicity. The lovers have carved their names in "*bloody lines*" on one another's hearts (II.iii.1237; II.iv.1383). They have exchanged a fidelity that will reach fulfilment through death.

Caraffa's multiple threats of violence at the end of the dream sequence amount to a variation on the rape metaphor. Since the duke's dream leaves him in bewildered uncertainty, he determines to discover the truth by severing human flesh to expose the vital organs which contain the mysteries of love. Thus, his threats enlist all of the associations that have been built up in previous scenes of emotional duress. Furthermore, the rhetoric of blood and violence prefigures the moment of truth in which Biancha's physical wounds will reveal the sanctity of her love for Fernando.

The most important linguistic pattern in terms of the play as a whole may be called the language of erotic martyrdom. And indeed Caraffa suggests this level of imagery in his dream report, for as soon as the dream-duke realizes his disgrace, Biancha and Fernando are concealed in "a rocke of fire" and "Guarded by ministers of flaming hell." The duke is reporting a nightmare, so it is natural that he should equate the burning rock with a demonic world of endless torture. From this point of view the rock burns with flames that scorch the souls of the lovers in punishment for sin, and the ministers of hell are devils who keep the damned in perpetual captivity. But there is at least a strong likelihood that Caraffa is misinterpreting his dream in the very act of reporting it. Like the clergy in *Saint Joan*, Caraffa believes that sin must be punished with fire; but as Joan's heart is not consumed by earthly flames, so Biancha's soul will be refined and at last sanctified on the altar of love. The rock of fire in the duke's dream is a miraculous occurrence, and miracles traditionally accompany martyrdom. Furthermore, it recalls both the "rocke of torment" (a martyrdom symbol) and the "fierie Piller" (a miraculous event) of *Christes Bloodie Sweat* (sigs. B1ᵛ, I1ᵛ). The burning rock which hides Biancha and Fernando is certainly religious in character, since it bears a striking resemblance both to the biblical rock of salvation (Isa. xxxii.2) and to the red rock of *The Waste Land*. Though fire is an instrument of cruel torture, in the context of martyrdom it becomes the agent which purifies the ascending soul. The "ministers" may well be a heavenly escort for the upward journey. In his subconscious dream world, Caraffa sees Fernando and Biancha not only as lovers, but as martyrs to love. His fantasy looks forward to the scene of death at the end of the play, where the lovers will be sheltered from Caraffa again in the actual rock of the tomb.

The images, metaphors, and rhetorical devices of the duke's dream are important in themselves, for the richness and intensity of the blank verse depends on such poetic techniques. But much more important, the verbal texture of this short speech reverberates with echoes from every level of the play's linguistic structure. Pauses, interjections, and enjambments underscore the emotional dynamics of the scene by suggesting the turbulence within Caraffa's soul. Monarchial images support the theme of illusion; the accusation of treason builds on the system of lovers' vows; threats of violence ring a change on the pervasive rape metaphor; and the rock of fire complements the pattern of martyrdom. The dream sequence, then, functions as a play within the play, or better still, as a dream within the dream. Since Ford's dramatic interests find their centre in the suffering human heart, the stuff that dreams are made on can furnish ideal verbal substance for expressing his subjective vision.

CHAPTER FIVE

GREAT MEN AND WORTHY OF REPORT

An Essay on Massinger, Fletcher, Shirley, and Otway

IN describing Ford as a baroque dramatist I have repeatedly emphasized the very qualities of theme, structure, and language that separate his plays from the work of the principal Elizabethan and Jacobean playwrights. The baroque style of Ford's plays, I have argued, makes them distinctive and unusual in the history of English drama. It would be shortsighted and naïve, however, to conclude that Ford stands entirely aloof from the world of his contemporaries; in fact, he shares many baroque tendencies with several other leading dramatists of the seventeenth century. The most notable members of this baroque circle are Massinger, Fletcher, Shirley, and Otway.

On the surface Massinger appears to be the English dramatist who most clearly resembles Ford. The two men lived and moved within the same literary and theatrical environment. Like Ford, Massinger wrote plays both for the King's men and for Queen Henrietta Maria's company.[1] Ford contributed laudatory if deferential verses for the publication of two Massinger plays— *The Roman Actor* and *The Great Duke of Florence*. While such occasional poems do not prove any degree of intimacy, they do suggest that Ford admired his more experienced and more productive contemporary. Indeed, Ford seems to emulate Massinger's dramatic practice in a more fundamental way: he borrows, adapts, and revises many of Massinger's favourite themes and situations. The incest theme is of central importance in *The Unnatural Combat*, as of course it is in *'Tis Pity*. Prolonged separation of husband and wife leads to jealousy and suspicion in *The Picture*, much as it does in *The Lady's Trial*. In *A Very Woman* Massinger introduces a skilful physician, Dr. Paulo, who stages an elaborate psychological cure for the melancholy which afflicts young Cardenes; Ford amplifies and deepens the significance of this device in *The Lover's Melancholy*. Massinger deals obliquely with the Spanish pretender Don Sebastian in the surviving version of *Believe as You List*; Ford adroitly transposes this theme to an English setting in *Perkin Warbeck*.[2]

The resemblance of Massinger's *The Duke of Milan* to Ford's *Love's Sacrifice* is a particularly telling instance of the close relationship between the two drama-tists. Both plays show the destructive results of consuming, irrational, and possessive sexual jealousy. Like Caraffa in Ford's play, Sforza has married an excessively beautiful woman of whom he feels inordinately proud. During a birthday celebration in honour of the duchess, Sforza publicly boasts that marriage has not "cloyd" his sexual palate: he still enjoys Marcelia's body every night.[3] When political events require his departure from Milan, Sforza's primary concern is that Marcelia might make love to someone else in his absence. He leaves her in the care of his favourite courtier, Francisco, with the sworn proviso that in case of political or military disaster, Marcelia must be put to death. The duke's ego cannot tolerate even the possibility of his wife achieving happiness other than the happiness he gives her.

Quite understandably, a vivacious and intelligent woman like Marcelia feels deprived and confined by her status as Sforza's duchess. Like Ford's Biancha she resents the sense of ownership which her marriage to a powerful, dominant, older man implies. But, again like Biancha, she remains technically chaste in spite of Francisco's best efforts to seduce her. When Sforza returns from his diplomatic mission, he is misled by the gossip of the court and by Marcelia's unusually cold behaviour into assuming that she has been unfaithful. In order to test her chastity, Sforza tells Marcelia that he has killed her supposed lover, Francisco. Marcelia's response bristles with vigorous feminine hauteur:

> Thou hast kil'd then
> A man I doe professe I lov'd, a man
> For whom a thousand Queenes might well be rivals.
>
> (IV.iii.281–83)

Through this defiant reaction to Sforza's accusation, above all, Marcelia betrays her close kinship to Biancha. In a similar moment of crisis Biancha tells her suspicious husband that she chose Fernando as her lover because of his graceful charm and his sexual appeal. Both women confront their husbands with a specific kind of emotional truth, even though the means of stating this truth is a technical lie; both women insist on asserting their emotional integrity, even though they realize that the price of integrity is death.

The similarities between *The Duke of Milan* and *Love's Sacrifice* stand out all the more clearly by comparison with Shakespeare's development of a parallel situation in *Othello*. Desdemona shows not the slightest inclination to liberate herself from the conventions that govern sexual behaviour. She has hardly had the time or the occasion to grow resentful; she would not understand Marcelia's misgivings about becoming a mere sexual object or Biancha's inner debate about the restrictions of marriage and the laws of love. The only spokesman for the rights of women in *Othello* is Emilia, and she represents a superficially libertine rather than a genuinely liberated attitude. Furthermore, the tragic lovers in Shakespeare's play are separated from the beginning and drawn further apart by a series of objective circumstances: a permanent racial barrier, Brabantio's disapproval, the fateful handkerchief, and Iago's machinations. In both Massinger and Ford, the principal causes of tragic action are by contrast internal and psychological. The conflict between good and evil recedes to make way for a less clearly drawn struggle between complex and contrasting emotional pressures: the desire for absolute loyalty, the need for independence, the craving for inner security, the quest for sexual gratification. To judge by Desdemona's behaviour, we may assume that Shakespeare would have applauded Paula Tanqueray's grand and remorseful capitulation. On the evidence of Marcelia's attitudes or Biancha's, we may suppose that Massinger and Ford could have given poor Paula just the sort of emotional consistency and theatrical vigour that Shaw so eloquently demanded.[4]

On the whole Massinger's female characters are sensitively drawn, though few of them achieve the proud independence of Marcelia. More typical of Massinger is the recurring figure of the forsaken woman. This unfortunate victim suffers betrayal and rejection at the hands of one of the male protagonists. She hovers mysteriously at the fringes of the dramatic action until very near the conclusion, when at last she reveals the secret cause of her disgrace just in time to precipitate the tragic catastrophe or to solve the tragicomic riddle. Massinger's forsaken woman, it would appear, is the conventional model on which Ford based his portrait of Penthea.

Eugenia is the discarded mistress of Sforza in *The Duke of Milan*. She makes no physical appearance until the last act, but by this time her spiritual presence has already become part of the world of the play. While the duke himself is blindly devoted to the joys of the present, the court of Milan is alive with rumours about the past. In an attempt to bury his love affair with Eugenia in silence, Sforza has promoted her brother Francisco to a position of special prominence. Rival courtiers are quick to notice the duke's motives, especially since Eugenia has obligingly retired from the court for a period of three years. These unsavoury reminders of Sforza's past leave the audience in some doubt concerning the blissful happiness of the duke's present life. As soon as Sforza has killed Marcelia in an outburst of jealous fury, the sins of the past return with a vengeance. Eugenia comes back to court, disguised as a man, in order to gain justice for the insult she has endured. In concert with Francisco she transforms her song of complaint into a cry for revenge.

Old Malefort's first wife in *The Unnatural Combat* occupies a structural position precisely parallel to that of Eugenia. Young Malefort gives an incomplete but tantalizing explanation of his resentment toward his father: we learn that Malefort's wife has been the victim of a dark and unforgivable act of betrayal. After Malefort's full career of crime, his wife makes her first appearance, and then only as a ghost with a face afflicted by leprosy. This theatrical device has made verbal complaint quite unnecessary, so the leper-lady appears and disappears in silence. Meanwhile, in a frenzied attempt to repent, Malefort confesses the guilt of the past: he poisoned his first wife long ago because he had fallen in love with another woman. The spots of leprosy on the discarded woman's face are stigmata which convict Malefort of the "impious wrongs" (V.ii.284) which he has tried to conceal.

Pathetic as they are, Massinger's forsaken women are not restricted to tragedy. In *The Bondman*, Statilia takes the suitably humble disguise of a Persian slave in order to hide her sexual disgrace. At the end of the play she declares her identity and prepares to marry her contracted lover, Leosthenes. This tragicomic pattern is developed more successfully in *The Bashful Lover*. Here Maria is the forsaken woman who has been seduced and betrayed by Alonzo. Disguised as the page boy "Ascanio," Maria faints when her former lover makes an unexpected visit to the court of Mantua. The waiting women recall Ascanio's wistful temperament and emotional sensitivity:

He would be very pensive, and then talk
So feelingly of love, as if he had
Tasted the bitter sweets of't.

(II.i.19–21)

The conventions of tragicomedy allow Alonzo to repent before it is too late, and while he confesses his guilt Maria appears, dressed in white, pretending to be the ghost of past wrongs. Of course the "shadow" becomes "substance" (IV.ii.114–17) and the lovers leave the mournful past behind to embrace the joys of marriage.

The distinctively plaintive resonance of Massinger's forsaken women is a note to which Ford is especially responsive. Penthea is more complex by far than her tragic sisters in Massinger's plays, but she shares their lovelorn sensibility and their submerged desire for revenge. She has not been directly betrayed by her lover, as Massinger's women have been, but she feels more deeply than they do the helplessness of being cut off from the richness and promise of the past. As if to draw attention to the class of women to which Penthea belongs, Ford glosses her name with its appropriate quality, "*Complaint.*" In *The Lover's Melancholy*, Eroclea takes the part corresponding to Massinger's Statilia and Maria. Even before Eroclea appears on stage we have already heard her characteristic tone of voice through Menaphon's lyrical description; dressed in the obligatory page's costume, "Parthenophill" sings his melancholy song in competition with the nightingale. This is the keynote of Eroclea's character. Until she regains the embraces of Prince Palador, she will be a forsaken maiden in whom "Rare pity and delight are sweetly mixt" (V.i.2633).

Although Massinger habitually shares Ford's thematic concerns, only occasionally does he adopt baroque principles of dramatic structure. His most fully baroque play in this respect is a tragicomedy—*The Maid of Honour*. The principal action involves the relationship between Camiola, who plays the title role, and Bertoldo, a knight of Malta. From the outset Camiola makes it clear that she wishes to marry Bertoldo, but since the Order of Malta requires a solemn vow of celibacy, Camiola cannot accept her lover on completely honourable terms. At length she abandons her scruples, rescues Bertoldo from captivity, and indicates that she is prepared for marriage regardless of Bertoldo's vow. But by this time Bertoldo has foolishly pledged himself to another woman—Aurelia, the Duchess of Siena. Nevertheless the preparations for marriage go forward. Father Paulo is summoned to officiate at the wedding, and only at the last possible instant does he disclose that Camiola has chosen to renounce the world in favour of the spiritual joys of a monastic life. "This is the marriage!" Camiola explains:

> Fill my spreading sayles
> With the pure wind of your devotions for me,
> That I may touch the secure haven, where
> Eternall happinesse keepes her residence.
>
> (V.ii.267–71)

With ironic symmetry Massinger circumvents Bertoldo's vow of chastity only to have Camiola defeat all expectations with another religious oath. The real and external obstacles to love are withdrawn, to be replaced with less apparent but far more permanent barriers.[5]

Thus the action of *The Maid of Honour* illustrates the open form of baroque tragicomedy. A confident social solution to the problems of love is simply not available to the characters of Massinger's world. In *Twelfth Night* or *A Midsummer Night's Dream* the confusions of the past are removed with the arrival of social stability, but for Camiola the dilemmas of love are resolved through an emotional impulse that removes her from society. Nor does Massinger end his play with the harsh distributive justice characteristic of Jonson or Marston. *The Maid of Honour* concludes with a purely psychological resolution of the central problem: Camiola's erotic desire has been sublimated, has become a desire for the sublime. And by means of thematic subordination, similar laws are applied to subsidiary characters. Bertoldo himself is restored to good standing in his knightly order; he will complement Camiola's resolve by accepting again the celibate regimen of his knighthood. The self-sacrificing suitor Adorni may continue his worship of woman, but only from a respectable distance. The foppish suitor, Signior Sylli, is consigned by definition to a life of frustration. In characteristic baroque fashion, the dominant motif of the main action gives shape and significance to the subordinate levels of the play.

Taken as a whole, Massinger is by no means so pure an example of baroque dramatic style as Ford. *The Duke of Milan* and *The Maid of Honour* are his nearest approaches to baroque drama, but they are not entirely representative of Massinger's artistry. To selectively outline the similarities between Massinger and Ford, then, is to risk considerable distortion. At his best and most typical,

Massinger betrays an honest middle-class bias which is totally alien to Ford, and which would appear quite out of place in most baroque writers. Social status generates the central conflict in *A New Way to Pay Old Debts* and *The City Madam*; both Sir Giles Overreach and Luke Frugal violate the accepted standards of bourgeois behaviour, but in both cases the norm remains intact. Even in less overtly didactic plays Massinger's middle-class outlook frequently prescribes a moralistic couplet which summarizes the ethical significance of the action. At the close of *The Unnatural Combat* the governor of Marseilles pauses to explicate the implied meaning of Malefort's miraculous death:

> There cannot be a want of power above
> To punish murther, and unlawfull love.
>
> (V.ii.342–43)

This relentlessly moralistic habit of mind is less objectionable in Massinger than it might be, because it is expressed ingenuously and openly. It would be unfair to require from Massinger a degree of sophistication that he does not aspire to, but it is only accurate to remark that his simple and middle-class ethical outlook separates him from the mainstream of the baroque literary tradition.[6]

Massinger's undistinguished verbal style is a second crucial way in which he fails to qualify as a fully baroque writer. Seldom does he exploit the subtle and evocative figures of speech that characterize Ford's verbal idiom. For Massinger's characters the language of emotion is a rather transparent medium; even at the highest points of emotional pressure they tend to describe rather than express their feelings.[7] Sforza kneels over the body of his murdered wife, and delivers an oratorical pronouncement that affirms but does not reflect the torment of his soul. Sir Giles Overreach becomes magnificent in his madness, but his language remains undeniably vigorous and lucid. Perhaps, as Eliot implies, Massinger simply lacks the imagination of a poet. His complicated sentences (well-furnished with subordinate clauses, parenthetical elements, and phrases in apposition) are a better medium for abstract thought than for emotional expression and response.

Both Massinger's moralism and his linguistic habits are the result of his unusually bold confidence in the virtue and power of reason. Here again he is certainly not baroque. His view of the human soul is by no means distinctive, since it is built up of the standard Stoical doctrines concerning the warfare between man's baser passions and his noble reasoning faculties. If human reason has been corrupted, for Massinger at least it has not lost its decisive influence on the lives and affairs of men. In *The Roman Actor*, Paris makes a sustained apology for the theatre which depends entirely on the techniques of logical argument and presupposes the rational capabilities of his auditors. When virtuous actions are "done to the life" on stage, Paris argues, they will inspire moral courage in the spectators (I.iii.90–95). Conversely, a well-drawn scene of vice will dissuade men from vicious actions. Amazingly, the enemies of the theatre are susceptible to such a rational appeal; for the moment at least Paris has won his case. And meanwhile he has stated as clearly and reasonably as possible a doctrine of aesthetics that Massinger appears to endorse. The actor, like any other artist, submits to his mimetic responsibility. For Massinger, a good imitation of "life" is the reasonable goal toward which art strives. For baroque artists and writers, the imagination creates a world beyond reality and above the expectations of reason.

Beaumont and Fletcher claim a special place in any discussion of English baroque drama, and indeed several critics have independently outlined the apparently baroque dimensions of the Beaumont and Fletcher world. In a series of articles on the subject, Marco Mincoff argues that the famous collaborators share neither the positive assumptions of their Elizabethan predecessors, nor the pessimism of the Jacobeans; rather, they initiate a wave of "early baroque" drama that soon gains a dominant position in the English theatre and leads eventually to the heroic plays of Dryden. The courtly tone of the Beaumont and Fletcher plays, the artificial gestures and attitudes of their characters, the unstable fluctuations of emotional impulses—these, according to Mincoff, are hallmarks of the baroque style.[8] This argument gains support from the less systematic reflections of critics who appear to stumble as if by chance into very similar positions. André Koszul, for example, defines the baroque nature of the Beaumont and Fletcher plays by listing such qualities as as theatricality, extravagance, and apparent insincerity.[9] Eugene M. Waith defends the structural vagaries of *Women Pleased* by appealing to baroque principles of construction: "Fletcher's is a baroque art," he contends, "in which distortion is a legitimate part of the elaborate design."[10] And for William W. Appleton, the more pathetic scenes of *The Maid's Tragedy* come to life through a "baroque heightening" reminiscent of Bernini's dramas in marble.[11]

In a loosely impressionistic way these judgments do manage to suggest the flavour of Beaumont and Fletcher's dramatic art, but they must be qualified in one important respect. The Beaumont and Fletcher plays are, on the whole, at least as close to the world of mannerism as to the baroque. Theirs is not the biting, caustic mannerism of Webster and Middleton, but rather the elegant, refined mannerism of a more sophisticated and more courtly milieu. In a book dealing principally with the visual arts, John Shearman characterizes mannerism as "the stylish style," and applies the term to "works of art which are polished, rarefied and idealized away from the natural."[12] The touchstone of the style is outward grace of form and address; its key exemplars are Parmigianino, Bronzino, Benvenuto Cellini, and the School of Fontainebleau. In his enthusiasm for "the stylish style" Shearman vigorously attacks the more generally accepted notion of mannerism as a crisis of nervous doubt and unresolved tension. Without presuming to solve the debates among art historians, it is possible to suggest that the two views of mannerism are not as diametrically opposed as the partisans on each side might pretend. Decorative elegance and nervous tension may have a great deal in common; both may be appropriate artistic responses to the skeptical climate that replaces the assurance of the high renaissance. In the English drama it is indeed the case that the darkness of Webster and the grace of Fletcher grow to maturity side by side in the same crucial transitional period. "The stylish style," then, may be taken as one of the basic trends within the larger context of mannerism. And it is to this elegant world of mannerism that Beaumont and Fletcher primarily belong.

Since the sheer bulk of the Beaumont and Fletcher canon rules comprehensive treatment quite out of the question, I have chosen to concentrate on three representative plays: *The Mad Lover, A Wife for a Month,* and *The Maid's Tragedy.* The first two of these are tragicomedies, written entirely by Fletcher. The third is perhaps the highest achievement of the dramatists working in collaboration. I have selected these three plays because of their intrinsic merits, because of their relation to Ford's drama, and because they seem closer to the baroque style than most of the plays in the canon. Since Fletcher's is the dominant name both in the canon as a whole and in the three works I wish to discuss, I shall adopt the convenient shorthand of referring to "Fletcher's drama" and "Fletcher's style" instead of repeatedly insisting on both collaborators as separate individuals.

The Mad Lover announces in its title a subject that Ford would later develop in a number of plays, beginning with The Lover's Melancholy. But in Fletcher there is little of the psychological complexity that one finds in such grief-stricken lovers as Palador, Fernando, and Orgilus. The central character of Fletcher's play is Memnon, a military man of great achievement and prestige, who during a peaceful interlude in his warlike career falls desperately in love with Calis, the princess of Paphos. Unfortunately Memnon lacks all of the social gifts required by the courtship situation, so he bungles his first interview with Calis disastrously. At first he kneels to her and stares at her totally unable to speak, and when he recovers his senses he can muster nothing more eloquent than the brief declaration, "I love thee Lady," or the brusque imperative, "Good Lady kiss me" (I.i).[13] Complete dedication to the life of the soldier has left Memnon a social cripple; hence, he is unable to function in the world of the court. His madness is a fairly simple form of social dislocation; as a result, most of the symptoms of madness are comic rather than pathetic.[14]

Memnon's distinguishing characteristic is the verbal flat-footedness already evident from his initial attempt at courtship. And much of the action of the play is generated by his habit of reading even the most fanciful conceits of the Petrarchan tradition as if they were literal statements. When Calis doubts the integrity of his "truly loving heart," Memnon insists that his tangible, physical heart could prove his emotional condition:

> I would you had it in your hand, sweet Lady,
> To see the truth it bears you.
>
> (I.i, p. 16)

Not satisfied with verbal literalism, Memnon calls a surgeon and gives strict orders to have his heart cut out of his body and sent to his mistress. Polydore, Memnon's brother, in fact delivers to the princess a physical heart in a transparent cup, calling it "the Legacie of Love" (III.i, p. 41). This heart is of course no more than a contrivance in the game of love. The audience is soon reassured when Memnon enters in the next act and begins to ponder, again in a gravely literal-minded way, the doctrine of the happy afterlife where lovers will embrace forever.

Despite the absurdity of Memnon's conduct, two of his friends take his madness seriously and set out to devise a series of cures. The first attempted cure is an exquisite musical duet by Orpheus ("a supplicating tenor") and Charon ("a deep bass").[15] The singers warn Memnon not to believe in a blissful Elysium, but to face realistically the cruel and painful effects of unrequited love. To underscore the lesson, Orpheus conjures up a "Masque of Beasts" which includes a lion who died by the rules of chivalry and a dog "that hung himself for love" (IV.i, p. 49). The final attempted cure is a burlesque version of the bed trick: a young whore is tarted up to resemble the princess Calis, and Memnon discovers the difference between the two only by using his sense of smell. Like the "Masque of Melancholy" arranged by Corax in *The Lover's Melancholy*, these devices have very little influence on the state of mind of the patient. But Memnon never becomes a fully sympathetic victim of emotional pressures, in the way that Palador and Meleander do. Memnon's real cure in fact is no more than a return to military life at the end of the play, when he learns that Calis has chosen his brother Polydore as her lover and husband. He announces that the grand "imployment" of battle will be his new "Mistress" (V.i, p. 74), and there can be no doubt this time that he has chosen wisely and well.

Yet Memnon is not the only mad lover of the play. Through a pattern of thematic fusion very similar to Ford's practice, Fletcher presents a full spectrum of mad lovers ranging from the soldier Siphax to the princess Calis herself. Siphax strikes a pose as the sexually experienced realist who can easily see through the veil of Memnon's madness. He knowingly offers to act as the lovers' go-between, approaches Calis on Memnon's behalf, and promptly finds himself drawn into the same vortex of desire that has claimed his general. Siphax's responses, unpredictable and irrational as they are, lend a degree of credibility even to Memnon's absurdity. By the same token Calis falls violently and impulsively in love with Polydore during the very ceremony in which Memnon's supposed heart is being offered to her. She falls into a swoon ostensibly because the mad lover's heart has violated her refined sensibilities, but in fact because she herself has become vulnerable to Polydore's powerful appeal.

The affair of Calis and Polydore is resolved in yet another literal projection of

Petrarchan rhetoric. The supposed Oracle of Venus tells Calis that she is destined to embrace a dead man as her lover:

> And, for thou hast been stern and coy,
> A dead Love thou shalt enjoy.
>
> (V.i, p. 62)

In the final scene Polydore's body is carried on stage in a hearse. Feeling that the prophecy is now fulfilled, Calis weeps, mourns, and pledges never to forsake the tomb of her dead shepherd. At this point Polydore rises from his hearse to take his final and rightful position at the side of the princess. The action has given theatrical substance and literal meaning to the supposed power of the lady to kill with a frown and restore life with a tear of pity.[16]

I have lingered over the events of *The Mad Lover* because they intersect so curiously with similar events in Ford's plays. The obvious parallel between Fletcher's play and *The Lover's Melancholy* is a matter of record and requires no further comment. More suggestive are the affinities between *The Mad Lover* and Ford's tragedies. The comic Oracle of Venus in Fletcher unites the living and the dead, just as the cryptic scroll in Ford calls for a union of the lifeless trunk of Ithocles and the broken heart of Calantha. Polydore rises out of the hearse to claim his love, just as Fernando rises from the tomb to join Biancha in erotic martyrdom. And of course the device of the lover's heart becoming flesh and blood gives the dagger scene in *'Tis Pity* its brilliantly rich and sensational colouring.

The difference between these events in Fletcher and their counterparts in Ford is partly, but only partly, the difference between tragicomedy and tragedy. It is also the difference between the surface elegance of mannerism and the deep intensity of the baroque. Actions of deviance and perversity in *The Mad Lover* are always defined and circumscribed by the social code which in the long run outlasts and may indeed assimilate such violations of decorum. Similar actions in *Love's Sacrifice* and *'Tis Pity* are expressions of individual fantasies which defiantly surge beyond social convention. If Memnon's heart remains transparent artifice, Annabella's heart becomes artistic truth. Fletcher's play depends for much of its effect on sustained but good-natured parody of the rhetorical conventions of courtly love. The result is a tone of *badinage* which appeals in particular to an informed and clever audience. Ford's plays transform the conventions once more, but this time in order to generate the grotesque horror and the sweet pathos of baroque tragedy.

A Wife for a Month is a clear example of Fletcher's tendency to design a plot that dominates the play at the expense of almost everything else.[17] In this case the key incidents are the result of a malicious and even sadistic scheme put in motion by Frederick, the usurping king of Naples. Frederick is frankly described as *"unnatural and libidinous"* in the *dramatis personae*; he provides the play with its initial complication by declaring that he wants Evanthe for his mistress. Because she lives by virtuous principles and because she intends to marry Valerio, her true lover, Evanthe haughtily declines the king's proposition. At this point Frederick sets up his game of cat-and-mouse. He permits Evanthe to marry Valerio, on the condition that he will be put to death after exactly one month; subsequently she must choose another husband on precisely the same terms, and so on and so on, indefinitely. She can break this cruel circle only by accepting Frederick as her lover. Yet Evanthe and Valerio agree to these terms and are married. On their wedding night, however, Frederick sends a messenger to Valerio to announce a change in the rules: Valerio must by no means make love to his wife; if he does, she will certainly be put to death; he is likewise forbidden to tell her the reason for his sexual restraint. On these new terms the bridal-night scene becomes an exercise in frustration for both lovers. Evanthe warmly invites her lover to bed, while he evades her first with a profession of rarefied spiritual love, finally with a bitter (though of course fraudulent) confession of physical impotence. There appears to be no way for the lovers to escape Frederick's artificially built madhouse. The situation changes only when Alphonso, Frederick's older brother, recovers from his prolonged melancholy and replaces Frederick as king. The true and wise ruler sentences his brother to a life of monastic renunciation; the path is now clear for Evanthe and Valerio to join in a marriage of souls *and* bodies.

The intensely frustrating situations which Fletcher contrives for his lovers give them ample opportunity to express a willingness to sacrifice the self, even a desire to die in the name of love. Thus Valerio, upon confronting the first sign of an obstacle in his quest for Evanthe, at once adopts the posture of the expiring victim: "if I dye for her," he sighs, "I am thy Martyr, Love, and time shall honour me" (I.i, p. 13). When he speaks these lines Valerio may indeed suspect the worst, but all he knows thus far is that his love-letters to Evanthe have been intercepted. His extreme reaction is almost an invitation to the hangman—an invitation which Frederick perversely honours by devising the terms of the marriage. Though on the whole Evanthe shows more of the instinct for self-preservation than her lover, she too can play the martyr when the situation demands. Her flirtation with death follows Valerio's disclosure of the real explanation for his "impotence": namely, the king's threat to take Evanthe's life. Far from expressing gratitude to her defender, Evanthe seems to resent his interference: "And was not I as worthy to dye nobly?" she asks (IV.i, p. 56). She continues to harangue him with a series of oxymorons designed to show how he has really destroyed her in the very act of saving her life. For Valerio and Evanthe, reality is far less important than the way they appear to themselves and to one another. In a sense this is true of all lovers, at least in moments of passionate involvement. But for Fletcher's lovers in this play masochistic fantasies have a way of becoming reality itself. If King Frederick didn't exist, one is tempted to say, Valerio and Evanthe would most certainly have invented him.

A Wife for a Month is a closer approach to baroque drama than *The Mad Lover*. No amount of barefaced manipulation is enough to deprive the central characters of a certain melting pathos when they confront a threat that seems insanely real to them. In this respect they look forward to so many of the distressed lovers in Ford—Palador, Penthea, Fernando, Biancha, Alphonso, Spinella. Taken as a whole, however, the play remains a specimen of the elegant, stylish mannerism of which Fletcher is the best example in English drama. The obstacles separating the lovers, despite a certain psychological articulation, remain obstacles of the surface that simply vanish when events in the external world take a turn for the better. *A Wife for a Month* is not a formally open play; indeed, the conclusion is artificially neat and precise. Where the baroque dramatist may suggest the movement of psychological forces beyond the ending of the play, the mannerist can cut off speculation by announcing arbitrarily that the rules of the game have been changed. The lustful tyrant will be mewed up in the monastery to make room for his benevolent brother. And in its total resemblance to a game above all—a refined, permissive, elegant, highbrow game of courtly dramatist and courtier audience—*A Wife for a Month* betrays its kinship with an artistic style that nourished the riddling allegories of Bronzino and the puzzling deceptions of Parmigianino. In both verbal and visual games the degree of polish and the level of sophistication are the values that ultimately please.

The nearest approach to baroque drama in the Beaumont and Fletcher canon is doubtless *The Maid's Tragedy*. The lyrical death-wish becomes both more pronounced and more suggestive in the context of tragedy; indeed, much as in Ford, the death-wish blends with the sexual impulse in distinctive moments of masochistic ecstasy. Aspatia, the forsaken maiden who gives the play its title, repeatedly longs for the tender embrace of death in a way that relates her intimately to Massinger's lovelorn women and of course to Penthea as well. Aspatia's register of complaints includes the hauntingly sweet song of death, ending with the line: "Upon my buried body lay lightly gentle earth" (II.i, p. 16). The apparently innocent adjective "gentle" electrifies this line of lament, defines the quality of Aspatia's death fantasy, and insists on the implied connection between the phantom of death and the lost bridegroom. Elsewhere Aspatia's death-wish decorates her corpse with flowers and vines, as if in sad remembrance of Ophelia's watery grave and Perdita's bank of love. When at last death does visit Aspatia, it comes as a "blessing" from the hand of her lover Amintor (V.iii, p. 72). Disguised as a young man, Aspatia provokes Amintor into physical combat. But her resistance is no more effective than the coyness of a bride: "thou spread'st thine arms," Amintor complains, "And tak'st upon thy breast" (V.iii, pp. 69–70). Fatally wounded by Amintor's sword, Aspatia is at last content:

> I have got enough,
> And my desire; there's no place so fit for me to die as here.
>
> (V.iii, p. 70)

The place designed for death, as a stage production would surley make visible, is in the arms of her once-contracted lover. The picture of Aspatia dying in Amintor's embrace is the supreme instance of a conceit becoming a literal truth; the two meanings of the verb "to die" are conflated in a theatrical pun that blends the figures of lover and killer into one.[18]

Aspatia is not the only victim of erotic death. Even the notorious King dies by the hand of his mistress in a scene that makes up in cruelty for what it may lack in pathos. Evadne ties the sleeping King to his bed, wakes him, and after a prolonged interview stabs him in self-righteous passion. At first the King interprets his chains as a "pretty new device" (V.i, p. 61) in the sexual game between lovers. Evadne takes up his hint and expands it, for while she kills him she refers to the thrusts of her dagger as "love-tricks" invented for his delectation (V.i, p. 63). And she confronts her own death with an equally postured eloquence, almost as if she is still competing with Aspatia—this time in a reckless pursuit of death ecstasy. She kills herself in the belief that Amintor will love her "once again" (V.iii, p. 71).

For all of its baroque preoccupation with the sensuous pleasure of death, *The Maid's Tragedy* remains fundamentally a mannerist play. Among its typically mannerist qualities is a shocking moral ambiguity of the kind which pervades *The White Devil* and *The Changeling*. Evadne is of course the focus of ambiguity, for she bears the double burden of guilt and responsibility. She is both the cause of evil and the vehicle of retribution. After she has murdered the King, she returns to Amintor with blood-stained hands that seem to cleanse her of past wrong. "Looks not *Evadne* beauteous with these rites now?" she asks (V.iii, p. 70); but Amintor can see only the ironic horror of sin piled upon sin. This scene completes the movement begun in Evadne's first ambiguous midnight meeting with Amintor—the wedding-night encounter. Evadne proposes that Amintor shall murder her undesirable lover, and in return she promises to "kiss the sin off from thy lips" (II.i, p. 19). Evadne is posing as the woman who can forgive a crime, even though Amintor has yet to learn how deeply stained with guilt she already is. To add to the irony, the murder victim Evadne has in mind is not the King but Amintor himself. In effect she is saying, "I'll forgive you if you kill yourself for my sake."

The external glitter of the courtly world in which these desperate characters move is both an additional source of ambiguity and another index of mannerism. The wedding masque is a showy and glamorous piece of courtly artifice, an elegant surface draped over an ugly substance. Dancing nymphs call on Night to "hide / the blushes of the Bride" (I.ii, p. 12). In retrospect even such a conventional and ceremonial appeal becomes ironic, because this bride has more than the usual reasons for blushing.[19] The discrepancy between superficial glitter and hideous truth applies to most of the key values of the play. Thus the sheer name of "King" carries an aura of magic that arrests Amintor before he can take the first step toward revenge, even though the real king is a selfish monster and a cruel tyrant. Amintor's own code of chivalric honour is attractive for its internal consistency and artificial elegance, but at length he must bitterly admit its failure to deal with real problems:

> The thing that we call Honour, bears us all
> Headlong into sin, and yet it self is nothing.
>
> (IV.ii, p. 60)

For an idealist like Amintor such disillusionment is more damning than for temperamental realists like Faulconbridge and Falstaff. Once the elegant surfaces of Amintor's world are eroded, no fundamental values remain untarnished.

One characteristic motif of mannerism in the visual arts is the *figura serpentinata*, in which visual design imitates the writhing of a live snake.[20] Even such a specifically spatial device finds a curious literary counterpart in *The Maid's Tragedy*. It occurs in Evadne's impassioned rejection of Amintor during their frustrated wedding-night interview. "You hear right," she assures Amintor:

> I sooner will find out the beds of Snakes,
> And with my youthful blood warm their cold flesh,
> Letting them curle themselves about my Limbs,
> Than sleep one night with thee.
>
> (II.i, pp. 19–20)

The image is disturbingly attractive, partly because Evadne expands it and lingers over it with such obvious relish. The connection between Evadne's figure of speech and the sculptured *figura serpentinata* by such artists as Giovanni Bologna may be purely coincidental, but the Sadean flavour in both verbal and visual mannerism is more than accidental. The serpent appears to have shaken off his old curse, for although he still carries the mystery of evil inside him, his outward form has become seductively beautiful once more.

The Maid's Tragedy remains a difficult play to classify with any assurance. The more one concentrates on Aspatia the more baroque it appears to be; the more one considers Evadne the more mannerist it becomes. The two women are rivals on more than one level. But on balance, like so much of Fletcher's drama, the play remains essentially within the mannerist style despite its occasionally baroque resonances. It concludes with the kind of distortion and fragmentation one expects in the tragedies of Webster and Tourneur. Melantius, the consistent spokesman for positive values, is left cruelly isolated at the close and robbed of every chance for decisive action. Even the ironic positive of suicide is denied him. Lysippus, the new king, draws an overly eager moral about the dangers of lust and the abuse of power, but he has done little in the play thus far to inspire confidence or to justify his moral stance. He has himself been preoccupied with the surfaces of the courtly world, while keeping his reputation clean throughout. Like the other great tragedies of the mannerist style, this one ends on a note of justifiable pessimism.

In general the plays of Beaumont and Fletcher may be classified either with *The Mad Lover* as fairly pure instances of mannerism, or with *The Maid's Tragedy* as principally mannerist plays with secondary baroque characteristics. To the first class belong works like *Philaster*, *The Loyal Subject*, *The Wild Goose Chase*, and many more. In each of these plays a superbly elegant courtly milieu sets the standards of behaviour for the major characters, and in consequence the action approximates the stages in a cleverly devised game played for its intrinsic enjoyment. *The Wild Goose Chase* in particular illustrates the resemblance between the witty elegance of mannerism and the social polish of comedy rococo in *The Way of the World*, *The Man of Mode*, and *The Beaux' Stratagem*. To the second class belong *A King and No King*, *The Knight of Malta*, and *Valentinian*. In each of these plays a consuming passion threatens to break through the brittle surface of the mannerist world. The attraction between Arbaces and Panthea, the tortured abstinence of Miranda and Oriana, the intense jealousy of Maximus—these are moments that would appear more at home in Ford's drama than in Fletcher's. The baroque impulses dominate only momentarily, to be submerged in Fletcher's habitual concern for courtly artifice and social convention. Because they are not after all brother and sister, Arbaces and Panthea need no longer violate the norm of proper conduct. A similar though less spectacular *volte-face* reduces the emotional pressure in each of the plays of this group, including *The Maid's Tragedy*. Were she a genuinely baroque heroine, Evadne would love her King with single-minded passion in defiance of the opinions of others or the rules of the courtly game. The measure of Evadne's adherence to the mannerist world is her forthright confession, "I love with my ambition, / Not with mine eyes" (III.i, p. 32). Here—as elsewhere in Fletcher's plays—is a clear victory of external courtly glitter over internal emotional truth.

Though Fletcher's works occupy only a fringe area of the baroque circle, he nevertheless deserves the importance I have given him in relation to the English baroque drama as a whole. During the seventeenth century Fletcher achieved a position of prominence and exercised a degree of authority that now seems wildly out of proportion to his actual merits as a dramatist. Thus, though few of his plays are in themselves baroque, they did influence decisively every future development in the direction of baroque drama. Just as the characteristic motifs and devices of mannerism in the visual arts are transformed by Rubens and Bernini, so too Fletcher's recurrent themes and stock characters take new life in Massinger and Ford. Not a fully baroque dramatist himself, Fletcher is in many ways responsible for creating the baroque tradition in English drama. It is with the school of Fletcher in mind, I believe, that Ford writes his rather equivocal eulogy "On the Best of English Poets, Ben Jonson, Deceased." Now that Jonson has achieved immortality, Ford argues, his rivals will have to be satisfied with merely mortal status:

> Great men, and worthy of *Report*, must fall
> Into their earth, and sleeping there sleepe *all*:
> Since *He*, whose *Pen* in every *straine* did use
> To drop a *Verse*, and every *Verse* a *Muse*,
> Is vow'd to *heaven*.[21]

No doubt Ford is modestly including himself among those who cannot aspire to Jonson's high rank, but he may be saying much more. In Fletcher especially Ford would recognize a dramatist of stature comparable to that of Jonson, yet with diametrically opposed principles and practices. Not all the great and worthy men of letters are sons of Ben; many of them, and in particular the baroque writers, would feel more welcome in the family of Fletcher.

James Shirley is the chameleon playwright of the Caroline theatre. His plays do reflect some baroque tendencies, but they also reflect such a profusion of different tendencies as to make any definition of the essential Shirley impossible. In the Prologue to *The Cardinal* Shirley warns his audience not to accept any single statement at face value, nor to expect any specific doctrine from the play: "I will say nothing positive; you may / Think what you please."[22] With very little exaggeration one might take this disclaimer as Shirley's most fundamental artistic principle; like Sidney's poet, "he nothing affirms, and therefore never lieth."[23] But what for Sidney is a central truth about the metaphysical status of poetic utterances becomes, in Shirley, a tactical excuse for endless shapeshifting. In short, Shirley's dramatic works are a map of theatrical fashion and very little more.

Because he lacks any profound sense of integrity as a dramatist, Shirley succumbs rather easily to the influence of his contemporaries—especially his successful contemporaries. Thus, at the beginning of his career he makes Jonson his model in a series of comedies including *The Wedding*, *The Witty Fair One*, and *Hyde Park*. In the dedication to *The Grateful Servant* this debt is made explicit, as Shirley takes a bow to his "acknowledged master, learned JONSON" (II, 3). But when Jonson's fortunes suffer an eclipse and Fletcher becomes the brightest planet in the theatrical galaxy, Shirley changes his orbit in response. *The Arcadia* follows the pastoral mode of *The Faithful Shepherdess*; *The Traitor* redevelops the passionate conflicts of *The Maid's Tragedy*; and *The Young Admiral* sets up and resolves the dilemmas of love and honour in the manner of *Philaster*, *The Loyal Subject*, or *A Wife for a Month*. By the time he makes his address "To the Reader" in the opening pages of the first Beaumont and Fletcher folio (1647), Shirley's transference of loyalty is complete. Now he treats the "cold contemplative knowledge" of the Jonson tradition with diffidence, and exalts the "soft purling passion" of Beaumont and Fletcher to the highest pinnacle of excellence. To read the Beaumont and Fletcher plays, Shirley contends, is to "tast the best wit that ever trod our English Stage."[24] And to read the sequence of Shirley's plays, one might add, is to follow at a second remove the progress from Jonson's caustic intellectual wit to the elegant courtly wit of Fletcher.[25]

A playwright so susceptible to contemporary pressures would be unlikely to escape Ford's influence entirely. From internal evidence alone *Love's Cruelty* and *The Duke's Mistress* appear to be Shirley's most complete responses to Ford's baroque style, and indeed the coincidences of theatrical history support such a conjecture. Shirley's career and Ford's happen to intersect in or around 1630, about a year prior to the licensing of *Love's Cruelty*. Shirley is at this time the leading dramatist of Queen Henrietta Maria's men at the Phoenix, the company to which he remains almost exclusively loyal from 1624 to 1636.[26] Meanwhile, Ford's early association with the King's men comes to an end in 1630, after which he contributes his remaining plays to the repertoire of Queen Henrietta Maria's company.[27] Shirley's dedicatory poem for the publication of *Love's Sacrifice* (1633), known largely for its ruthless attack on William Prynne, also contains a public gesture of admiration for his fellow dramatist.[28] The external evidence, then, confirms the view that shortly after 1630 Shirley is decisively aware of Ford's stature as a playwright, and particularly sensitive to his influence.

Love's Cruelty is the first of Shirley's plays to bear the mark of his association with Ford. It is by no means an extremely good play—even for Shirley—except for the lusty, vigorous, and morally ambiguous role of the central female character, Clariana. The principal action is built around a standard adultery situation: Clariana marries a virtuous young lover (Bellamente), only to find that what she really wants is an affair with a cynical young rake (Hippolito). After lengthy and complex preliminaries the lovers come to an agreement, and Act IV opens with the following stage direction: "*Enter Hippolito and Clariana upon a bed.*"[29] With a similar flair for shocking sexual intimacy, Ford sets the stage for the closet scene in '*Tis Pity*: "*Enter* Giovanni *and* Annabella *lying on a bed*" (V.v.2299). Both dramatists are working with the same company of actors and the same indoor theatre;[30] inevitably a production of either play would recall the parallel scene in its counterpart.

Furthermore, both dramatists exploit the bedroom setting as a vehicle for developing intimate conversational exchanges that border on the perverse. Giovanni, despite the gathering tension and the clear threat of death, accuses Annabella of enjoying her "night-games" with Soranzo rather more than she ought (V.v.2301). By remaining obsessively loyal to his vow of incestuous love, Giovanni has become quite naturally and yet perversely jealous of his sister. In the parallel scene from *Love's Cruelty*, Hippolito laments that the pleasures of adultery are "not lawful," only to have Clariana contradict him at once:

> Lawful! that would take much from the delight
> And value; I have heard some gentlemen,
> That want no venison of their own,
> Swear they had rather strike their neighbour's deer
> Than hunt in their own park.
>
> (IV.i, p. 238)

Clariana believes that danger increases desire. Her psychological principles may be morally suspect, but they do account beautifully for much of her behaviour toward Hippolito. Her sexual interest in Hippolito dates from the moment she learns of his reputation as a libertine, reaches the breaking point as soon as she has married Bellamente, and erupts with volcanic intensity when she discovers his involvement with another woman. Like Ford, Shirley can be fair to internal fantasies even when they violate the prescribed norm. And again like Ford, he arranges the visual spectacle of the bedroom scene as a way of exploring obsessions and impulses that seldom surface in more pedestrian circumstances.

If the titles by themselves are not enough to suggest an affinity between *Love's Cruelty* and *Love's Sacrifice*, the theme of marital jealousy certainly strengthens the connection. Bellamente resists the first temptation to jealousy and mistrusts the evidence of his servant on idealistic grounds: the names of "friend" and "wife" are "sacred" to him, "like the heads of saints, and holy martyrs" (III.i, p. 235). His desire to believe in absolute fidelity recalls Caraffa's mental image of himself as "a Monarch of felicitie" (I.i.217). Bellamente goes through a series of vacillations even more protracted than Caraffa's; both jealous husbands require the immediate stimulus of clear and outrageous guilt before they can act on their desire for revenge. And in both plays the guilty lovers are drawn together in the ecstasy of death. In order to prevent by anticipation the vengeance of her husband, Clariana stabs her lover and receives a mortal wound from him in return. The sexual undertones of this exchange receive support frcm the masochistic flavour of her language:

> Thy sword was gentle to me; search't again,
> And thou shalt see how my embracing blood
> Will keep it warm, and kiss the kind destroyer.
>
> (V.ii, p. 264)

Like Aspatia in *The Maid's Tragedy*, like Biancha, Annabella, and Penthea, Clariana interprets death as the ultimate consummation of her sexual wishes, desires, and dreams. Bellamente does not meet a violent death, but follows the example of Calantha instead and dies of a broken heart.

In *The Duke's Mistress* Shirley recreates the tone of *Love's Cruelty* even though he is now working within the conventions of tragicomedy. From the opening moments of the play the court bristles with rumours about a love affair between the Duke and his supposed mistress, Ardelia. The central situation allows Shirley to develop two supporting roles with considerable pathos. Bentivolio, the honourable young man who deeply loves Ardelia, finds himself tormented by jealousy; Euphemia, the Duke's wife, responds to her disgrace with eloquence borrowed from the forsaken maidens of Massinger. In Act III the audience learns that Ardelia has not yet fallen prey to the Duke's lust, and the rest of the play weaves out a complex pattern of reconciliation for the two pairs of lovers. At the critical instant the Duke restores Euphemia to his loving embrace and sanctions the marriage of Bentivolio and Ardelia. Two fairly inconsequential courtiers (Valerio and Leontio) must sacrifice their lives to bring about the happy result, but their deaths are not enough to alter the shape of the tragicomic design.

The sensuous but technically chaste relationship between Ardelia and the Duke is a variation on the theme of *Love's Sacrifice*. But while Ford's frustrated lovers create an emotional reality above and beyond the facts of the case, Shirley's Duke and mistress recede into comfortable marriages just as if nothing had ever passed between them. The resolution of *The Duke's Mistress* in fact illustrates what is both Shirley's greatest strength and most damaging weakness: his undisputed skill at constructing a plot. Complex motives, obsessions, fantasies, and frustrations are pared away with amazing dexterity when the time comes for a decisive and theatrical finish.[31] Whenever Shirley has a technical problem to solve he manages brilliantly. Whenever he confronts a problem not exclusively of a technical kind, he is sadly out of his depth.

Enough has been said to locate Shirley's place in the baroque dramatic tradition. Even his finest tragedy, *The Cardinal*, can only provide additional supporting evidence. The relationship between Rosaura and Alvarez does generate a baroque pathos that recalls Penthea and Orgilus, but the effect is momentary. The same is true of *Love's Cruelty* and *The Duke's Mistress*. Shirley exploits themes and verbal patterns borrowed from Massinger, Fletcher, and Ford, but he is only too willing to abandon baroque tendencies whenever they do not fit the demands of his technical craftsmanship. As a result, he seldom achieves the larger baroque structural effects that characterize Ford's plays. When he works with multiple spheres of action the connections between one level and another tend to be adventitious rather than organic; when he laces up the loose ends of a plot the skill of his workmanship prevents the suggestion of open form. Swinburne's estimate of Shirley, vituperative though it may be, remains largely true. "Once or twice the writer may remind you of Jonson—with all the sap squeezed out of him, or of Fletcher—with all his grace evaporated"; but in general Shirley finds himself "in a field reserved for steeds of finer blood and higher mettle."[32] Once or twice he may remind you of Ford—with most of his passion spent; and in these moments Shirley continues the baroque style though he lacks the genius to transform it.

Thomas Otway is the last significant playwright of the English baroque tradition. In the Restoration setting—among such peers and rivals as Dryden, Rochester, and Wycherley—Otway's proverbially tender voice is very much an anomaly. A baroque dramatist by talent and temperament, he struggles unsuccessfully to conform to the rigours of classicism, clumsily mimics the agile gestures of the rococo, and discovers his true métier at last in *The Orphan* and *Venice Preserv'd*. The chronological gap of some forty years which separates his plays from those of the Caroline dramatists should not be allowed to obscure the more fundamental relations between Otway and his predecessors in the baroque style. Indeed, many critics have remarked that in his finest work Otway is a throwback to the earlier world of Elizabethan and Jacobean drama.[33] This critical commonplace requires only slight modification: Otway is the true heir not of Shakespeare or Webster, but of Massinger, Fletcher, and Ford.

Otway's first tragedy, *Alcibiades*, is very much an apprentice play. Under the spell of French models and current theories of heroic drama, Otway tries his hand at a classical form which is not at all congenial to his particular abilities. The rhymed couplets are laborious without being elevated; the central character is pompous without being heroic. Only in the figure of Timandra, the self-sacrificing mistress of Alcibiades, does the playwright begin to show his true colours. In her pathetic loyalty to the man who has wronged her, Timandra anticipates Otway's greater heroines, Monimia and Belvidera. *Don Carlos* is both a considerable improvement over *Alcibiades*, and a major step in the direction of baroque tragedy. Though he still uses the rhymed couplet as his medium, though he still thinks of himself as writing heroic drama, Otway is now independent enough to follow his special talent for creating exquisitely passionate scenes. The Queen and Don Carlos, deprived of mutual happiness in the real world, embrace each other at last in the glorious *Liebestod* that crowns the play. In emulation of Orgilus, Don Carlos opens his veins to release life, and expires in rapture while leaning on his lady's breast.

If Otway never fully acclimatized himself to the world of heroic drama, his exploratory ventures in the comedy of manners were even less successful. *Friendship in Fashion*, the first of his comedies, illustrates clearly enough that Otway lacks the light touch and the social grace of the rococo style. The play consists largely of the sort of verbal fencing that Etherege can manage with such aplomb, but there is none of Etherege's wit. *The Soldier's Fortune* and *The Atheist* are slight improvements, but still fall far below the standards set for the genre by Wycherley, Congreve, or Farquhar. In scenes of slapstick and parody Otway can be funny, but his darts of satire are simply too heavy, his social irony too savage; in the fragile world of Restoration comedy Otway is little better than a blustering buffoon.

In *The Orphan* and *Venice Preserv'd* Otway discovers his genuine talent and his true style. Perhaps it is only coincidence that the period of Otway's mature tragedies should correspond to the period of Mrs. Barry's maturity as an actress of tragic roles. In any case it is a productive coincidence: Mrs. Barry's sensuous and pathetic style of acting appears to have left a permanent mark on the characters of Otway's heroines.[34] Just as Mrs. Barry was admired by her contemporaries for a special ability to bring tears to the eyes of her audiences, so Otway's distinctive gift, according to literary observers, was a genius for stirring the emotions. Even Dryden can afford to give Otway legitimate though guarded praise, once his own classical reputation is beyond doubt. "I will not defend everything in his *Venice Preserved*," Dryden writes; "but I must bear this testimony to his memory, that the passions are truly touched in it, though perhaps there is somewhat to be desired, both in the grounds of them, and in the height and elegance of expression."[35] Dryden's reservations are clearly based on the classical assumptions of decorum and gravity. Almost in spite of himself, he admires Otway for his ability to arouse the pathos and ecstasy of baroque tragedy.

Monimia stands at the structural and emotional centre of *The Orphan*. As the title indicates, she is a woman cut loose from her social moorings and set adrift in a vortex of passion. The external events of the play conspire against Monimia to place her in a position that Penthea might have been describing in her paradoxical lament:

> There is no peace left for a ravish'd wife
> Widdow'd by lawlesse marriage.
>
> (BH IV.ii.1953–54)

For Penthea this complaint is an expression of sorrowful fantasies; for Monimia it would be almost a literal statement of her circumstances. She marries Castalio, the man she loves, only to be deceived into spending her wedding night with his rakish brother Polydore. In this sense she is literally violated, just as Penthea has been figuratively raped. Any possibility for a tranquil emotional life disappears for Monimia as soon as she discovers what has occurred. Now she is forever estranged from both of her lovers, because one of them is no better than a rapist and the other is forever barred from her by the powerful incest barrier. Monimia responds to the dilemma by fainting, and the remainder of her life is but a slow preparation for death.

Again like Penthea, Monimia finds herself buffeted back and forth by one male ego after another. Chamont, Monimia's brother, behaves in an irrationally protective manner that recalls Ithocles: he schemes and plots to prevent Monimia from marrying the man she loves. Castalio is wounded to the core of his being when he finds himself unable to enter the bridal chamber, and to compensate for the hurt he roundly abuses Monimia on the following morning. The physical relation between Monimia and Castalio, then, corresponds precisely to the psychological relation between Penthea and Orgilus: both lovers must remain forever in the ambiguous position of being "married Bachelours" (*BH* IV.ii.1938). Since her marriage has turned out so wretchedly, it is not surprising that Monimia also shares Penthea's obsessive desire to return to the innocence of the past. She tells Castalio that she can never see him again, for happiness is a condition they cannot hope to recover:

> Oh! were it possible that we could drown
> In dark Oblivion but a few past hours,
> We might be happy.
>
> (V.211–13)[36]

It is but a short metaphorical step from the desire for oblivion to the desire for death; since the past can never return, death is the highest promise that the future holds. At the end of her sad journey, Monimia "talks of dying with a Voice so sweet, / That life's in love with it" (V.200–201). Her death-wish is not as persistent or as pronounced as Penthea's, only because her miseries have matured more quickly and more urgently.

If Monimia's character and situation are the strongest link between *The Orphan* and *The Broken Heart*, in more general terms the masochistic tone of so many scenes in the play is the decisive indication of Otway's baroque style. Even before she learns the truth about her wedding night, Monimia fears that something has gone sadly wrong. She describes her feelings to Chamont in what can only be described as a masochistic fantasy:

> When in some Cell distracted, as I shall be,
> Thou seest me lye; these unregarded Locks,
> Matted like Furies Tresses; my poor Limbs
> Chain'd to the Ground, and 'stead of the delights
> Which happy Lovers taste, my Keeper's stripes . . . .
>
> (IV.209–13)

When you find me in this lamentably forlorn position, she says to Chamont, think of me with pity. And she concludes with a direct admission of the pleasure she derives from sorrow: "Let me enjoy this thought" (IV.217). So in a sense Monimia is compatibly matched with Polydore, for his "malicious pleasure" in seducing her complements her "belov'd Despair" at being seduced (III.419; IV.163). The language of the play intensifies the tone of masochism by alluding repeatedly to Monimia's trembling limbs and panting breasts. From Dryden's classical point of view such emotional ecstasies are insufficiently grounded in reality; for the baroque dramatist they are a means of creating an erotic pathos that is entirely justified for its own sake. Otway proudly observes in the Preface to *Don Carlos* that his play has "never fail'd to draw Tears from the Eyes of the Auditors, I mean those whose Souls were capable of so Noble a pleasure" (I, 174). The playwright's aims appear to have been perfectly served by the talents of his principal actress, for Mrs. Barry reputedly never failed to draw forth her own tears when she spoke the line, "Ah poor *Castalio!*" (V.298).[37]

Like so many baroque artists in all media, Otway brings to life the sweetness of intolerable suffering, the rich pathos of heartfelt pain.

The characteristic baroque thematic patterns are developed with even greater intensity in Otway's undisputed masterpiece, *Venice Preserv'd*. Jaffeir is never a political revolutionary in more than an external sense; his quintessential nature is the rarefied substance that distinguishes the passive martyrs of baroque tragedy. Each sacrifice he makes is motivated by his experience of love. When he is obliged to yield Belvidera as a political hostage, he imaginatively places Pierre into the position of intimacy that Belvidera usually occupies. If only you were she, he says to Pierre, I could confess everything to you:

> How I could pull thee down into my heart,
> Gaze on thee till my Eye-strings crackt with Love,
> Till all my sinews with its fire extended,
> Fixt me upon the Rack of ardent longing.
>
> (II.425–28)

Jaffeir's imagery speaks worlds about his relationship to Belvidera. Even his most casual references to his wife are heavy with sexual resonance, and in this instance the "fire extended" of his imagined longing is clearly an erotic fantasy. Furthermore, Jaffeir's concept of sexuality includes the sensation of pain: the wheel of torture becomes the "Rack of ardent longing." When he discovers that Belvidera has betrayed his political confidences, he responds with submissive passivity. He asks to be led "like a tame Lamb / To Sacrifice" (IV.87–88) and imagines himself revelling in the delights of a bloody ritual:

> *Till by Her, bound, Hee's on the Altar layn;*
> *Yet then too hardly bleats, such pleasure's in the pain.*
>
> (IV.93–94)

These are the words of a man who recognizes the immense power that sexual love exercises over his every word and action, who acknowledges in short "The soft Authority of *Belvidera*" (III.ii.26). By reasonable standards Jaffeir may be weak, vacillating, even perverse;[38] but there is an exquisite sensitivity in his responses that goes beyond the limits of reason. In his imagination he is already approaching the climax of an action that might best be described as "love's sacrifice."

Jaffeir's masochistic reactions to adversity are matched by Belvidera's recurrent and passionate death-wish. While making her deliciously prolonged explanation of Renault's attempt to rape her, Belvidera pauses to invite death at her lover's hands. "Fetch, fetch that Dagger back," she says with an accent of urgency; "strike it / Here to my heart" (III.ii.68–70). As in *The Maid's Tragedy*, *'Tis Pity*, and *The Ecstasy of St. Teresa*, the weapon of death takes on a distinctively sexual colouring. In another of her fantasies Belvidera wonders how Jaffeir's "kind Dagger" will look when it pierces her heart (IV.24); and when he draws the dagger on her in a moment of passion she madly embraces him and prepares to "die in joys" (IV.518). In their last scene together, Belvidera makes an explicit connection between sexual ecstasy and the climax of death. She begs for death, promising to kiss Jaffeir even as he wounds her:

> Yes, and when thy hands,
> Charg'd with my fate, come trembling to the deed,
> As thou hast done a thousand thousand dear times,
> To this poor breast, when kinder rage has brought thee,
> When our sting'd hearts have leap'd to meet each other,
> And melting kisses seal'd our lips together,
> When joyes have left me gasping in thy armes,
> So let my death come now, and I'll not shrink from't.
> (V.243–50)

Coming as he does at the end of the baroque tradition, Otway brings to the surface what so many of his predecessors had revealed only through implication. Perhaps the open sensuality of Belvidera's outburst is the inevitable product of a baroque dramatic style combined with a theatre that allows actresses to play women's parts. In any event, the mysterious connection between eros and death remains mysterious, even when it flares up in the white heat of Belvidera's urgent appeal. Of course Belvidera is not being reasonable. Hers is a private vision of emotional truth, a vision that will lead at last to madness. Love isolates Jaffeir and Belvidera from the controls of the real world, until the only value that remains is the subjective reality of the one experience they share so bravely and so passionately.

The structure of *Venice Preserv'd* furnishes a good example of unity achieved through baroque fusion of disparate elements. The Nicky-Nacky scenes, as the shrewdest of Otway's critics have demonstrated, are thematically related to the principal action.[39] On the surface there appears to be no greater contrast than the one that separates the virtuous wife from the opportunistic courtesan, or the devoted husband from the lecherous patrician. But, like their more noble counterparts, Aquilina and Antonio participate in a private world of sexual fantasy that removes them from the real and the mundane. Though the very social fabric of Venice is in danger of imminent collapse, Antonio, one of its guardians, is crawling about on his knees and howling like a dog while his favourite whore whips him into a goatish frenzy. And while the lives of Pierre and his fellow conspirators are hanging in the most precarious balance, Antonio can think of nothing but his pressing desire to be kicked by Aquilina's "fragrant foots and little toes" (V.207). Clearly these are repulsive fantasies, aesthetically if not morally distinguishable from the masochism of Jaffeir and Belvidera. Yet, the theme of pleasure mingled with pain has the curious effect of bringing the tragic lovers and the comic lechers dangerously close together. At the end of the first Nicky-Nacky scene, Aquilina whips Antonio out of doors and remarks laconically to the audience that she is making a "*Sacrifice*" of her "*Fool*" in order to be free to entertain her lover (III.i.145). At once Belvidera enters, announcing her disgraceful treatment at Renault's hands in the same terms: "I'm Sacrific'd! I'm sold! betray'd to shame!" (III.ii.1). This equivocation on the word "sacrifice" insists on the relation between the two plots, and Renault's actions are additional evidence that lecherous old men are not confined to any single political camp or social stratum. The world of *Venice Preserv'd*, however, is not simply a nightmare of deliberately perverse and irresponsible distortions. The one quality that rescues Jaffeir and Belvidera from this house of mirrors is their ability to *share* one another's fantasies and desires. Theirs alone is the isolation of the mutual embrace.

Although Venice has been preserved at the end of the play there is no evidence whatever to suggest that she has been redeemed. From the outset the city is personified as "the *Adriatique* Whore" (II.292), and the ambivalent nature of the political action tends to confirm the suspicion that whores do not reform. The political impasse on which the play ends is of course consistent with the baroque tendency toward open form. The revolution has failed, society remains unregenerate, and the only possible triumph occurs at the personal and emotional level. Thus the conspirators, though their own motives and tactics have been clouded in corruption and scandal, can achieve at least a psychological victory over their environment by facing death with courage.

And in their shared death scene Pierre and Jaffeir reach a pinnacle of absolute trust that defies the limits of real experience. "Now thou hast indeed been faithful," Pierre can say to his friend at last (V.467). Though life has been a series of betrayals, bribes, and broken oaths, death rises above it all as the one moment of pure fidelity. For Belvidera death comes by means of a lucid madness which allows her to share in the triumph of Jaffeir and Pierre. When Priuli's servants forcibly restrain her, Belvidera wishes only to be taken to her husband: "Are all things ready? shall we dye most gloriously?" (V.366). Her own tortured spirit answers the question in the affirmative, for her final speech is a private illusion in which she imagines herself embracing Jaffeir in the climax of death. It is a glorious vindication of her first promise: "Oh I will love thee, even in Madness love thee" (I.371).

Otway's language in *Venice Preserv'd* is richer and more vibrant than in any of his other writings, largely because he exploits many of the characteristic devices of the baroque idiom. The flesh-ripping metaphor, for example, plays a major part in scenes that develop the idea of loyalty. Jaffeir takes his oath of allegiance to the cause of revolution by calling on Pierre, at the slightest sign of wavering faith, "to rip this Heart of mine / Out of my Breast, and shew it for a Cowards" (II.190–91). As in *Love's Sacrifice* and *'Tis Pity*, the physical action of tearing open the bosom will reveal emotional truth. Indeed, when the conspirators show signs of suspecting Jaffeir, Pierre offers first to tear the secret out of Jaffeir's breast (II.311–15), then challenges them to search his own heart with their swords (III.ii.410–11). As the two friends approach the scaffold, Pierre prepares for the moment of death by asking the simplest question: "Dost thou love me?" (V.437). Jaffeir's answer depends on a rhetorical figure that both men understand: "Rip up my heart, and satisfie thy doubtings" (V.438). With this verbal gesture the scene has been set for an action of ultimate sacrifice; in a few moments Jaffeir will in fact sever both his friend's flesh and his own with the point of his dagger. The metaphor has become emotionally and theatrically real in a way that recalls the shocking climax of *'Tis Pity*.

Tears, blood, wounds, and instruments of torture are Otway's favourite images for creating the sensation of suffering. When Belvidera uses these key images, she adds to them a sensual colouring that creates a highly erotic effect. She distracts Jaffeir from his revolutionary purpose by describing the victims of murder and rape in richly provocative terms (IV.48–58). She screws up Jaffeir's courage by dwelling on her own tearful, throbbing confrontation with attempted rape (III.ii.181–86). Jaffeir can use much the same imagery with similar eloquence; he recalls how he came to Pierre "With eyes o'rflowing and a bleeding heart" (IV.440), only to receive a humiliating blow in return for his sorrow. The language of tears and blood is slightly more stylized in Otway than in Ford, but the effect remains almost the same. In Ford's scenes of intense suffering, sacramental associations cling to his imagery to create an effect bordering on the mystical. In Otway, an ideal of childhood innocence takes the place of religion. Jaffeir, for example, explains that he cannot bear to be parted from Belvidera, because:

> every moment
> I am from thy sight, the Heart within my Bosom
> Moans like a tender Infant in its Cradle
> Whose Nurse had left it.
>
> (III.ii.17–20)

The naïve sensitivity of the tender infant ensures a response of unblemished intensity to the language of suffering. Like Ford, Otway has mastered the rhetoric of pathos.

Otway's two major tragedies, despite the intervening accidents of theatrical history, show a closer kinship to Ford's baroque style than virtually any other plays in the English dramatic tradition.[40] Massinger explores baroque themes and baroque form in a somewhat tentative way, Fletcher moves flirtatiously between mannerist and baroque styles, and Shirley exploits the baroque just as he would any other fashion. Only with Otway does the English theatre produce another fully baroque dramatist of genuine stature. And even in Otway's case the baroque resurgence is a short-lived affair. Dryden's overpowering prestige is already moving tragedy in the direction of disciplined classicism, while Etherege and Wycherley are setting in order the playful and fragile conventions of comedy rococo. Otway himself escapes the pressures of his immediate literary and theatrical environment only in *The Orphan* and *Venice Preserv'd*. There are further echoes of Otway's influence, but no more than echoes, in such plays as *The Mourning Bride*, *The Fair Penitent*, and *Jane Shore*. The world of the domestic she-tragedy, however, is too thoroughly sentimental to belong to the baroque style in any meaningful sense. The English baroque drama ends principally with Otway, just as it begins primarily with Ford. This alone does not make them great men, but it does make them eminently worthy of report.

CHAPTER SIX

TRIAL NOW MORE FORTUNATE

An Essay in Criticism

FORD remains an elusive and baffling figure for the literary critic. In so many ways his short and eccentric career as a dramatist defies access from the usual quarters, and frustrates those who dig with the usual critical tools. Only a few biographical traces have survived—all of them trivial. Attempts to base criticism on Ford's refusal to pay the buttery bill or on the melancholy tilt of his hat in the *Elegy on Randolph's Finger* come under the heading of prose fiction.[1] The canon of Ford's writings is by no means a fixed entity, and hardly even a unified corpus. His early prose and poetry show little promise, and no dramatic subtlety at all. One can hardly say that the author of *Fames Memoriall* (1606) develops or matures into the dramatist of the 1630s, because there is little in *Fames Memoriall* worth developing or capable of maturing. The playwright who wrote '*Tis Pity* and *The Broken Heart* seems to have very little to learn from the sincere but tedious young versifier who preceded him. Contrary to romantic notions about the way artists are revealed to the world, Ford did not have a precocious development; in fact he did not produce a single play of his own until he was over forty.

If Ford frustrates the biographer, he is no more congenial to the historian—whether of the literary, cultural, or theatrical variety. With the exception of *Perkin Warbeck*, Ford does not use narrative or dramatic sources, although he borrows freely here and there whatever seems to suit his present need. With the same exception again, Ford makes very few telling allusions to the political, social, or religious controversies of his day. The theatre historian encounters almost the same dearth of factual evidence. Aside from the oblique reference to a player-king called *Warbeck* in Shirley's *The Constant Maid* (III.ii), there would appear to be no indication that Ford's drama created a great stir on the Caroline stage.[2] We have only the usual title page advertisement to assure us that this or that play was "acted" by the King's Servants or the Queen's Servants at Blackfriars or the Phoenix. It will be an unexpected luxury to learn, as we may in the case of *Love's Sacrifice*, that the play was not only "acted," but "received generally well."

So, without the aid of biographical data and with very little historical material, the critic must approach the startling content and puzzling form of the plays themselves. There is the incest motif, the frequency of mental imbalance, the theatricality of the death scenes, the questionable humour of the subplots, the occasional attempt to deceive or trick the audience. And there is the special quality of Ford's poetry—its musical voluptuousness, its religious pathos, its surrender to emotion for emotion's sake. The accidents of history have not left a well-charted series of documents, and the process of artistic creation has certainly not left an easily palatable body of literary work.

Ford's elusiveness in the face of standard scholarly and critical methods is not simply the result of insufficient information, or of theatrical sensationalism, or of moral turpitude. It is a matter of artistic style, if we understand the word "style" in its broadest sense. To suggest that Ford is the baroque dramatist of the English tradition, is to claim for him an artistic integrity and a stylistic unique-ness that previous critical approaches have not on the whole been able to reckon with. And once this claim has been made, even if it is not unanimously endorsed, it is bound to affect the topography of the critical map. If Ford can be accurately described and fruitfully analyzed as a baroque dramatist, then this in itself becomes a new datum of criticism; as such it may help to revise, modify, refute, or confirm the standard assumptions held by Ford's critics.

The point of view that has dominated critical thinking for the past century or so—and still dominates in circles where a class distinction is drawn between the "scholar" and the "critic"—may be described as the progressive evolutionary theory. Most literary histories depend at least in part on an evolutionary view of their subject which expresses itself in metaphors drawn from the natural sciences. The English drama of the sixteenth and seventeenth centuries seems particularly susceptible to evolutionary treatment, under such headings as "origins," "flowering," and "decay." Shakespeare is the full flowering of the genre, of course, and next to him it is only too easy to make almost any dramatist look like a dark origin or a sad decline. Basic assumptions of this sort may be found in the standard surveys by A. W. Ward, W. A. Neilson, E. K. Chambers, Felix E. Schelling, Allardyce Nicoll, and Hardin Craig. Schelling's statement of the theory as it applies to the English theatre deserves quotation, at least for its succinctness. According to Schelling and many subsequent historians, English drama had its origins in church rite and gradually won its independence as a species with the early Tudor interludes. "With these stages of initial growth behind it," Schelling continues, "the drama became an art; and more, it grew to be the peculiar art in which the worldly and vigorous yet ideal and poetical age of Elizabeth found its most lasting and characteristic expression. For English drama reached in the days of Shakespeare a diversity of species combined with a rare and pervading quality of literary excellence unsurpassed in the literature of other ages and countries; and it finally subsided into a paucity of form and poverty of content by the Restoration which is surprising in view of its previous history."[3] Here we find nearly all of the evolutionary principles in action. The drama grows from certain "initial stages" of life (presumably the *Quem quaeritis* corresponds to the single living cell) into ever more complex species. Elizabethan drama—the highest form of life—flourishes for a season, decays, and dies. The organic analogy is held in a muted, implied form. It is never explicit enough to invite exposure or censure, but it is nevertheless a decisive influence on critical thought.

The spirit of controversy which used to polarize debates between fashionable critical theorists and old-line literary historians seems to have settled at last, so it should now be possible to assess the habit of evolutionary thinking with greater fairness and objectivity. As a working hypothesis, as a way of looking at literature, the evolutionary view may be as valuable as any theory yet devised. What must be condemned is not the theory itself, but its tendency to parade as fact. This tendency is particularly dangerous where the issue of artistic merit arises, for despite its scientific dress the evolutionary view in effect prejudges many questions of value. Given the schematic outline suggested by Schelling and held by numerous literary scholars to be accurate, it becomes temptingly easy to move from the relative chronological position of any play to a judgment of the play which will confirm the theory. As a result, historians tend to overvalue such important "firsts" as Bale's *Kynge Johan*, *Gorboduc*, and *Ralph Roister Doister*; these plays receive artificial praise because they are the first English specimens of their kind in each case, and because they begin a tradition that leads directly up to the major Shakespearean genres. On the other hand, Peele and Greene are thrown into an artificial depression in the evolutionary scheme. They are neither the crucial "firsts" of the tradition, nor yet its finest flowering; and intermediate stages of development seldom attract the highest praise, or even the closest attention. Still more damaging, plays that come after the pre-determined period of highest development are either empty reworkings of Shakespearean forms with very little new material added, or else hysterical perversions of the old materials to cater to the new debauchery of taste. It is here that Ford has suffered his harshest treatment, under the organically damning label of "decadence."

The classic charge of decadence in Ford's works may be found in the scattered writings of S. P. Sherman, particularly in the essay entitled "Forde's Con-tribution to the Decadence of the Drama." Sherman's attack is frankly and outspokenly moralistic: "Forde, like his fellows in those latter days of the drama, sinned in his subject matter." Ford sins by confining his dramatic attention to sexual relationships, by exalting romantic love above the claims of conventional morality, by freeing the individual from the restraints of society, and by dressing up "the last ugliness of unnatural lust...in a veil of divine illusion."[4] The first meaning of "decadence," then, is moral decline. The dramatists of the Elizabethan age showed us plenty of sin, of course, but they disapproved of it and referred it to the judgment of God and of society. Gradually this tough moral fibre softened and turned sour, until in Caroline England the dramatists positively enjoyed the sins they put on stage. It is not sin itself that condemns a man, the exponents of this view would have us believe, but the capacity to enjoy sin.

Of the many replies Ford criticism has offered to Sherman's charges, two are of special interest in the present context. The first counter-strategy accepts Ford's sin and explains it in terms of historical causes; the second denies the sin on extra-literary grounds. G. F. Sensabaugh's work might be described as an historical apology for the sins of Ford's theatre. Sensabaugh grants all the premises of Sherman's argument. Yes, Ford's lovers do act in defiance of a social and moral code, and Ford approves of their defiance. But in the playwright's defence, Sensabaugh brings forward the complementary doctrines of Burtonian psychology and Platonic love. Thus, Giovanni cannot be blamed for his actions because he is a pathological case of love-melancholy from the pages of Burton's *Anatomy*. Fernando and Biancha can also escape the laws of society by appealing to the fashionable cult of Platonic love at the court of Queen Henrietta Maria. "The whole meaning of Ford's plays," runs Sensabaugh's rather confident conclusion, "rests on the supremacy of love over all, on the belief that beauty and love should command more respect than convention and law; he could not brook custom that might judge against beauty, or conceive any crisis of unsatisfied passion, adultery, or incest where love should not conquer."[5] Thus Ford is rescued from the slough of decadence only to be seated rather uncomfortably on the throne of ethical revolution. For Sensabaugh, Ford is not so much the seditious exponent of crime who must be shunned for the good of society, as the clairvoyant revolutionary who anticipates prophetically the moral dilemmas of the modern world.

After Sensabaugh's blatant romanticism, Mark Stavig's return to the world of prose and sense comes almost as a shock. In *John Ford and the Traditional Moral Order* Stavig makes a detailed and systematic reply to the traditional attack on Ford's morality.[6] Stavig denies Sherman's premises one by one. First, Ford's character is rescued from ill-repute, as on the evidence of his early prose and poetry he becomes "a traditional and quite orthodox Christian who was deeply influenced by classical ethics." Then, in each of Ford's plays we discover that sin is not glorified, society not condemned. The "moral deterioration" of characters like Giovanni, Fernando, and Biancha is cited as proof of sin; and the "satiric undercutting" which these characters encounter indicates that Ford does not approve of sin. The discussion of *'Tis Pity* ends with a statement of Stavig's position. "We should pity the lovers since their situation was difficult and since passions are hard to control, but I can find no historical justification for romanticizing their love as something noble and transcendent."[7] Admirably hard-headed as this view may appear, it tells us much more about traditional ethics than about the play in question. The critic who wishes to settle matters of nobility and transcendence in any artistic medium had best not restrict himself to methods of "historical justification."

Both of these replies to Sherman's charges fail, because both of them accept the dichotomy between conventional morality and the individual will as the fundamental concern of Ford's plays. Sensabaugh solves the problem by perpetrating an equivocation so large and so preposterous that it almost escapes detection: he merely reverses the value signatures which Sherman attached to conventional society and individual will. If society is by definition immoral, and lovers by definition moral, then Ford is absolved from the charge of having created immoral lovers. Stavig returns the value signatures to their old positions—positive for society and negative for the lovers. Then he turns the plays upside down, arguing on historical grounds that any seventeenth-century author must approve of society and disapprove of the lovers. Again Ford's moral nature is cleared, this time by converting plays like 'Tis Pity and Love's Sacrifice into didactic pamphlets on ethical questions.

If the excesses of historical interpretation confine the meaning and flatten the texture of Ford's plays, the same is by no means true when similar methods are applied with dexterity and caution. At their best, Clifford Leech's essays on Ford show the positive results of historical learning and critical sensitivity combined in a judicious and illuminating way. *John Ford and the Drama of his Time* is principally a critical study of the major plays, but a study in which the critic's eye remains always aware of the historical and theatrical milieu. Leech argues, for example, that 'Tis Pity shares affinities both with preceding Jacobean models and with subsequent Caroline developments in tragedy. Giovanni's violent egotism is "the surest link between this play and the tragedies of Ford's predecessors, while Annabella belongs rather with the heroines of the plays that were to come."[8] Such delicate distinctions are possible only for the critic who has absorbed the Jacobean and Caroline plays without diluting them into lesser versions of the Elizabethan ideal. Leech is unusual among historical critics for his ability to use the resources of scholarship to serve the interests of criticism.

In general, however, it remains true that the historical method and the evolutionary view have placed Ford in the awkward position of failing to meet the ethical standard set by Shakespeare and the other Elizabethans. To deal with Ford from the point of view of the baroque style is a helpful way of answering the charge and avoiding the unacceptable expedients proposed by Sensabaugh and Stavig. The baroque artist, even when his religious enthusiasm and his mystical fervour are at their highest pitch, does not treat ethical matters as a primary concern. Renaissance artists picture man in action or man in society, and thus ethical concerns are their stock-in-trade. In the baroque phase we see man suffering, man exultant, or man distressed, but always man plunged in emotional turbulence. The baroque artist's first concern is to explore the emotional nature of man with all the tools and techniques he can muster, presumably on the assumption that moral philosophy is someone else's business. We are invited to take a more specialized view of the human soul than the broad and unified style of the renaissance can offer us. It is enough to probe to the depths of human sorrow, pain, frenzy, or excitement, without referring at once to a moral framework. It is enough to understand, without at once attaching praise or blame.

Like Bernini's Teresa, Ford's martyrs die in the atmosphere of sweet, voluptuous pain, and not in the world of pressing ethical concerns. Their language is religious, their rhetoric ecstatic, their vision mystical, but they are not primarily concerned with questions of right and wrong action. The sufferings of guilt and repentance may be the result of an ethical dilemma, but the emotional experience itself demands our sympathy; the moral cause is secondary, almost incidental. The spiritual intensity of the moment sweeps Ford's lovers upward, as the marble cloud bears up St. Teresa, into a world where only the vivid sensation of ecstasy matters.

Once the baroque qualities of Ford's style have been fairly grasped, it becomes impossible to dismiss him as a decadent heir of renaissance conventions. Ford's 'Tis Pity must not be judged by the standards of Romeo and Juliet, because the two plays are different not only in moral purpose, but in artistic kind. To describe Ford as "baroque" rather than "decadent" is a way of recommending a small but important adjustment of the critical and historical perspective. The adjustment is important because it prevents facile value judgments, because it implies that Ford's plays should be accepted or rejected on their own terms, and because it insists on a "properly complicated" sense of literary history.[9] The term "baroque," in short, is by no means a calculated affront to the historical approach; it is merely a good substitute for one of the most harmful clichés of the evolutionary scheme.

A second group of critics finds that Ford sins not so much in the moral content of his work as in his style. L. G. Salingar's brief but eloquent account of this second point of view is fairly representative. Ford's "prevailing mood" may rise to "anguish," Salingar concedes, but "more generally, it keeps to the listless, nostalgic cadence of *The Broken Heart*." Some of his scenes show a "mannered perversity," particularly the "entirely self-pitying and theatrical" scenes of death and torment. Ford's "obsessive monotony" is the mark of a man who has closed his eyes to "public values" and "turned his back on life." Although he is the best of the Caroline dramatists, Ford's work does not deserve to be ranked with Milton's *Comus*; rather, "it marks the dissolution of tragedy as an art, since the poet has no objective standard of judgement remaining to check his liquefying emotions." [10]

Salingar's particular observations in this essay are clearly compatible with the theoretical principles of the critical school to which he belongs. This is the school of F. R. Leavis, L. C. Knights, and the other members of the *Scrutiny* group. The orientation is to some extent still historical, but emphatically not evolutionary. Since the critic's primary responsibility is to define and maintain the vitality of the great tradition in English literature, his principal activities are not research and scholarship, but discrimination and evaluation. The sensitive critic, Leavis would argue, has a right and indeed a duty to decide which works of literature qualify as masterpieces, and which may be justly forgotten.

When the critic's goal is to select those poems, novels, and plays that deserve membership in an exclusive club, then it becomes unusually important to discover the criteria by which such judgments are made. The first requirement, on the evidence of Leavis's own writings, would seem to be the "intense moral preoccupation" which springs from "an unusually developed interest in life." [11] Like Arnold's high seriousness, this moral interest implies that the artist must be involved with the great issues of his day, that he must grapple intellectually with the problems of his culture and his country. The second requirement—arising quite naturally from the first—is an audience. Some writers of considerable stature, such as Blake and Hopkins, have done fairly well without one, but the greatest writers, Leavis argues, speak not to themselves but to their contemporaries. A man like Bunyan, who by himself could have achieved nothing, reached near-greatness by "participating in a rich traditional culture." [12] It follows that some audiences are better than others, and the better the audience the more likely they are to have a great poet, novelist, or dramatist address them.

The third criterion is not quite so easy to summarize, because it is never directly stated as a theoretical principle. But it is clearly applied over and over again to actual cases in Leavis's practical criticism, and it clearly has something to do with language and style. One may find hints about the nature of this third criterion in the scattered comments on language in *The Common Pursuit*. For example, Leavis praises *Macbeth* for the "control" and "concreteness" of its poetry. He selects a short passage from *Cymbeline* (V.iii.43–46) to illustrate "strength" of imagery: "In 'like fragments in hard voyages' and 'back-door' we have, in imagery, the business-like and intense matter-of-factness...that gives the speech its highly specific and dramatically appropriate tone."[13] Of all the images available to illustrate the quality of poetry in *Cymbeline*, Leavis chooses "fragments in hard voyages" and "back-door," because even in a romantic world it is "business-like" language that matters to him. To belong to the great tradition a writer must use a realistic, concrete language, for it is language of this sort that best conveys an attitude of serious moral concern with the public problems of real life.

The linguistic criterion of the great tradition school becomes explicit in the writings of Leavis's American counterpart, Yvor Winters. According to Winters, the "statement" a poem makes "will be more or less rational," so the standard for judging the merit of a poem is equally based on reason. "In so far as the rational statement is understandable and acceptable, and in so far as the feeling is properly motivated by the rational statement, the poem will be good."[14] This principle of evaluation makes allowance for the emotional content of poetry, but only negatively; feeling is permitted if and only if reason remains in control of verbal style. In Winters' rapid survey of the English lyric from Wyatt to Traherne we see the practical results of this doctrine of discrimination. Highest praise belongs to poets of the plain style—Gascoigne, Greville and above all Ben Jonson. In poets of the aureate style, in much metaphysical poetry, and supremely in Crashaw's religious lyrics, Winters can find little more than a "fragmentary brilliance" vitiated by "confusion."[15]

Given a theoretical background such as this, it becomes much easier to understand L. G. Salingar's accusations. Indeed Ford does not deal primarily with moral or rational problems, as Salingar has acutely noticed. To a devoted traditionist it follows that he has "turned his back on life." Ford does not write for a broad cross-section of society, and his work cannot be located in the context of national glory or cultural resurgence. Thus, by the first two standards of discrimination, Ford fails. The third criterion, the linguistic one, is for Salingar the most important. It is precisely in the baroque qualities of Ford's language that he discovers "mannered perversity," "obsessive monotony," and an "entirely self-pitying and theatrical" tone. To clinch his point about Ford's language, Salingar offers the following description: "The air is warm with the altar-smoke and tears of amorous devotion, with the steam of transfixed and bleeding hearts."[16] To the uninitiated this is merely a fine statement of the effect baroque poetry can produce, but to the confirmed traditionist it is evidence enough on which to base a final negative judgment. To the builders of the great tradition, Ford is just another stone to be rejected.

T. B. Tomlinson offers a somewhat fuller account of Ford's plays from a similar point of view. He clarifies the traditionist position on Ford by adding to his practical discussions a short disclosure of his theoretical views. These include a pronouncement on "the real business" of dramatic literature: "to see the difficulty, toughness and vulgarity of life as a source of spiritual and intellectual food." The "lack of fibre" which Tomlinson finds in the verse of the decadent dramatists is a symptom of their inability to face squarely the serious issues of real life and experience. In Ford's case, Tomlinson discovers all of the classic faults of the traditionist system. *Love's Sacrifice* is marred by moral confusion; *The Broken Heart* wavers between sentimentality and melodrama; and in *'Tis Pity*, Ford is "enjoying it all immensely and has forgotten even a pretence of critical comment." The result of all this is a decay of poetic language. At times Ford's lines are "stiff and rhetorical," at other times "softly sentimental" or "exhibitionist" or "opportunist rather than critically directed." The virtue which Ford's style lacks is "toughness." His error is not only a matter of the subjects he chooses, but also of the style with which he paints them. "The cloying texture" of Ford's verse is the price he pays for his failure to face "the toughly intractable nature of everyday living."[17]

If the evolutionists run the risk of hyperopia, great tradition critics have more to fear from astigmatism. At any rate, this is how one is tempted to diagnose a point of view that makes "toughness" the supreme poetic virtue. There is an explanation (though no excuse) for this mote in the critical eye. One must remember that Leavis's chief concern as a practical critic has always been the novel. His standards of judgment have been formed by his preference for low mimetic writers such as George Eliot, Dickens, Conrad, and Lawrence. And given the context of social realism, of course, it is natural and right to expect plain, concrete language that comes from direct contact with ordinary experience. But it is not a criterion that works well in the case of lyric, tragedy, or romance. To praise Spenser for the "toughness" of his verse, for example, would be a decided insult; to require "toughness" in such a fragile masterpiece as *The Eve of St. Agnes* would be absurd.

If the Leavis criterion for poetic language does not work for all genres or all modes, it works no better for all literary styles. Baroque language is by no means plain language, and it does not aspire to the state of toughness. Once again the analogy between poetry and painting functions as a corrective. How would one react to a critic of the visual arts who set up toughness of plastic texture as a criterion for good art, regardless of period, style, or function? Surely he would be challenged by everyone who has found pleasure in any of the more delicate artistic modes or forms—in medieval manuscript illumination, or rococo furniture, or Pre-Raphaelite painting. Above all he would be challenged by the filmy otherworldliness of Rubens' mythological canvases, and by the sinuous smoothness of Bernini's marble draperies. Baroque visual style does not aim at toughness, and there is no reason why we should expect baroque verbal style to do so.

When defining a great tradition becomes the central business of criticism, then the anomalies and exceptions of literature are bound to suffer either misjudgment or neglect. There are always a number of works that somehow command the highest critical respect and deserve the closest critical attention, but yet fail to fit into the pattern which a selected tradition imposes. In English drama one could cite such instances as Henry Medwall's *Fulgens and Lucrece*, poised tantalizingly on the borderline (real or imaginary) between the medieval world and the renaissance. Or Addison's *Cato*, which seems to resist kinship either with Dryden's classicism or with George Lillo's sentimentalism. If the small minorities deserve protection from a tradition that hardens imperceptibly into orthodoxy, then the great exceptions need their advocates just as badly. Ford is one of the great exceptions. Under unusual circumstances and during an unusually late period of life, he produces a unique body of drama in a style not native to English soil. To assess Ford's work with a fixed picture of the select English tradition already in mind is another way of confirming the orthodox by condemning the exception. To describe Ford's achievement in terms of the baroque style is a way of insisting on the value of the great exception, even at the expense of the traditional rule.

Those critics who specialize in verbal analysis are frequently attacked for myopia—the inability to see beyond detail. Where this is true, it seems to me the fault of the individual critic and not of the theory. Contentious rallies under such banners as the intentional and affective fallacies or the heresies of para-phrase and pure sound appear to be a thing of the past. Members of the verbal analysis school still insist on the primary importance of explication, even though they are now more willing to allow for such supplementary activities as the description of historical context or the discussion of comparative merit.[18] Under these more liberal circumstances, myopia can have its positive advantages. If a literary text is carefully and systematically analyzed before the general "truths" about it are boldly put forward, then criticism is less likely to be conditioned in favour of some predetermined view about the growth and decadence of the English drama, or about the exclusive nature of a great tradition.

It comes as quite a surprise to discover that the impact of the verbal analysts has not yet reached Ford studies, except in the form of casual observations or brief, exploratory essays. William Empson turns momentarily to Ford when he introduces the fifth type of ambiguity, which "occurs when the author is discovering his idea in the act of writing." To illustrate, Empson quotes a passage from 'Tis Pity in which Giovanni prepares himself for the catastrophe by arguing that the Friar's morality should not subdue the "gall / Of Courage," and by comparing himself to "a well-growne Oake" which crushes the sur-rounding underbrush in its mighty fall (V.iii.2225–31). By means of a random series of word associations combined with flagrant neglect of the dramatic context, Empson establishes the ambiguity of the speech and demonstrates to his own satisfaction that Ford is not in control of the idea being expressed. The combination of the gall image and the oak image into "oak-galls" (an excrescence produced by parasites on oak trees) must surely rank among the most fanciful tricks of Empson's alchemy. If this is the method of analysis, it is easy to see why Empson must at last condemn the speech as a "turgid piece of writing."[19]

Donald K. Anderson, Jr., makes a much more promising start in the analysis of Ford's language; he isolates two significant image patterns in Ford's most famous tragedies, and argues that much of what we would ordinarily call the effect or meaning of the plays depends on these images.[20] The heart is tradition-ally the seat of man's emotions and the mainspring of life. In 'Tis Pity Ford gives us a shockingly visual heart image in the notorious dagger scene, but he has built up to this point by saturating the language of the play with references to the heart, and with imagery drawn from the physical and emotional nature of the heart. Then, there is the complementary pattern of banquet imagery. Again we have a physical counterpart—the marriage feast to celebrate the union of Soranzo and Annabella. But this feast turns sour because it celebrates a marriage without love, while the banquet image is traditionally associated with domestic happiness and mutual affection.

Anderson finds the same scheme varied for different purposes in *The Broken Heart*. Penthea starves not for want of food, but for want of love. The theme of frustration is realized metaphorically as a "never-tasted feast." And of course it is again the heart—the emotional life of man—that cracks under the pressure of frustration. Thus, "in both plays the heart is destroyed, but for opposite reasons: in *'Tis Pity*, because the banquet is eaten; in *The Broken Heart*, because it is not." And we are not dealing here with mere decoration, Anderson warns: "The imagery is sustained, contributing to the unity and reinforcing the theme of each play; it is dynamic, progressing from the figurative to the literal; and it often is ironic."[21]

"Sustained," "dynamic," and "often...ironic." From the verbal analyst's point of view this is high praise indeed. It implies a degree of complexity and organic integrity in Ford's language that previous methods of critical enquiry would never have suspected. Yet, Anderson's contribution to Ford criticism lies not so much in what he finds in these two plays, as in what by implication he leaves undiscovered. If Ford's language is as rich as his essay implies, then it must follow that the other plays stand in need of fresh examination from this point of view, and that the two plays he does examine may yield other rewards to the critic who is prepared to look hard enough and long enough.

More recently G. Wilson Knight has taken a similar approach to the major plays, and again we are invited to see the heart as a basic pattern in Ford's language. Wilson Knight hints suggestively at the life-in-death paradox, at the ambiguity of the marriage motif, and at the religious undertones of the death scenes. But his essay is a very informal survey, and Ford's language escapes once more with rather casual treatment. "Ford's diction is choice," Wilson Knight argues, "but never ostentatious; he eschews metaphor and imagery; no literary skills are allowed to fog his statements."[22] We are left with the feeling that *'Tis Pity* and *The Broken Heart* do not quite warrant the most energetic and careful attention of the critic.

Thus, if Ford has suffered at the hands of the verbal analysts, it is not by what they have said about his poetry, but by what they have left unsaid. The leaders of the verbal analysis school have shown little interest in Ford, with two disastrous results. First, it has become easy to assume that Ford's language is not particularly vital if it has not sustained the interest of a William Empson nor so much as attracted the attention of a Cleanth Brooks. Secondly—and here lies the real danger—the superficial generalities about Ford's poetry have been allowed to linger far longer than is critically useful or intellectually honest, simply because there has been no persistent challenge from the verbal analyst's direction.

Chief among these received ideas is the vague notion of Ford's stillness, calm, and restraint. One line from *The Broken Heart* has been taken up by critic after critic as if it were the central principle of Ford's poetic practice. It is Calantha's line, very near the close of her life and very near the end of the play: "They are the silent griefes which cut the hart-strings" (V.iii.2594). She refers in particular to her scene of unusual restraint—the dance scene—during which she displayed a shocking lack of response to the three reports of death. Now she confirms what several of the courtiers suspected: her behaviour was only a way of repressing emotions much too powerful for direct expression. This scene, so runs the usual argument, amounts to an allegorical statement of Ford's practice as a poet. His subjects are always coloured with the deepest human emotions, but his style constantly restrains, dampens, and tempers the turbulence of his material.

Charles Lamb is indirectly responsible for this blemish in critical perception; his remark on the relative scarcity of metaphor and imagery in Ford's verse becomes a point of departure for many subsequent estimates of Ford's poetic abilities. Swinburne repeats the suggestion, adding praise for the "quiet hand" with which Ford sets down even the most violent passions of the soul. And Eliot modifies these chance remarks into a general principle: we are asked to observe "that slow solemn rhythm which is Ford's distinct contribution to the blank verse of the period."[23]

In this case Eliot's pronouncement has created orthodoxy rather than controversy, for a long and distinguished line of scholars lends uncritical support to the quietness theory.[24] Thus Clifford Leech, despite his usual critical acumen, can admire the "weighted simplicity" of Ford's style without bothering too much about linguistic complexities. "There is imagery, of course," Leech admits, "but it is usually of a conventional sort." In a representative statement of this point of view Moody E. Prior contends that Ford's figures of speech are "auxiliary" rather than organic; they may lend "effectiveness and force to the expression" but they create no "additional depth of meaning."

These received ideas about Ford's poetic technique are largely untrue, for they are simply inconsistent with the results of serious verbal analysis. But perhaps more important, the orthodox line has discouraged critics from digging for subtleties of language with the same curiosity and vigour that are regularly applied to Webster, Tourneur, Jonson, and of course to Shakespeare. With the exception of Anderson's essay, there has been no direct and consistent critical focus on Ford's verbal technique; as a result, the poetry of a play like *Love's Sacrifice* has been virtually ignored. Critics appear to have been intimidated by Eliot's declaration that Ford "wrote enough plays for us to see the absence of essential poetry."[25]

I have already put forward a radically different assessment of Ford's poetic achievement, so this is hardly the place to review the verbal evidence in detail. Perhaps it is enough to observe that exponents of the quietness theory have overlooked nearly all of the linguistic patterns most characteristic of Ford's writing. Ford skilfully employs the techniques of metre and rhythm in order to produce the dynamic movement of his blank verse. He generates a special emotional power by exploiting the suggestive possibilities of paradox and metaphor. He creates a tone of religious pathos through the rhetoric of martyrdom, especially in those scenes where a cluster of liquid images prepares for the sweetness of death. In *Perkin Warbeck* a series of verbal paradoxes grows out of the central thematic and psychological paradox of the play. In *'Tis Pity* and *Love's Sacrifice*, metaphors of rape and images of martyrdom support organically the blending of eros and death. At its best, Ford's language develops and heightens the baroque tendencies inherent in the themes and design of his plays.

The contemporary verbal analyst may admit these qualities, but still deny the "essential poetry" of Ford's verse by arguing that he uses the wrong kind of figurative language. Indeed, such tactics of evasion could be supported by Cleanth Brooks's criterion for distinguishing good metaphors from bad. Since the metaphorical process requires "some degree of tension" between vehicle and tenor, Brooks observes, the successful metaphor will "possess a certain density and sharpness of outline."[26] Curiously, Brooks here describes the language of poetry in a metaphor of his own that might have been borrowed from Wöfflin's account of the linear technique in renaissance painting. If this preference for sharp outlines and verbal density is pushed to extremes, the analyst runs the risk of joining forces with the great tradition critics to condemn a large tract of poetry as "shimmering incoherence" or "mannered perversity."[27] In their eagerness to elucidate the tensions of poetic language, verbal analysts have made irony a virtual requirement of poetry. The pervasively ironic tone of modern literature may have obscured for us an alternate way of resolving poetic tensions—the method of ecstasy and rapture, or in short the method of the baroque style.

A more serious limitation of the verbal analysis critics is the strong leaning they show toward lyric poetry, often to the exclusion of drama, epic, or literary prose. A theory of criticism cannot rely too heavily on any one genre, unless it is willing to sacrifice claims to comprehensiveness. Above all, a critical theory begins to perpetrate its own fallacies when it imports the criteria of one genre into the examination of another. It would be a mistake to expect of Ford's plays the same kind of language, or the same linguistic compression, as one finds in the poems of Donne and Herbert. This is partly because of the distinction in genre: what applies to the lyric may not be true of the drama. But there is also the distinction in style. The mannerist language of Donne finds dramatic shape in Tourneur and Webster. The verbal analysts have made this sort of figurative language—the metaphysical conceit—a cornerstone of their theory. It will not do to censure or disregard Ford's verbal style simply because it is not as compressed, or as ironic, or as intellectual as the metaphysical style. In the materials he selects and the design he imposes on the drama, Ford shows decided characteristics of baroque style. If his language is also baroque, then that is certainly one of the explicable features of his style, but it is by no means a defect.

As in the case of the verbal analysis school, it is difficult to judge the effectiveness of the archetypal theory of criticism as an approach to Ford's plays, because so little practical discussion exists that might count as evidence. The only attempt seems to be R. J. Kaufmann's essay, "Ford's 'Waste Land': *The Broken Heart*."[28] The action of this play, according to Kaufmann, amounts to an elaboration of a single "botanical metaphor." This metaphor is of course a form of the wasteland archetype. The world of the play is a barren wilderness; "life and growth cannot continue to exist where the means of sustenance, the fertilizing energies, are cut off or diverted from their normal course." Thus, the pattern of growth and frustration of growth is the central mythic substance of the play. Among the numerous metaphoric realizations of the myth, the most important one occurs in the words of the oracle quoted by Tecnicus: according to the prophecy Calantha is destined to marry the "*livelesse Trunke*" of her lover Ithocles (IV.i.1778). Kaufmann notices a reference to the Phaethon myth during the trick-chair episode (IV.iii.2221–22). Ithocles has scorched Penthea's beauty and withered her life, just as Phaethon's runaway steeds ravaged the fertility of the earth with flames of destruction. Orgilus' engine of death, a chair which confines Ithocles' movements, also functions as an image of the play's action. To confine movement is to inhibit growth and prevent fertility, and in Ford's Sparta "each character is boxed in, entrapped, by the other characters." When all of the wasteland images are gathered together, we discover that *The Broken Heart* "depends upon a familiar mythic pattern—the vegetative myth of the dying king."[29]

This is a brave new step for Ford criticism to take. In the various images of growth, and images of perverted or stunted growth, Kaufmann does isolate an important new layer of poetic texture. Yet his attempt to apply archetypal theory falls short of one's expectations, for in many ways his essay draws connections between myth and literature that are rather too literal to be entirely satisfying. Kaufmann appears to be the victim of a superstition that has grown up around the fringes of archetypal criticism—the assumption that all the practical critic has to do is arm himself with *Bulfinch's Mythology* and track down the myths appropriate to the work he happens to be studying.

The case is of course much more complicated than this. For one thing, as soon as we accept even for the sake of argument that literature is displaced mythology, we surely begin to wonder about the exact nature of the peculiar process called "displacement." Frye's theoretical and synoptic scheme provides hints, but theory is only the skeleton, or in Fernando's words, the "lean anatomy" of criticism. The muscular tissue of critical debate will be a matter of individual literary works, their relationships to one another, and their relationships to the broad mythic patterns. In other words, myth displacement is not the final solution for every critical problem, but simply another way of asking the basic questions. If Ford's plays are displacements of mythic patterns, then in what respects do they differ from other displacements of the same myths? How does the archetype of stunted growth in *The Broken Heart* differ from the canker images in *Hamlet*, or the disease images in *The Revenger's Tragedy*? Why does Ford favour botanical imagery in *The Broken Heart*, and zoological imagery in *The Fancies*? As soon as we begin to analyze the relationship between pure myth and its displacement in these specific literary terms, we find ourselves talking about style.

It is at this point that our analogy with the visual arts comes to the forefront—almost unavoidably it seems—because the relationship between archetype and realized artifact is often more easily and more effectively illustrated from painting than from poetry.[30] Everyone knows that it would be quite possible to develop a very thorough introductory course on the history of style in post-Christian art simply by studying and comparing an intelligently selected sample of the various paintings and sculptures which depict the crucifixion scene. Such a course might begin with *The Gero Crucifix* in the cathedral at Cologne, of roughly the same vintage as *The Dream of the Rood*. It could reach into our own century with works such as George Rouault's *Head of Christ*, and the modern *Crucifixions* by Salvador Dali and Graham Sutherland. Between the extremes there would be plenty of material to choose from, including major works by Cimabue, Masaccio, Grünewald, Rubens, and Vouet. From any such study a general set of expectations about the crucifixion scene would emerge. If we prefer to think in terms of visual art alone, we might call this set of expectations the suffering Christ convention. If we think in terms of Christian mythology and its realizations, we would call this same pattern the crucifixion archetype. The relationship between the particular art object and the archetype tells us something about the angle from which the artist chooses to see the myth. The various approaches to a common myth, then, are different ways of seeing, or different artistic styles.

Now let us examine a similar situation in literature. We set out to study the suffering Christ convention in English poetry. We begin with *The Dream of the Rood* and selected pageants from *The Wakefield Plays*. We proceed at least as far as Hopkins, Eliot, and Auden. The intermediate stages include Southwell, Donne, Herbert, Crashaw, and Blake. I do not think it would take any great effort to convince our hypothetical teacher of art history and our hypothetical student of literature that they have something in common. They are studying the same myth, realized in different media. And they are bound to find that the angle of vision from which the myth is presented, or the artistic style, goes through broadly parallel phases in art and literature. Our two hypothetical specialists meet quite naturally as soon as they begin to study a common mythological source in its multifarious displacements.

A comparative study of the apotheosis archetype would not have the same broad comprehensiveness, but it would yield special results for the baroque stylistic phase. A literal apotheosis would be the same as turning into a god, but since Christian mythology is particularly uncompromising on this point, we have become accustomed to a looser form of the archetype. Enoch, Moses, and Elijah are conspicuous among the prophets who are gloriously translated into a higher existence at the moment of death. Elijah's case is of special interest, because he rides to heaven on a chariot of fire. In literature we find this pattern in *The Assumption and Coronation of the Virgin* in the York cycle, and in Pompilia's death scene in *The Ring and the Book*. But apotheosis has not become a favourite literary archetype, which explains why Mary's apotheosis in the York cycle seems like superimposed theology to many readers, and why Pompilia's seems like pure sentimentality.

In the visual arts apotheosis is much more common, especially during the baroque phase. Pozzo's ceiling fresco for St. Ignazio and Gaulli's for the nave of the Gesù illustrate the baroque tendency to picture the soul of the Christian martyr soaring triumphantly upward into infinity. Bernini's sculptures and Rubens' religious paintings are less literal but equally powerful versions of this motif. In the moment of death the human soul moves upward while the body reflects the triumph of the soul in sensual ecstasy. There are many examples of the apotheosis motif even without an overtly religious context, such as Rubens' *Apotheosis of James I*, painted for the ceiling at Whitehall. Here the same upward illusionism, the same projection into infinity, and the same triumph over death extend to a purely secular martyrdom.

The apotheosis archetype is a typically baroque way of realizing the larger myth of death and resurrection. Dramatic upward movement and sensuous enjoyment of death are features of style because they tell us something about the way in which the artist looks at his myth. In Ford's plays we find parallel qualities in a literary medium. Biancha's apotheosis, like James I's, is not an overtly religious event, but this does not prevent Ford from using all the religious imagery of the baroque style. The altars, flames, and incense of the last act are ways of intensifying, sustaining, and even celebrating the consummation of death.

To return to the marvellous "rocke of fire" in Caraffa's dream sequence, we find now that it supports the mythic pattern of death and resurrection. It has affinities with Elijah's chariot of fire, with the pillar of fire that guides the Israelites from bondage to the promised land, and with the sun imagery on the Mount of Transfiguration, where the Elijah story and the Moses story are united with Christ. The rock of fire is a purgatorial symbol; it stands at the very peak of human experience; it marks the point of epiphany at which martyrs are metamorphosed into saints. The baroque hero's quest (St. Teresa's, James I's, or Fernando's) turns out to be a disaster from a theological, political, or social point of view, and the result is tragedy. But it may be salvaged in part by the psychological illusion of personal triumph, even in death, and thus it often ends in apotheosis.

In other stylistic phases we tend to find the death and resurrection myth in less theatrical terms. Renaissance tragic heroes die in relative tranquillity and silence, just as renaissance martyrs in the visual arts die without grand gestures or histrionic posturing. If there is to be a revival after death, it will be taken care of by a theological world or by posterity, and it needs no psychological emphasis. There is simply more than one way of looking at death in literature, just as there is more than one angle of vision from which the painter may see the crucifixion myth.

The great advantage of the archetypal system is its pluralistic character. It starts from a basic hypothesis about the relationship between myth and literature, but it does not end in monism. Indeed, the modes, symbols, archetypes, and genres multiply almost bewilderingly as one reads the *Anatomy of Criticism*, until at times the system seems entirely too complicated to be of any use to the practical critic. But in the very nature of complexity an important principle has been established. Within one body of literature there are many different forms and levels at which the created artifact may take shape. The complex relationships between works of literature, between their modes, their symbols, and their styles, form the legitimate subject of critical debate. But these are not matters that can be laid to rest by marshalling chronological data, or by pronouncing value judgments. "A comes before B" and "A is better than B" are not critically useful statements, at least not in the sense that "A differs from B in such-and-such a way" is. A system which recognizes the plurality of literary value is bound to recognize the plurality of style as well. And the term "baroque" is one way of insisting on stylistic plurality, particularly in an area where "renaissance" has exercised an unusually troublesome tyranny.

In sketching the broad outlines of Ford criticism I have of course been selective rather than exhaustive, with the result that some of Ford's better critics have made but furtive appearances in this essay. I have all but ignored Robert Davril's carefully argued and richly documented study of Ford, because Davril's eclectic approach resists identification with any of the dominant theoretical positions in the critical spectrum. On similar grounds I have excluded Glenn H. Blayney's influential essay on *The Broken Heart*, Jonas A. Barish's thoughtful reading of *Perkin Warbeck*, and H. J. Oliver's concise and sensible assessment of the dramatist in *The Problem of John Ford*. Such regrettable omissions have however been necessary, in the interests of achieving a larger goal—the goal of demonstrating how the baroque interpretation of Ford's plays may affect the general shape of Ford criticism.

The baroque style of Ford's drama has historical, evaluative, descriptive, and comparative consequences for the literary critic. As a baroque playwright, Ford finds his proper theatrical context in the company of Massinger, Fletcher, and Otway, just as he finds his aesthetic roots in the dynamic and revolutionary environment of seventeenth-century visual art. Given the vitality of the baroque tradition as a whole, the standard historical charge of decadence may be discarded as basically misleading. In evaluative terms, Ford's drama emerges from the debates of the *Scrutiny* critics with its principal baroque qualities vibrantly intact. If the baroque Ford is the playwright who offends the austere moralist, he is also the playwright who attracts the zealous admiration of Antonin Artaud. From a descriptive or analytical point of view Ford's baroque style is again an argument in his favour, insofar as it hints at the range, complexity, and subtlety of his verbal texture. And in broadly comparative terms, Ford becomes the dramatist who exploits in characteristically baroque fashion the very archetypes that dominate the seventeenth-century mind. Penthea's complaint is a song of regret for the loss of innocence, Perkin's majesty is a tribute to the seductive appeal of illusion, and Biancha's ecstatic death is a fulfilment of the desire for apotheosis through martyrdom. Ford's approach to these archetypal patterns is in one sense his own, though in another sense it is also the approach of Bernini, of Rotrou, and of Crashaw. Ford's unique artistic outlook gives him a sharply individual style, just as the shared angle of vision draws him into the larger compass of the baroque tradition.

"It is an easie vanity," Ford writes in the early days of his career, "to be a conceited Interpreter, but a difficult commendation to bee a serious Author."[31] The story of Ford's critical fortunes might be told as a series of oscillations between these two extremes. On the whole, historical scholars and great tradition critics would rank Ford with the conceited interpreters, but the tentative commendations of verbal analysis and archetypal criticism have begun to discover a serious author. Ford returns indirectly to the subject of the artist's reputation at the very end of his career, in the Epilogue to his last play, *The Lady's Trial*. The actor who speaks the Epilogue continues the dominant courtroom analogy of the play, but reshapes it to apply to the relationship between playwright and audience. When the speaker implies a wish for "tryall now more fortunate" (2653), when he asks for "a gentle day" (2659), we realize that we have left Genoa and are back in Drury Lane. It is Ford who is on trial now, and the audience is the jury. With one more such transformation we can apply the same metaphor to the relationship between Ford and his critics. The verdict may never be unanimous, but the evidence of the baroque tradition should at least point us in the direction of Ford's artistic merits.

NOTES

NOTES TO CHAPTER ONE

1 Heinrich Wölfflin, *Renaissance and Baroque,* trans. from 1st ed. by Kathrin Simon (1888; reprint ed., London: Fontana, 1964), and *Principles of Art History : The Problem of the Development of Style in Later Art,* trans. from 7th ed. by M. D. Hottinger (1929; reprint ed., New York: Dover, 1950).

2 Wölfflin, *Principles,* pp. 18, 73, 124, 156–57, 197–98. Although "painterly" is not the most elegant translation of the German *malerisch,* it is more accurate than synonyms such as "pictorial" or "picturesque."

3 See René Wellek, "The Parallelism between Literature and the Arts," *English Institute Annual, 1941,* ed. Rudolf Kirk (New York: Columbia University Press, 1942), p. 58; Odette de Mourgues, *Metaphysical, Baroque and Précieux Poetry* (Oxford: Clarendon, 1953), p. 68; John Rupert Martin, "The Baroque from the Point of View of the Art Historian," *JAAC,* 14 (1955–56), 165; and Imbrie Buffum, *Studies in the Baroque from Montaigne to Rotrou,* Yale Romanic Studies, Second Series 4 (New Haven: Yale University Press, 1957), p. 240.

4 Erwin Panofsky, *Studies in Iconology : Humanistic Themes in the Art of the Renaissance* (1939; reprint ed., New York: Harper & Row, 1962), pp. 99, 123, 127.

5 See the F Prologue (ll. 226–38) in *The Works of Geoffrey Chaucer,* ed. F. N. Robinson, 2nd ed. (Boston: Houghton Mifflin, 1957), p. 487.

6 For an allegorical reading of the Temple of Venus passage see D. W. Robertson, Jr., *A Preface to Chaucer : Studies in Medieval Perspectives* (Princeton: Princeton University Press, 1962), pp. 370–73.

7 Sonnets 5 and 73, in *The Poems of Sir Philip Sidney,* ed. William A. Ringler, Jr. (Oxford: Clarendon, 1962), pp. 167, 203.

8 Richard Crashaw, *The Poems: English, Latin and Greek,* ed. L. C.Martin, 2nd ed. (Oxford: Clarendon, 1957), p. 407.

9 Aldous Huxley, "Death and the Baroque," *Horizon,* 19 (April 1949), 289.

10 See Werner Weisbach, *Der Barock als Kunst der Gegenreformation* (Berlin: Cassirer, 1921), pp. 20, 135–36; and Robert T. Petersson, *The Art of Ecstasy: Teresa, Bernini, and Crashaw* (London: Routledge, 1970), pp. 72–73.

11 *The Poems of Henry Constable,* ed. Joan Grundy (Liverpool: Liverpool University Press, 1960), pp. 191–92.

12 *Poems,* ed.Martin, pp. 319–20.

13 Eric Mercer, *English Art, 1553–1625,* The Oxford History of English Art, 7 (Oxford: Clarendon, 1962), pp. 241–46.

14 Theodore Spencer, *Death and Elizabethan Tragedy: A Study of Convention and Opinion in the Elizabethan Drama* (1936; reprint ed., New York: Pageant Books, 1960), pp. 220, 256–64. For further discussion of death in Beaumont and Fletcher, Massinger and Shirley, see chap. v, pp. 169, 177–78, 184–86.

15 Panofsky, *Iconology,* p. 229.

16 Descartes, *Discours de la méthode,* ed. Gilbert Gadoffre, 2nd ed. (Manchester: Manchester University Press, 1961), p. 31.

17 Wölfflin, *Principles,* pp. 21–22; *Renaissance and Baroque,* p. 30.

18 Wölfflin, *Principles,* pp. 198, 222.

19 *Poems,* ed. Martin, p. 195.

20 Jean Rousset, *La Littérature de l'âge baroque en France: Circé et le paon,* 2nd ed. (Paris: José Corti, 1954), p. 228. "Dans la querelle de l'être et du paraître, ceux qui sont du côté du Baroque se reconnaissent à l'accent qu'ils font porter sur le paraître."

21 Germain Bazin, *The Baroque: Principles, Styles, Modes, Themes,* trans. Pat Wardroper (Greenwich, Connecticut: New York Graphic Society, 1968), pp. 30, 35.

22 See Arnold Hauser, *Renaissance, Mannerism and Baroque,* rev. ed., *The Social History of Art,* 2 (London: Routledge, 1962), pp. 57–62.

23 See Anthony Blunt, *Art and Architecture in France, 1500 to 1700,* 2nd ed., The Pelican History of Art (Harmondsworth: Penguin, 1957), pp. 189–90; and Rudolf Wittkower, *Gian Lorenzo Bernini: The Sculptor of the Roman Baroque,* 2nd ed. (London: Phaidon, 1966), pp. 246–47.

24 See Wylie Sypher's discussion of "Renaissance Composition" in *Four Stages of Renaissance Style: Transformations in Art and Literature, 1400–1700* (Garden City, New York: Doubleday, 1955), esp. pp. 57–63. See also Erwin Panofsky, *Meaning in the Visual Arts* (1955; reprinted., Harmondsworth: Penguin, 1970), pp. 119–22.

25 Manfred F. Bukofzer, *Music in the Baroque Era: From Monteverdi to Bach* (New York: Norton, 1947), pp. 3–4.

26 Preface to *Troilus and Cressida,* "Containing the Grounds of Criticism in Tragedy," *Essays of John Dryden,* ed. W. P. Ker (Oxford: Clarendon, 1900), I, 228.

27 The standard reference works demonstrate an unusually high proportion of anonymous and collaborative plays during the 1590s; see the listings for these years in Alfred Harbage and S. Schoenbaum, *Annals of English Drama, 975–1700,* 2nd ed. (Philadelphia: University of Pennsylvania Press, 1964). See also Gerald Eades Bentley, *The Profession of Dramatist in Shakespeare's Time, 1590–1642* (Princeton: Princeton University Press, 1971), pp. 14–15.

28 See Rudolf Wittkower, *Art and Architecture in Italy, 1600 to 1750,* 2nd ed., The Pelican History of Art (Harmondsworth: Penguin, 1965), pp. 105–106.

29 See Bukofzer, *Music in the Baroque Era,* pp. 5–7.

30 See Frank J. Warnke, *Versions of Baroque: European Literature in the Seventeenth Century* (New Haven: Yale University Press, 1972), p. 158.

31 C. S. Lewis, *English Literature in the Sixteenth Century, Excluding Drama,* The Oxford History of English Literature, 3 (Oxford: Clarendon, 1954), pp. 64–65.

32 I do not mean to imply in the progression from renaissance to rococo any neat chronological sequence, since each of the categories overlaps with its neighbours from time to time, and of course stylistic phases do not spring up simultaneously in every European capital. For discussions of the chronology of styles see Jean Alazard, "Spätrenaissance, contre-réforme, et baroque," *Bulletin of the International Committee of Historical Sciences,* 10 (1938), 620–22; Bukofzer, *Music in the Baroque Era,* pp. 16–19; Rousset, *L'Age baroque,* pp. 233–35; Helmut Hatzfeld, "The Baroque from the Viewpoint of the Literary Historian," *JAAC,* 14 (1955–56), 156–64; and Walter Friedlaender, *Mannerism and Anti-Mannerism in Italian Painting* (New York: Columbia University Press, 1957), pp. 1–5.

33 Sypher, *Four Stages,* pp. 101–105, 180–81. See also Arnold Hauser, *Mannerism: The Crisis of the Renaissance and the Origin of Modern Art* (London: Routledge, 1965), I, 6–11.

34 Giuliano Briganti, *Italian Mannerism,* trans. Margaret Kunzle (London: Thames and Hudson, 1962), p. 24.

35 See Hauser, *Mannerism,* I, 270; and Friedlaender, *Mannerism and Anti-Mannerism,* pp. 7–9.

36 *The Complete Poetry of John Donne,* ed. John T. Shawcross (New York: New York University Press, 1968), p. 130.

37 See Hauser, *Mannerism,* I, 23–27; and Bazin, *Baroque,* pp. 18–19.

38 John Donne, *Selected Prose,* ed. Evelyn Simpson et al. (Oxford: Clarendon, 1967), p. 91.

39 Robert Burton, *The Anatomy of Melancholy,* ed. Floyd Dell and Paul Jordan-Smith (New York: Tudor Publishing Company, 1927), p. 220.

40 See Morris W. Croll's discussion of the *stile coupé* and the loose style in "The Baroque Style in Prose," *Studies in English Philology: A Miscellany in Honor of Frederick Klaeber,* ed.

Kemp Malone and Martin B. Ruud (Minneapolis: University of Minnesota Press, 1929), pp. 432–36, 442–43.

41 See Una Ellis-Fermor, *The Jacobean Drama: An Interpretation,* 4th ed. (London: Methuen, 1958), pp. 17–25. See also Cyrus Hoy, "Jacobean Tragedy and the Mannerist Style," *ShS,* 26 (1973), 53–57.

42 John Webster, *The Duchess of Malfi,* ed. John Russell Brown, The Revels Plays (London: Methuen 1964). In taking Webster as a primary example of mannerism I follow Sypher (*Four Stages,* p. 123) and run counter to Ralph Berry's attempt to deal with Webster as a baroque dramatist. Berry dismisses the concept of mannerism rather too cavalierly; see *The Art of John Webster* (Oxford: Clarendon, 1972), p. 7.

43 Jean de Rotrou, *Théâtre choisi,* ed. Félix Hémon (Paris: Garnier, n.d.), p. 323.

> J'ai souhaité longtemps d'agréer à vos yeux;
> Aujourd'hui je veux plaire à l'empereur des cieux;
> Je vous ai divertis, j'ai chanté vos louanges;
> Il est temps maintenant de réjouir les anges,
> Il est temps de prétendre à des prix immortels,
> Il est temps de passer du théâtre aux autels.
> Si je l'ai mérité, qu'on me mène au martyre:
> Mon rôle est achevé, je n'ai plus rien à dire.

44 F. P. Wilson, *Elizabethan and Jacobean* (Oxford: Clarendon, 1945), p. 95.

45 "Der ewigkeiten cron" (V.448), in Andreas Gryphius, *Werke,* ed. Hermann Palm and F. W. Wentzlaff-Eggebert (Hildesheim: Georg Olms, 1961), II, 465.

46 See Gonzague de Reynold, *Le XVIIᵉ siècle: Le Classique et le baroque* (Montreal: Editions de l'Arbre, 1944), pp. 155–56; Pierre Kohler, "Le Baroque et les lettres françaises," *Cahiers de l'association internationale des études françaises,* 1 (1951), 14–16; and Henri Peyre, "Common-Sense Remarks on the French Baroque," *Studies in Seventeenth-Century French Literature Presented to Morris Bishop,* ed. Jean-Jacques Demorest (Ithaca, New York: Cornell University Press, 1962), pp. 1–19.

47 See Rousset, *L'Age baroque,* p. 246; and Bazin, *Baroque,* p. 102.

48 *The Complete Poetry of Robert Herrick,* ed. J. Max Patrick (New York: New York University Press, 1963), p. 105.

49 *The Poems of John Dryden,* ed. James Kinsley (Oxford: Clarendon, 1958), I, 389.

50 Sypher, *Four Stages,* pp. 262–63, 271–73, 277–78, 282–96. Though I consider his term "late-baroque" inconvenient, I wish to imply only a slight qualification of Sypher's imaginative synthesis.

51 See Bazin, *Baroque,* pp. 120–21.

52 Wittkower, *Art and Architecture,* p. 304.

53 Milton, *Complete Poems and Major Prose,* ed. Merritt Y. Hughes (New York: Odyssey, 1957), p. 100.

54 Roy Daniells tries to make a mannerist poem out of *Comus,* but in order to do so he is forced to deny the manifest triumph of virtue in the dance that concludes the masque; see *Milton, Mannerism and Baroque* (Toronto: University of Toronto Press, 1963), pp. 32–37.

55 *The Dramatic Works of Sir George Etherege,* ed. H. F. B. Brett-Smith (Oxford: Blackwell, 1927), II, 248–49.

56 *The Poems of Alexander Pope,* ed. John Butt et al. (New Haven: Yale University Press, 1939–69), II, 166.

57 *Lessings Werke,* ed. Kurt Wölfel et al. (Frankfurt am Main: Insel, 1967), III, 114. "Körperliche Schönheit entspringt aus der übereinstimmenden Wirkung mannigfaltiger Teile, die sich auf einmal übersehen lassen. . . . Der Dichter, der die Elemente der Schönheit nur nacheinander zeigen könnte, enthält sich daher der Schilderung körperliche Schönheit, als Schönheit, gänzlich."

58 Svetlana and Paul Alpers, "*Ut Pictura Noesis?* Criticism in Literary Studies and Art History," *New Literary History,* 3 (1971–72), 457.

59 For an incisive critique of Lessing's theory of art see Rensselaer W. Lee, *Ut Pictura Poesis: The Humanistic Theory of Painting* (1940; reprint ed., New York: Norton, 1967), pp. 20–23.

60 Edgar Wind, *Pagan Mysteries in the Renaissance,* rev. ed. (New York: Norton, 1968), p. 43.

61 Northrop Frye, *A Natural Perspective: The Development of Shakespearean Comedy and Romance* (New York: Columbia University Press, 1965), p. 9.

62 See Wellek, "Parallelism," pp. 50–58; and Rosemond Tuve, "Baroque and Mannerist Milton?" *Essays by Rosemond Tuve: Spenser, Herbert, Milton,* ed. Thomas P. Roche, Jr. (Princeton: Princeton University Press, 1970), pp. 264–65.

63 *The Complete Plays of Christopher Marlowe,* ed. Irving Ribner (New York: Odyssey, 1963), p. 411. All Marlowe citations refer to this edition.

64 Rotrou, *Théâtre choisi,* ed. Hémon, p. 335.

> Ne plaignez point, Madame, un malheur volontaire,
> Puisqu'il l'a pu franchir et s'être salutaire,
> Et qu'il a bien voulu, par son impiété,
> D'une feinte en mourant faire une vérité.

65 For the terms "harmony" and "fusion" see Roy Daniells, "Baroque Form in English Literature," *UTQ,* 14 (1944–45), 396.

66 Sypher, *Four Stages,* p. 21.

67 Margaret Whinney and Oliver Millar, *English Art, 1625–1714,* The Oxford History of English Art, 8 (Oxford: Clarendon, 1957), pp. 4, 71.

68 See Friedrich Wild, "Zum Problem des Barocks in der englischen Dichtung," *Anglia,* 59 (1935), 414–15; and Austin Warren, *Richard Crashaw: A Study in Baroque Sensibility* ([Baton Rouge]: Louisiana State University Press, 1939), pp. 4–10.

69 Whinney and Millar, *English Art, 1625–1714,* p. 123.

70 See Alfred Harbage, *Cavalier Drama: An Historical and Critical Supplement to the Study of the Elizabethan and Restoration Stage* (New York: MLA, 1936), pp. 11–13, 19.

71 See Bukofzer, *Music in the Baroque Era,* pp. 183–84.

72 See Gerald Eades Bentley, *The Jacobean and Caroline Stage* (Oxford: Clarendon, 1941–68), I, 252–59.

73 James Howell, *Epistolæ Ho-Elianæ: The Familiar Letters,* ed. Joseph Jacobs (London: David Nutt, 1890), p. 165.

74 Whinney and Millar, *English Art, 1625–1714,* p. 70.

75 See Terence Heywood, "Some Notes on English Baroque," *Horizon,* 2 (November 1940), 267; Rudolf Stamm, "Englischer Literaturbarock?" *Die Kunstformen des Barockzeitalters: Vierzehn Vorträge,* ed. Stamm (Bern: Francke, 1956), pp. 383–88; Helen C. White, "Southwell: Metaphysical and Baroque," *MP,* 61 (1963–64), 159; and Mario Praz, "Baroque in England," *MP,* 61 (1963–64), 169–70.

76 Whinney and Millar, *English Art, 1625–1714,* pp. 69, 121.

77 Dedicatory verse to Richard Brome's *The Northern Lasse: A Comoedie* (London, [1632]). sig. A3ᵛ.

78 "Ein Hervorbrechen des barocken Stilprinzips" (Wild, "Problem des Barocks," 418).

79 Roy Daniells, "English Baroque and Deliberate Obscurity," *JAAC,* 5 (1946–47), 118.

80 Clifford Leech, *John Ford and the Drama of his Time* (London: Chatto & Windus, 1957), p. 23.

81 Warnke, *Versions of Baroque,* p. 200.

NOTES TO CHAPTER TWO

1 *John Ford's Dramatic Works,* ed. Henry de Vocht, Materials for the Study of the Old English Drama, NS 1 (Louvain: Uystpruyst, 1927). All quotations from Ford's plays refer to the reprints in this series. The other relevant volumes are: *John Fordes dramatische Werke,* ed. W. Bang, Materialien zur Kunde des älteren englischen Dramas, 23 (1908); and *The Queen, or the Excellency of her Sex,* ed. Bang, Materialien, 13 (1906). Act and line numbering follows the practice of Bang and de Vocht; for convenience I insert the scene numbering used by Gifford and subsequent editors.

2 C. S. Lewis, *The Allegory of Love: A Study in Medieval Tradition* (Oxford: Clarendon, 1936), p. 42.

3 See Louis L. Martz, *The Poetry of Meditation: A Study in English Religious Literature of the*

Seventeenth Century, rev. ed., Yale Studies in English, 125 (New Haven: Yale University Press, 1962), esp. pp. 78–79.

4 Luis de la Puente, *Meditations upon the Mysteries of our Holie Faith, with the Practise of Mental Prayer Touching the Same,* trans. John Heigham (St. Omer, 1619), I, sig. F1.

5 Ibid., I, sig. 3D3ᵛ. Marginal notes direct us to Cant. i.1 and v.4 (i.2 and v.4 in the Authorized Version).

6 Wylie Sypher, *Four Stages of Renaissance Style,* pp. 186–89.

7 John Ford, *Honor Triumphant, or the Peeres Challenge, by Armes Defensible, at Tilt, Turney, and Barriers* (London, 1606), sig. E2ᵛ.

8 Ibid., sigs. E2ᵛ–3. The words in square brackets are my emendations for *conuinction* and *sent.*

9 Putana's name is of course derived from romance-language slang for "prostitute"; compare the Spanish word *puta* and the French *putain.* Elsewhere, Ford himself translates "*Huio di puto*" as "*sonne of a whore*" (*LT* IV.ii.1982–83). In this connection see also *'Tis Pity She's a Whore,* ed. Derek Roper, The Revels Plays (London: Methuen, 1975), p. 6, n.

10 S. P. Sherman, "Forde's Contribution to the Decadence of the Drama," in *Werke,* ed. Bang, p. xii. See also Mark Stavig, *John Ford and the Traditional Moral Order* (Madison: University of Wisconsin Press, 1968), pp. 96–101, 119.

11 *Religio Medici* I.ix, in *The Prose of Sir Thomas Browne,* ed. Norman Endicott (New York: New York University Press, 1968), p. 14.

12 The flagrantly erotic tone of so many scenes in *Love's Sacrifice* may indicate that Ford considers the organization of the standard repertory company of his time obsolete. A boy actor could hardly play Biancha's part to full advantage, since stage directions twice call for her appearance in bedroom attire, and one of her most important speeches requires a "naked" bosom (V.i.2529). It is probable that while writing *Love's Sacrifice* Ford visualized an ideal performance with actresses, even though the regular theatres could not yet furnish such conditions. This conjecture is strengthened by Fernando's enthusiastic account of "women Anticks" (actresses) whom he had observed in Brussels (III.ii.1570–77). According to Gerald Eades Bentley, Ford may be making an oblique reference to the excitement generated by Henrietta Maria's personal appearance in private theatrical productions; the celebrated rehearsals for *The Shepherd's Paradise* drew a barrage of comment and speculation during the period of five months (Sept. 1632 to Jan. 1632/33) immediately prior to the entry of *Love's Sacrifice* in the Stationers' Register (21 Jan. 1632/33). See *The Jacobean and Caroline Stage,* III, 452–53; IV, 917–20.

13 Katherine has only a walk-on role in Ford's primary source, Sir Francis Bacon's *The Historie of the Reigne of King Henry the Seventh,* 2nd ed. (London, 1629), sig. X1. For detailed discussion of Ford's deviation from his sources on this point see Emil Koeppel, *Quellen-Studien zu den Dramen George Chapman's, Philip Massinger's und John Ford's,* Quellen und Forschungen zur Sprach- und Culturgeschichte, 82 (Strassburg: Karl J. Trübner, 1897),

pp. 193–94; Robert Davril, *Le Drame de John Ford,* Bibliothèque des Langues Modernes, 5 (Paris: Didier, 1954), pp. 180–81; and Peter Ure, ed., "Introduction," *The Chronicle History of Perkin Warbeck: A Strange Truth,* The Revels Plays (London: Methuen, 1968), pp. xl–xli.

14 I use the letters *a* and *b* to correct the error of redundancy in de Vocht's line numbering for *The Fancies.*

15 *The Queen* (published anonymously in 1653) was first added to the Ford canon by Bang in 1906 on the basis of internal evidence alone. Fifty years later Bentley could claim that "all subsequent Ford students of any standing have agreed with Bang's attribution" (*Jacobean and Caroline Stage,* III, 457), and indeed much the same assertion would hold true today. The principal reasons for accepting *The Queen* as Ford's work are as follows: the thematic treatment of sexuality is typical of Ford; the character of Muretto strongly resembles Corax in *The Lover's Melancholy*; the influence of Burton's *Anatomy* is apparent in this play and in Ford's work as a whole; and many of Ford's characteristic verbal patterns occur in *The Queen.* This last point could be expanded indefinitely, but two examples must suffice. With "married Batchelor" (*Queen* I.ii.678) compare "married Bachelours" (*BH* IV.ii.1938). With "new revive," "new marry," and "new torment" (*Queen* V.ii.3448, 3663, 3815) compare "new reviv'd" (*FW* I.i.236), "new marry" (*BH* V.iii.2585), and "new kisse" (*LS* I.ii.533).

16 Sonnet 144, in *The Complete Works,* ed. Alfred Harbage et al., rev. ed. (Baltimore: Penguin, 1969). All Shakespearean citations refer to this edition. Of course it is dangerous to assume that Shakespeare is entirely typical of renaissance style, especially in his later plays. In general I restrict my Shakespearean references to texts written before 1600, because it is in these early works that Shakespeare shares most with his renaissance contemporaries. On the problem of classifying Shakespeare's style as renaissance, mannerist, or baroque, see Oskar Boerner, "Shakespeare und der Barock," *Germanisch-romanische Monatsschrift,* 25 (1937), 368–81; Levin Ludwig Schücking, "The Baroque Character of the Elizabethan Tragic Hero," *Proceedings of the British Academy,* 24 (1938), 111; Patrick Cruttwell, "Shakespeare and the Baroque," *Shakespeare Jahrbuch,* 97 (1961), 100–108; Arnold Hauser, *Renaissance, Mannerism and Baroque,* pp. 156–58; Edith M. Roerecke, "Baroque Aspects of *Antony and Cleopatra,*" *Essays on Shakespeare,* ed. Gordon Ross Smith (University Park: Pennsylvania State University Press, 1965), pp. 182–95; Janine Bauduin, "Les Eléments baroque dans *Macbeth* et leur utilisation," *Etudes anglaises,* 24 (1971), 1–21; and Frank J. Warnke, *Versions of Baroque,* pp. 45–46.

17 *The Works of Thomas Kyd,* ed. Frederick S. Boas (Oxford: Clarendon, 1901), V.ii.91.

18 Ford acknowledges Burton's influence in *The Lover's Melancholy* with a marginal note: "*Vid. Democrit. Junior*" (III.i.1255–57). For further discussion, see pp. 59–62 and n. 35.

19 *The Lyf of the Mother Teresa of Jesus,* trans. W.M. (Antwerp, 1611), sig. 2F4ᵛ.

20 "Eine Sensualisierung religiöser Stoffe geht in Literatur und bildender Kunst parallel" (Weisbach, *Der Barock,* p. 33).

21 See Mary Edith Cochnower, "John Ford," *Seventeenth Century Studies,* ed. Robert Shafer (Princeton: Princeton University Press, 1933), p. 273; T. S. Eliot, "John Ford," *Selected Essays,* 3rd ed. (London: Faber, 1951), p. 204; H. J. Oliver, *The Problem of John Ford* (Carlton, Victoria:Melbourne University Press, 1955), pp. 70, 84; and T. B. Tomlinson, *A Study of Elizabethan and Jacobean Tragedy* (Cambridge: Cambridge University Press, 1964), pp. 274–76.

22 *The Golden Meane,* 2nd ed. (London, 1614), sigs. H4ᵛ–5. Convincing external evidence in support of Ford's authorship is advanced by M. Joan Sargeaunt, *John Ford* (Oxford: Blackwell, 1935), pp. 13, 16. Subsequent critics confirm Sargeaunt's judgment; see Davril, *Le Drame,* pp. 87–88; Oliver, *The Problem,* pp. 14–15; and Stavig, *Moral Order,* p. 21.

23 See Clifford Leech, *John Ford and the Drama of his Time,* p. 26; and Samuel Anthony Caldwell, "John Ford and Seventeenth-Century Stoicism," Diss. Harvard 1968, pp. 99–109.

24 See R. J. Kaufmann, "Ford's Tragic Perspective, "*Texas Studies in Literature and Language,* I (1959–60), 525–29.

25 For critics who damn her death scene, see William Hazlitt, *Lectures on the Dramatic Literature of the Age of Elizabeth* (1818; reprint ed., New York: Wiley and Putnam, 1845), pp. 112–13; Wallace A. Bacon, "The Literary Reputation of John Ford," *Huntington Library Quarterly,* 11 (1947–48), 186; and Oliver, *The Problem,* pp. 69–70. For those who praise it, see Charles Lamb, ed., *Specimens of English Dramatic Poets Who Lived about the Time of Shakespeare,* new ed. (London: Bohn, 1854), p. 228; A. C. Swinburne, "John Ford," *Essays and Studies,* 5th ed. (London: Chatto & Windus, 1901), pp. 285–86; Davril, *Le Drame,* pp. 256–58; and Charles O. McDonald, "The Design of John Ford's *The Broken Heart*: A Study in the Development of Caroline Sensibility," *SP,* 59 (1962), 152–55.

26 For example, see her address "To Virgin wives, such as abuse not wedlocke / By freedome of desires" (III.v.1573–74). This passage and similar figures of speech are discussed in detail in chap. iv, pp. 136–39.

27 See Bacon, *Henry the Seventh,* sigs. 2C1ᵛ–2. Ford's characteristic treatment of death is also detectable in *The Witch of Edmonton* (1621), a play written in collaboration with Dekker and Rowley. When Frank Thorney stabs the second of his two wives, Susan Carter, she embraces death with eager submission: "I did not think that death had been so sweet; Nor I so apt to love him" (III.iii.58–59). After Frank's crimes of bigamy and murder have been exposed, his first wife Winnifride stands by him until he is led away to execution, just as Katherine stands by Perkin. Winnifride is sure that Frank's repentance has made him "white as innocence," and wishes that she could reclaim her husband after death: "might our Souls together / Climb to the height of their eternity, / And there enjoy what earth denied us, Happiness" (V.iii.95–99). See *The Dramatic Works of Thomas Dekker,* ed. Fredson Bowers (Cambridge: Cambridge University Press, 1953–61), III, 531, 560. In general, I have chosen to exclude from consideration Ford's ventures in collaborative writing (principally *The Witch of Edmonton* and *The Sun's Darling*), on the grounds that these works of apprenticeship raise complicated questions of no strict relevance to the present argument.

28 *The Works of George Herbert,* ed. F. E. Hutchinson, rev. ed. (Oxford: Clarendon, 1945), pp. 185–86.

29 Robert Wilmot, *The Tragedie of Tancred and Gismund,* ed. W. W. Greg (London: Malone Society, 1914), V.ii.1725. For comment on Wilmot's treatment of death, see Lenora Leet Brodwin, *Elizabethan Love Tragedy, 1587–1625* (New York: New York University Press, 1971), pp. 41–43.

30 See Lawrence Babb, *The Elizabethan Malady: A Study of Melancholia in English Literature from 1580 to 1642* (East Lansing: Michigan State College Press, 1951), pp. 1–5.

31 C. S. Lewis uses the *Lucrece* example in his discussion of the rational soul; see *The Discarded Image: An Introduction to Medieval and Renaissance Literature* (Cambridge: Cambridge University Press, 1964), pp. 156–61.

32 *The Works of Edmund Spenser: A Variorum Edition,* ed. Edwin Greenlaw et al. (Baltimore: Johns Hopkins Press, 1932–47), II, 156.

33 Blaise Pascal, *Pensées et opuscules,* ed. Léon Brunschvicg (Paris: Hachette, 1961), pp. 457–58. "Tout notre raisonnement se réduit à céder au sentiment....La raison s'offre, mais elle est ployable à tous sens....Le cœur a ses raisons, que la raison ne connaît point.... C'est le cœur qui sent Dieu, et non la raison" (*Pensées* iv.274–78).

34 Burton, *The Anatomy of Melancholy,* p. 147.

35 Ford's treatment of abnormal psychology, though of primary importance, is by no means so clinical as the "medical" school of criticism has argued. See S. Blaine Ewing, *Burtonian Melancholy in the Plays of John Ford,* Princeton Studies in English, 19 (Princeton: Princeton University Press, 1940); G. F. Sensabaugh, *The Tragic Muse of John Ford* (Stanford: Stanford University Press, 1944), pp. 34–70; Babb, *The Elizabethan Malady,* pp. 113–27; and Robert Rentoul Reed, Jr., *Bedlam on the Jacobean Stage* (Cambridge: Harvard University Press, 1952), pp. 132–53. For a balanced assessment of this approach to Ford's plays see Davril, *Le Drame,* pp. 223–33.

36 Ewing, *Burtonian Melancholy,* pp. 36–39.

37 Burton, *Anatomy,* p. 798.

38 See Leech, *Ford and the Drama,* p. 114.

39 See Glenn H. Blayney, "Convention, Plot, and Structure in *The Broken Heart,*" *MP,* 56 (1958–59), 7; and Alan Brissenden, "Sexual Themes in Jacobean Drama with Special Reference to Tourneur, Webster, Middleton and Ford," Diss. University College (London) 1962, pp. 156–58.

40 See Winston Weathers, "*Perkin Warbeck*: A Seventeenth-Century Psychological Play," *SEL,* 4 (1964), 218–20.

41 Thomas Kyd, *The Spanish Tragedy,* ed. Philip Edwards, The Revels Plays (London: Methuen, 1959), III.xiii.140.

42 For comparisons of the various versions, see T. O. Beachcroft, "Crashaw—and the

Baroque Style," *Criterion,* 13 (April 1934), 413–19; and Austin Warren, *Richard Crashaw,* pp. 105–10.

43 *The Life and Works of George Peele,* ed. Charles Tyler Prouty et al. (New Haven: Yale University Press, 1952–70), III, 69.

44 See Swinburne, *Essays and Studies,* p. 297; Ewing, *Burtonian Melancholy,* pp. 47–48; and Stavig, *Moral Order,* p. 81. For a rejoinder see Peter Davison, "La Dramaturgie en Angleterre à la veille de la guerre civile: John Ford et la comédie," *Dramaturgie et société: Rapports entre l'œuvre théâtrale, son interprétation et son public aux XVIe et XVIIe siècles,* ed. Jean Jacquot (Paris: Centre National de la Recherche Scientifique, 1968), II, 806–807.

45 See Oliver, *The Problem,* p. 114.

46 See Peter Ure, "Cult and Initiates in Ford's *Love's Sacrifice,*" *Modern Language Quarterly,* 11 (1950), 301; Oliver, *The Problem,* pp. 77–79; Leech, *Ford and the Drama,* p. 80; and Tomlinson, *A Study,* pp. 269–70.

47 Il a "préféré laisser à cette décision tout son mystère" (Davril, *Le Drame,* p. 248).

48 Gerard Langbaine, *An Account of the English Dramatick Poets* (Oxford, 1691), p. 222.

NOTES TO CHAPTER THREE

1 Northrop Frye, *Anatomy of Criticism: Four Essays* (Princeton: Princeton University Press, 1957), pp. 209–10.

2 See Travis Bogard, *The Tragic Satire of John Webster* (Berkeley: University of California Press, 1955), pp. 128–31; and Alvin Kernan, *The Cankered Muse: Satire of the English Renaissance,* Yale Studies in English, 142 (New Haven: Yale University Press, 1959), pp. 242–46.

3 Cyril Tourneur, *The Revenger's Tragedy,* ed. R. A. Foakes, The Revels Plays (London: Methuen, 1966), V.iii.125.

4 Frye, *Anatomy of Criticism,* p. 187.

5 See Camille Cé, "Le Drame incestueux chez John Ford," *Cahiers du sud,* 10, special no. (1933), 225; M. Joan Sargeaunt, *John Ford,* p. 124; H. J. Oliver, *The Problem of John Ford,* pp. 86–88; Robert Davril, "Shakespeare and Ford," *Shakespeare Jahrbuch,* 94 (1958), 124–26; S. Gorley Putt, "The Modernity of John Ford," *English,* 18 (1969), 47; and Arthur C. Kirsch, *Jacobean Dramatic Perspectives* (Charlottesville: University Press of Virginia, 1972), pp. 121–23.

6 See E. M. W. Tillyard, *The Elizabethan World Picture* (London: Chatto & Windus, 1943), pp. 94–99.

7 See T. S. Eliot, *Selected Essays,* p. 194; Sargeaunt, *John Ford,* p. 153; Robert Davril, *Le Drame de John Ford,* pp. 323–25; Oliver, *The Problem,* p. 57; and Robert Ornstein, *The Moral Vision of Jacobean Tragedy* (Madison: University of Wisconsin Press, 1960), pp. 201–203.

8 See Nicholas Grimald's "Of Friendship" (no. 154) in *Tottel's Miscellany* (*1557–1587*), ed. Hyder Edward Rollins, rev. ed. (Cambridge: Harvard University Press, 1965), I, 106.

9 See Clifford Leech, *John Ford and the Drama of his Time,* p. 60; Irving Ribner, *Jacobean Tragedy: The Quest for Moral Order* (London: Methuen, 1962), pp. 164–65; and Larry S. Champion, "Ford's *'Tis Pity She's a Whore* and the Jacobean Tragic Perspective," *PMLA*, 90 (1975), 84.

10 But Giovanni's emphasis on Annabella's *"face"* indicates the sensuality of his paradise in a way that Antony's speech does not. Indeed, such "Immortal longings" (V.ii.280) are exceptional in Shakespeare.

11 Maud Bodkin, *Archetypal Patterns in Poetry: Psychological Studies of Imagination* (London: Oxford University Press, 1934), pp. 85–86.

12 See Mark Stavig, *John Ford and the Traditional Moral Order,* p. 126; and Juliet McMaster "Love, Lust, and Sham: Structural Pattern in the Plays of John Ford," *RenD,* NS 2 (1969), 161.

13 See Richard Levin, *The Multiple Plot in English Renaissance Drama* (Chicago: University of Chicago Press, 1971), pp. 109–16.

14 See Penthea's use of this phrase (*BH* IV.ii.1938).

15 G. Wilson Knight, "John Ford: Dramatist of the Heart," *Devonshire Association Report and Transactions,* 103 (1971), 10.

16 See Glenn H. Blayney, "Convention, Plot, and Structure in *The Broken Heart,*" 6–8; and Juliet McMaster, "John Ford, Dramatist of Frustration," *English Studies in Canada,* 1 (1975), 269–70.

17 See Davril, *Le Drame,* p. 279; Stavig, *Moral Order,* pp. 158–59; and Tucker Orbison, *The Tragic Vision of John Ford,* Salzburg Studies in English Literature: Jacobean Drama Studies, 21 (Salzburg: Institut für englische Sprache und Literatur, 1974), pp. 121–22.

18 Friar Bonaventura makes an equally hasty departure from Parma (*TP* V.iii.2217–22).

19 See Jonas A. Barish, "*Perkin Warbeck* as Anti-History," *EIC,* 20 (1970), 158–59.

20 Social rebirth is given special emphasis in *Henry V* and *Richard III,* the concluding plays of the two tetralogies. In both cases a proposed royal marriage is a decisive closing symbol. Of course Shakespeare's history plays do dovetail into one another, as many scholars have shown, and in this sense the conclusion of one play points forward to the beginning of another. But this linking technique should not be confused with open form.

21 See M. C. Bradbrook, *The Growth and Structure of Elizabethan Comedy* (London: Chatto & Windus, 1955), pp. 67–70.

22 See Eugene M. Waith, *The Pattern of Tragicomedy in Beaumont and Fletcher,* Yale Studies in English, 120 (New Haven: Yale University Press, 1952), esp. pp. 70–75.

23 This play ran through the remarkable total of ten editions in the first 28 years of its

known history; see Gerald Eades Bentley, *The Jacobean and Caroline Stage*, VII, 63. I refer throughout to the first edition (London, 1598). A modern edition of the 1610 version may be consulted in *Elizabethan and Stuart Plays*, ed. Charles Read Baskervill et al. (New York: Holt, Rinehart and Winston, 1934), pp. 527–52.

24 Northrop Frye, *A Natural Perspective*, p. 72.

25 For a similar treatment of the conventions of renaissance comedy, see C. L. Barber, *Shakespeare's Festive Comedy: A Study of Dramatic Form and its Relation to Social Custom* (Princeton: Princeton University Press, 1959), pp. 11–15.

26 See Frye, *A Natural Perspective*, p. 93; and *Anatomy of Criticism*, pp. 175–76.

27 See S. Blaine Ewing, *Burtonian Melancholy in the Plays of John Ford*, p. 39; and Lawrence Babb, *The Elizabethan Malady*, pp. 163–64.

28 See Davril, *Le Drame*, p. 158.

29 Denis de Rougemont, *Passion and Society*, trans. Montgomery Belgion, rev. ed. (London: Faber, 1956), pp. 36–42.

30 Waith, *Pattern of Tragicomedy*, pp. 32–36.

31 He might just as easily have drawn his examples from contemporary dramatists: Flamineo helps to make the match between his sister Vittoria and Bracciano (Webster, *The White Devil* I.ii); Gratiana is quite willing to act as factress for her daughter (Tourneur, *The Revenger's Tragedy* II.i); Sir Charles Mountford resolves to sell his sister's virginity to pay off his gambling debts (Heywood, *A Woman Killed with Kindness* xiv); both Leantio and his mother obligingly close their eyes while Bianca becomes the Duke's mistress (Middleton, *Women Beware Women* III.ii); Sorano promises to procure the body of his sister Evanthe for King Frederick (Fletcher, *A Wife for a Month* I.i); and Sciarrha twice plays the pander's role— once in jest and once in earnest—for his sister Amidea (Shirley, *The Traitor* II.i, V.i).

32 See Juliet McMaster, "Platonic Love in Ford's *The Fancies, Chaste and Noble*," *SEL*, 7 (1967), 303–308.

33 See Peter Davison, "Ford et la comédie," *Dramaturgie et société*, ed. Jacquot, II, 809.

34 Levin, *Multiple Plot*, pp. 85–87. See also McMaster, "Love, Lust, and Sham," 158–59.

35 Most scholars concede Ford only a minor share in *The Sun's Darling*; see Sargeaunt, *John Ford*, pp. 57–63; and Oliver, *The Problem*, pp. 39–40.

36 *The Dramatic Works and Poems of James Shirley*, ed. William Gifford and Alexander Dyce (London: Murray, 1833), VI, 366.

37 Andreas Gryphius, *Werke*, ed. Palm, II, 234.

> Tod: Rechtschaffne liebe wird nur in dem tod erkennet.
> Liebe: Wer liebt, wird durch den tod von liebe nicht getrennet.
> Tod: Der liebt ohn alles falsch, wer biss zum tode liebt.
> Liebe: Wer liebend stirbet, wird nicht durch den tod betrübt.

38 "Willkommen süßer tod!" (V.119).

1 See Heinrich Wölfflin, *Principles of Art History*, pp. 18–22; and Wylie Sypher, *Four Stages of Renaissance Style*, p. 19.

2 For a discussion of the cartoon and its various copies, see Roy Strong, *Holbein and Henry VIII* (London: Routledge, 1967), esp. pp. 2–4, 39–43.

3 See Friedrich Blume, *Renaissance and Baroque Music: A Comprehensive Survey*, trans. M. D. Herter Norton (London: Faber, 1968), pp. 19–26.

4 See Manfred F. Bukofzer, *Music in the Baroque Era*, pp. 20–25; and Alec Harman and Anthony Milner, *Late Renaissance and Baroque Music*, rev. ed., *Man and his Music*, 2 (London: Barrie and Rockliff, 1969), pp. 8–24.

5 See Bukofzer, *Music in the Baroque Era*, pp. 388–89; and Claude V. Palisca, *Baroque Music* (Englewood Cliffs, New Jersey: Prentice-Hall, 1968), pp. 3–5.

6 See Blume, *Renaissance and Baroque Music*, pp. 90–95; and Harman and Milner, *Late Renaissance and Baroque Music*, pp. 128–33.

7 See Rosemond Tuve, *Elizabethan and Metaphysical Imagery: Renaissance Poetic and Twentieth-Century Critics* (Chicago: University of Chicago Press, 1947), pp. 281–84; and Wilbur Samuel Howell, *Logic and Rhetoric in England, 1500–1700* (1956; reprint ed., New York: Russell, 1961), p. 4.

8 Thomas Wilson, *The Arte of Rhetorique*, ed. Robert Hood Bowers (1553; reprint ed., Gainesville, Florida: Scholars' Facsimiles & Reprints, 1962), sig. A1.

9 Ibid., sigs. D1, Q2^v, R4^v.

10 See Howell, *Logic and Rhetoric*, pp. 147–50, 165.

11 Dudley Fenner, *The Artes of Logike and Rethorike* ([Middleburg], 1584), sig. E2.

12 John Smith of Montague Close, *The Mysterie of Rhetorique Unvail'd* (London, 1657), sig. B1.

13 Ibid., sigs. G5^v, K4, K6^v, L2^v, R8^v, S5^v.

14 Ibid., sig. S5^v.

15 Dedicatory epistle to *Hydriotaphia or Urne Buriall*, in *The Prose of Sir Thomas Browne*, ed. Endicott, p. 245.

16 *Religio Medici* II.xiii, in *Prose*, ed. Endicott, p. 88.

17 Smith, *Mysterie of Rhetorique*, sig. K6^v.

18 For parallel examples see Penthea's description of Orgilus as "unkinde: ô most unkinde" (*BH* III.v.1627), and Spinella's expostulation: "*Auria* unkinde, unkinde" (*LT* V.ii.2496).

19 Wilson, *Arte of Rhetorique*, sigs. Z3^v–4.

20 George Puttenham, *The Arte of English Poesie*, ed. Edward Arber (1589; reprint ed., London: Constable, 1906), p. 189.

21 See the Life of Cowley, in Johnson's *Lives of the English Poets,* ed. George Birkbeck Hill (Oxford: Clarendon, 1905), I, 20.

22 See Una Ellis-Fermor, *The Jacobean Drama: An Interpretation,* p. 234; David Cecil, *The Fine Art of Reading and Other Literary Studies* (London: Constable, 1957), p. 87; and T. B. Tomlinson, *A Study of Elizabethan and Jacobean Tragedy,* p. 271. Standing apart as he does from the mainstream of criticism, Antonin Artaud describes the grotesque aspects of this scene with unflinching admiration. Giovanni's behaviour is perfectly in tune with Artaud's definition of the theatrical ideal: "an immediate gratuitousness provoking acts without use or profit." See *The Theater and its Double,* trans. Mary Caroline Richards (New York: Grove Press, 1958), pp. 24–29.

23 *The Plays and Poems of Philip Massinger,* ed. Philip Edwards and Colin Gibson (Oxford: Clarendon, 1976), II, 210.

24 *The Poems & Letters of Andrew Marvell,* ed. H. M. Margoliouth, 2nd ed. (Oxford: Clarendon, 1952), I, 27.

25 Crashaw, *The Poems: English, Latin and Greek,* ed. Martin, p. 307.

26 Luis de la Puente, *Meditations,* I, sig. 4H3; II, sigs. V2–2ᵛ.

27 See Werner Weisbach, *Der Barock als Kunst der Gegenreformation,* pp. 144–48; and Emile Mâle, *L'Art religieux de la fin du XVIᵉ siécle, du XVIIᵉ siècle et du XVIIIᵉ siècle: Etude sur l'iconographie après le Concile de Trente,* 2nd ed. (Paris: Armand Colin, 1951), pp. 122–45.

28 *Christes Bloodie Sweat* (London, 1613), sig. B1ᵛ. This poem was attributed to Joseph Fletcher in the nineteenth century, but modern scholars follow M. Joan Sargeaunt, who assigns it to the Ford canon (*John Ford,* pp. 8–11). See Clifford Leech, *John Ford and the Drama of his Time,* pp. 22–24; and G. D. Monsarrat, "John Ford's Authorship of *Christes Bloodie Sweat,*" *English Language Notes,* 9 (1971–72), 20–25.

29 *Christes Bloodie Sweat,* sig. F4.

30 John Webster, *The White Devil,* ed. John Russell Brown, 2nd ed., The Revels Plays (London: Methuen, 1966).

NOTES TO CHAPTER FIVE

1 See Gerald Eades Bentley, *The Jacobean and Caroline Stage,* IV, 754–55; and T. A. Dunn, *Philip Massinger: The Man and the Playwright* (London: Thomas Nelson, 1957), pp. 28–29.

2 See Philip Edwards, "The Royal Pretenders in Massinger and Ford," *Essays and Studies,* NS 27 (1974), 18–36.

3 *The Plays and Poems of Philip Massinger,* ed. Edwards and Gibson, I, 225–26. Subsequent references are to this edition, specifically to volumes I (*The Maid of Honour*), II (*The Unnatural Combat*), III (*The Roman Actor*), and IV (*The Bashful Lover*).

4 For a slightly overstated account of Massinger's "feminism" see Maurice Chelli, *Le Drame de Massinger* (Lyon: Audin, 1923), pp. 310–12.

5 For divergent interpretations of Camiola's conduct, see Chelli, *Le Drame,* pp. 241–42; and Peter F. Mullany, "Religion in Massinger's *The Maid of Honour,*" *RenD,* NS 2 (1969), 154–56. With Camiola's announcement, compare Fabricio's equally surprising renunciation of the world (*Fancies* V.iii.2574–76).

6 For analysis of Massinger's "social morality" see L. C. Knights, *Drama & Society in the Age of Jonson* (London: Chatto & Windus, 1937), pp. 276–92. See also Dunn, *Massinger,* pp. 142–47.

7 See T. S. Eliot, "Philip Massinger," *Selected Essays,* pp. 211–14; D. J. Enright, "Poetic Satire and Satire in Verse: A Consideration of Jonson and Massinger," *Scrutiny,* 18 (1951–52), 220; and Dunn, *Massinger,* pp. 250–52, 265–66. For a wavering defence of Massinger's poetic technique see John O. Lyons, "Massinger's Imagery," *Renaissance Papers* (1955), pp. 47–53.

8 See Marco Mincoff, "The Social Background of Beaumont and Fletcher," *English Miscellany,* 1 (1950), 1–30; "Fletcher's Early Tragedies," *RenD,* 7 (1964), 70–94; and "Shakespeare, Fletcher and Baroque Tragedy," *ShS,* 20 (1967), 1–15.

9 André Koszul, "Beaumont et Fletcher et le baroque," *Cahiers du sud,* 10, special no. (1933), 212–14.

10 Eugene M. Waith, *The Pattern of Tragicomedy in Beaumont and Fletcher,* p. 156.

11 William W. Appleton, *Beaumont and Fletcher: A Critical Study* (London: Allen & Unwin, 1956), p. 40.

12 John Shearman, *Mannerism* (Harmondsworth: Penguin, 1967), p. 19.

13 *The Works of Francis Beaumont and John Fletcher,* ed. Arnold Glover and A. R. Waller (Cambridge: Cambridge University Press, 1905–12), III, 5–6. Subsequent references are to this edition, specifically to volumes I (*The Maid's Tragedy*) and V (*A Wife for a Month*).

14 See Joseph T. McCullen, Jr., "Madness and the Isolation of Characters in Elizabethan and Early Stuart Drama," *SP,* 48 (1951), 208–209.

15 See John P. Cutts, "Music and *The Mad Lover,*" *Studies in the Renaissance,* 8 (1961), 242.

16 For a discussion of Beaumont and Fletcher's technique of constructing theatrical scenes based on Petrarchan conceits, see John F. Danby, *Poets on Fortune's Hill: Studies in Sidney, Shakespeare, Beaumont & Fletcher* (London: Faber, 1952), pp. 170–75.

17 See Una Ellis-Fermor, *The Jacobean Drama: An Interpretation,* pp. 206–12; and Clifford Leech, *The John Fletcher Plays* (London: Chatto & Windus, 1962), pp. 38–39.

18 See Robert Ornstein, *The Moral Vision of Jacobean Tragedy,* p. 176.

19 See Michael Neill, "'The Simetry, Which Gives a Poem Grace': Masque, Imagery, and the Fancy of *The Maid's Tragedy,*" *RenD,* NS 3 (1970), 120–31.

20 Shearman, *Mannerism,* pp. 81–90.

21 *Ben Jonson,* ed. C. H. Herford, Percy and Evelyn Simpson (Oxford: Clarendon, 1925–52), XI, 466.

22 *The Dramatic Works and Poems of James Shirley*, ed. Gifford and Dyce, V, 275. Subsequent references are to this edition, specifically to volumes II (*The Grateful Servant, Love's Cruelty*) and IV (*The Duke's Mistress*).

23 Sir Philip Sidney, *A Defence of Poetry,* ed. J. A. Van Dorsten (London: Oxford University Press, 1966), p. 52.

24 Beaumont and Fletcher, *Works*, ed. Glover and Waller, I, xi–xii.

25 See Arthur Huntington Nason, *James Shirley, Dramatist: A Biographical and Critical Study* (1915; reprint ed., New York: Benjamin Blom, 1967), esp. pp. 241–42.

26 Bentley, *Jacobean and Caroline Stage*, V, 1068.

27 There is no reliable way of dating Ford's plays with accuracy; my account follows Bentley's sensible and conservative argument (*Jacobean and Caroline Stage*, III, 436–37). The plays written for the King's men (probably before 1630) are *The Lover's Melancholy*, *The Broken Heart*, and *Beauty in a Trance* (lost); those written for Queen Henrietta Maria's men (probably after 1630) are *Love's Sacrifice*, *'Tis Pity*, *Perkin Warbeck*, *The Fancies*, and *The Lady's Trial*. *The Queen* is not assigned to any company. The only one of these plays for which a precise date can be fixed is *The Lover's Melancholy* (1628).

28 The first stanza of this poem flatters Ford by imitation, through the use of such characteristic images as "altar" and "flames ascending." The second stanza is an ill-tempered rebuke: "be vext / To read this tragedy," Shirley advises Prynne, "and thy owne be next" (*LS*, ll. 37–44). For the fortunes of Prynne and a summary of the *Histriomastix* controversy, see Alfred Harbage, *Cavalier Drama*, pp. 14–17.

29 James Shirley, *Loves Crueltie: A Tragedy* (London, 1640), sig. F3. I quote the quarto rather than Dyce's abbreviated stage direction.

30 For an informative account of the design of the Phoenix theatre, see Glynne Wickham, *Early English Stages, 1300 to 1660* (London: Routledge, 1959–72), II.ii, 82–89.

31 See M. C. Bradbrook, *Themes and Conventions of Elizabethan Tragedy* (Cambridge: Cambridge University Press, 1935), pp. 261–67.

32 A. C. Swinburne, "James Shirley," *Contemporaries of Shakespeare*, ed. Edmund Gosse and Thomas James Wise (London: Heinemann, 1919), pp. 278, 281–82.

33 See Bonamy Dobrée, *Restoration Tragedy, 1660–1720* (Oxford: Clarendon, 1929), p. 142; William H. McBurney, "Otway's Tragic Muse Debauched: Sensuality in *Venice Preserv'd*," *Journal of English and Germanic Philology*, 58 (1959), 399; and Thomas B. Stroup, "Otway's Bitter Pessimism," *SP*, ES 4 (1967), 75.

34 See Aline Mackenzie Taylor, *Next to Shakespeare: Otway's* Venice Preserv'd *and* The Orphan *and their History on the London Stage* (Durham, North Carolina: Duke University Press, 1950), pp. 80–82. For the story of Otway's alleged infatuation with Mrs. Barry, see Roswell Gray Ham, *Otway and Lee: Biography from a Baroque Age* (New Haven: Yale University Press, 1931), pp. 82–90.

35 "A Parallel of Poetry and Painting," *Essays of John Dryden,* ed. Ker, II, 145.

36 *The Works of Thomas Otway: Plays, Poems, and Love-Letters*, ed. J. C. Ghosh (Oxford: Clarendon, 1932), II, 75. Subsequent references are to this edition.

37 Taylor, *Next to Shakespeare*, p. 80.

38 See Gordon Williams, "The Sex-Death Motive in Otway's *Venice Preserv'd*," *Trivium*, 2 (1967), 64–65.

39 See Williams, "Sex-Death Motive," 59–61; Ronald Berman, "Nature in *Venice Preserv'd*," *ELH*, 36 (1969), 541; and Derek W. Hughes, "A New Look at *Venice Preserv'd*," *SEL*, 11 (1971), 449–53.

40 The special relationship between the two dramatists has been recognized by Dobrée in his discussion of *The Orphan*: "In the sort of emotion which this play contains he [Otway] is almost unmatchable; almost, because Ford still overtops him" (*Restoration Tragedy*, p. 142).

NOTES TO CHAPTER SIX

1 For the buttery bill controversy see M. Joan Sargeaunt, "John Ford at the Middle Temple," *Review of English Studies*, 8 (1932), 69–71. One couplet which presumably characterizes Ford may be found in William Hemminge's *Elegy on Randolph's Finger*, ed. G. C. Moore Smith (Oxford: Blackwell, 1923), as follows:

> Deep In a dumpe Jacke forde alone was gott
> With folded Armes and Melancholye hatt. (ll. 81–82)

2 See Gerald Eades Bentley, *The Jacobean and Caroline Stage*, III, 434–35; V, 1096.

3 Felix E. Schelling, *Elizabethan Drama, 1558–1642* (Boston: Houghton Mifflin, 1908), I, xxiii-xxiv.

4 In *John Fordes dramatische Werke*, ed. Bang, pp. vii, xii.

5 G. F. Sensabaugh, *The Tragic Muse of John Ford*, p. 165.

6 For roughly similar attempts to "read conventional morality into" Ford's plays, see Cyrus Hoy, "'Ignorance in Knowledge': Marlowe's Faustus and Ford's Giovanni," *MP*, 57 (1959–60), 154; Robert Ornstein, *The Moral Vision of Jacobean Tragedy*, pp. 220–21; and Irving Ribner, *Jacobean Tragedy: The Quest for Moral Order*, pp. 154–55.

7 Mark Stavig, *John Ford and the Traditional Moral Order*, pp. 35, 96, 136, 119.

8 Clifford Leech, *John Ford and the Drama of his Time*, p. 63.

9 The phrase is from Lionel Trilling's still pertinent essay, "The Sense of the Past," in *The Liberal Imagination*: *Essays on Literature and Society* (1950; reprint ed., Garden City, New York: Doubleday, 1953), pp. 183–89.

10 L. G. Salingar, "The Decline of Tragedy," *The Age of Shakespeare*, ed. Boris Ford, A Guide to English Literature, 2 (Harmondsworth: Penguin, 1955), pp. 438–39.

11 F. R. Leavis, *The Great Tradition: George Eliot, Henry James, Joseph Conrad*, 2nd ed. (London: Chatto & Windus, 1960), pp. 7–9.

12 F. R. Leavis, *The Common Pursuit* (London: Chatto & Windus, 1952), p. 189.

13 Ibid., pp. 124, 178.

14 Yvor Winters, *Forms of Discovery: Critical & Historical Essays on the Forms of the Short Poem in English* ([Chicago]: Swallow, 1967), p. xvii.

15 Ibid., pp. 80, 92.

16 Salingar, "Decline of Tragedy," p. 438.

17 T. B. Tomlinson, *A Study of Elizabethan and Jacobean Tragedy*, pp. 266–77.

18 The "verbal analysis school" would seem to be a suitable replacement for the unfortunate label—New Critics. For an index of the broadening attitude among theorists of this school, compare W. K. Wimsatt's early manifesto, "Explication as Criticism," with his less doctrinaire formulation of similar principles in "What to Say about a Poem." See respectively *The Verbal Icon: Studies in the Meaning of Poetry* (Lexington: University Press of Kentucky, 1954), pp. 235–51; and *Hateful Contraries: Studies in Literature and Criticism* (Lexington: University Press of Kentucky, 1966), pp. 215–44.

19 William Empson, *Seven Types of Ambiguity*, 3rd ed. (London: Chatto & Windus, 1953), pp. 155–56.

20 Donald K. Anderson, Jr., "The Heart and the Banquet: Imagery in Ford's '*Tis Pity* and *The Broken Heart*," *SEL*, 2 (1962), 209–17. Disappointingly, Anderson's recent book does very little to continue his interest in verbal analysis; see *John Ford*, Twayne's English Authors Series, 129 (New York: Twayne, 1972), pp. 75–76.

21 Anderson, "The Heart and the Banquet," 216–17.

22 Wilson Knight, "John Ford: Dramatist of the Heart," 4.

23 See respectively Charles Lamb, ed., *Specimens of English Dramatic Poets*, p. 228; A. C. Swinburne, *Essays and Studies*, p. 277; and T. S. Eliot, *Selected Essays*, p. 195.

24 Among the offenders are M. C. Bradbrook, *Themes and Conventions of Elizabethan Tragedy*, pp. 250–51; Una Ellis-Fermor, *The Jacobean Drama: An Interpretation*, pp. 235–37; Moody E. Prior, *The Language of Tragedy* (New York: Columbia University Press, 1947), pp. 148–50; Clifford Leech, *John Ford*, Writers and their Work, 170 (London: Longmans, 1964), pp. 14–15; Alan Brissenden, "Impediments to Love: A Theme in John Ford," *RenD*, 7 (1964), 96–97; Brian Morris, ed., "Introduction," *The Broken Heart*, The New Mermaids (London: Benn, 1965), p. xxvii; and David Malouf, "The Dramatist as Critic: John Ford and *The Broken Heart*," *Southern Review* (Adelaide), 5 (1972), 202–205. For tentative reservations about this pervasive notion, see George C. Herndl, *The High Design: English Renaissance Tragedy and the Natural Law* (Lexington: University Press of Kentucky, 1970), pp. 278–80; and Anderson, *John Ford*, pp. 138–39.

25 Eliot, *Selected Essays*, pp. 203–204. There are several technical accounts of Ford's

metre, versification, vocabulary, and rhetorical devices, but none of these contains a coherent and synthetic treatment of the poetic language of the plays. See Eduard Hannemann, *Metrische Untersuchungen zu John Ford*, Diss. Vereinigten Friedrichs-Universität 1888 (Halle: C. A. Kaemmerer, 1888), pp. 50–62; Robert Davril, *Le Drame de John Ford*, pp. 425–71; and Thelma N. Greenfield, "The Language of Process in Ford's *The Broken Heart*," *PMLA*, 87 (1972), 397–405.

26 Cleanth Brooks, "Metaphor, Paradox, and Stereotype," *British Journal of Aesthetics*, 5 (1965), 323.

27 Brooks, "Metaphor," 323; and Salingar, "Decline of Tragedy," p. 439.

28 R. J. Kaufmann, "Ford's 'Waste Land': *The Broken Heart*," *RenD*, NS 3 (1970), 167–87.

29 Ibid., 169–76.

30 It is revealing that Frye finds it difficult to introduce the subject of literary archetypes without using the visual art analogy. See *Anatomy of Criticism*, pp. 133–34; "The Archetypes of Literature," *Fables of Identity: Studies in Poetic Mythology* (New York: Harcourt, 1963), p. 14; and "Design as a Creative Principle in the Arts," *The Stubborn Structure: Essays on Criticism and Society* (London: Methuen, 1970), pp. 56–65.

31 John Ford, *A Line of Life: Pointing at the Immortalitie of a Vertuous Name* (London, 1620), sig. A2ᵛ.

INDEX

Ford's plays are listed separately by title. All other works will be found under the author's name, wherever this is known.

Abnormal psychology: as outlined by Burton, 30, 59; prominence of in Ford's plays, 59, 196, 226n35; in relation to comedy of humours, 63; *see also* Melancholy

Actresses, 191, 223n12; *see also* Barry, Elizabeth

Addison, Joseph: *Cato,* 205

Alpers, Paul, 26

Alpers, Svetlana, 26

Anderson, Donald K., Jr., 206–207, 209, 235n20

Apotheosis: as an archetypal pattern, 213–14; of chastity in *Comus,* 23–24, 221n54; in relation to baroque tragedy, 78, 86, 89, 101, 213–14; treatment of in baroque style, 19, 213

Appleton, William W., 171

Arden of Faversham, 82

Aristotle, 142

Arnold, Matthew, 202

Artaud, Antonin, 215, 231n22

Assumption and Coronation of the Virgin, The; see York cycle

Auden, W. H., 212

Bach, Johann Sebastian, 22

Baciccio; *see* Gaulli, Giovanni Battista

Bacon, Sir Francis, 72: *The Historie of the Reigne of King Henry the Seventh,* 223n13

Bale, John: *Kynge Johan,* 198

Bang, W., 224n15

Barish, Jonas A., 215

Baroque style: definition of, 1; as distinct from classicism, 19–22, 189; as distinct from mannerism, 14–19; as distinct from renaissance, 1–13; as distinct from rococo, 22–25; dynamic movement as characteristic of, 16, 20–21; expression of pathos in, 6, 58–59, 67–68, 76, 132, 136,

Baroque style: (cont.)
175–76, 189–90, 200–201; fusion
achieved in, 2, 29–30, 79; in music
history, 11, 131–33; open form of,
2, 28–29, 31, 78–79, 110, 115, 168;
painterly technique of, 1, 8, 27–28,
31, 129–30, 154; psychological
emphasis in, 6, 28, 59, 129–33,
140, 145; recessional movement of,
2, 28, 31; relative clarity of, 2, 8,
31, 154; typical imagery of, 150–51;
virtuosity as an ideal in, 10–13
Barry, Elizabeth, 187, 189, 233n34
Beaumont, Francis, and Fletcher, John,
8, 107, 120: compared with Ford,
171–77, 180–81; general relation to
baroque style, 170–71, 178–81;
general relation to mannerist style,
171, 178–81; *A King and No King*,
180; *The Knight of the Burning Pestle*,
12; *The Maid's Tragedy*, 57, 171,
177–80, 182, 184, 191; *Philaster*,
180, 182; *Valentinian*, 180
Beauty in a Trance; *see* Ford, John
Bellini, Giovanni, 31, 79: *St. Francis in
Ecstasy* (pl. 2), 4–5, 9, 15, 28
Bentley, Gerald Eades, 223n12, 224n15,
233n27
Beowulf, 6
Bernini, Gianlorenzo, 10–12, 31, 47,
79, 171, 181, 205, 213, 216:
Baldacchino (pl. 13), 22–23; *The
Ecstasy of St. Teresa* (pl. 1), 3–4, 6, 9,
13, 15, 28–29, 38, 191, 201; *The
Rape of Persephone* (pl. 20), 30, 85
Berry, Ralph, 220n42
Blackfriars theatre, 196
Blake, William, 70, 202, 212
Blayney, Glenn H., 215
Bodkin, Maud, 89
Bologna, Giovanni, 179
Borromini, Francesco, 11
Botticelli, Sandro, 129: *The Birth of
Venus* (pl. 16), 27, 70, 130
Boy actors, 88, 223n12

Boyle, Elizabeth, 9
Bramante, Donato, 31: *The Tempietto*
(pl. 5), 8–9
Briganti, Giuliano, 14
Broken Heart, The, 34, 75, 195, 202,
204, 212
INDIVIDUAL CHARACTERS: Bassanes,
42–43, 51–52, 66–67, 90, 97–100,
113, 136–38, 155–56; Calantha,
53–54, 97–101, 127–28, 155,
174, 208, 211; Christalla, 99;
Crotolon, 52; Euphranea, 127;
Groneas, 99; Hemophil, 99;
Ithocles, 43, 54, 65–66, 97–101,
149, 155, 174, 188, 211;
Nearchus, 101; Orgilus, 42–43,
51–53, 65–67, 97–101, 136–38,
172, 187–88, 211, 230n18;
Penthea, 42–43, 52–54, 65–67,
97–101, 136–40, 155, 166–67,
176–77, 184, 188–89, 207, 211,
215, 228n14, 230n18; Philema,
53, 99; Phulas, 66; Prophilus, 127;
Tecnicus, 60, 90, 99, 125, 211

MAJOR THEMES: death and
martyrdom, 51–54, 101;
inhibition, 66, 98–101, 211;
jealousy, 43, 66–67, 99–100;
madness, 65–67; sexuality, 42–43,
97–98

STRUCTURE, 97–101: figure of the
pedant, 60, 99, 125; the masque
within the play, 127; pattern of
honour and restraint, 98–101,
139, 211; unity achieved through
fusion, 100

VERBAL TECHNIQUE: imagery, 155–56,
207, 211; metaphor, 149, 211;
paradox, 136–39

Brome, Richard: *The Northern Lasse*,
222n77
Bronzino, Agnolo, 171, 176
Brooks, Cleanth, 2, 142, 208–10

Browne, Sir Thomas, 40, 59: *Religio Medici*, 135; *Urne Buriall*, 135
Browning, Robert: *The Ring and the Book*, 213
Bukofzer, Manfred F., 11
Bunyan, John, 202
Burton, Robert, 79, 125, 132: *The Anatomy of Melancholy*, 17, 30, 46, 59–62, 199, 224n15, 224n18

Caravaggio, Michelangelo da, 11
Carracci family, 11
Cavalier poets, 13, 31
Cavendish, William, Duke of Newcastle, 33
Cellini, Benvenuto, 171
Chambers, E. K., 197
Chapman, George, 7–8, 48: *Bussy D'Ambois*, 126
Charles I: as arbiter of taste, 32; courtship of the Spanish Infanta, 33; as depicted by Van Dyck, 32, 140; marriage to Henrietta Maria, 32–33; as a patron of art, 32; as portrayed by Gryphius, 19
Chastity: deflation of in rococo style, 24–25; as a dramatic theme, 44–45, 49, 71, 93, 98, 112–13, 115, 167–68; in relation to marriage and betrothal, 137–38; treatment of in *Comus*, 23–24
Chaucer, Geoffrey: *The Knight's Tale*, 3 61; *The Legend of Good Women*, 3; *The Merchant's Tale*, 66; *Troilus and Criseyde*, 78
Christes Bloodie Sweat; see Ford, John
Christian Stoicism; see Stoicism
Chronicle History of Perkin Warbeck, The; see *Perkin Warbeck*
Ciceronian prose, 16, 28, 133, 143
Cimabue, 212
Classicism: as distinct from baroque, 19–22, 189; restraint as characteristic of, 20–21

Cockpit in Drury Lane; *see* Phoenix theatre
Comic structure: in baroque drama, 19, 115–16, 119–20; in mannerist drama, 19, 120; in renaissance drama, 107–111, 114, 117–20
Congreve, William, 187: *The Mourning Bride*, 194; *The Way of the World*, 180
Conrad, Joseph, 204
Constable, Henry: "To St. Mary Magdalen," 4–5
Cornaro Chapel, 4, 13
Corneille, Pierre: *Le Cid*, 21; *L'Illusion comique*, 19, 69; *Polyeucte*, 19
Cortona, Pietro da, 31: *Santa Maria in Via Lata* (pl. 7), 8–9; *The Triumph of Divine Providence* (pl. 15), 23, 68
Courtly love, 3, 37, 174
Craig, Hardin, 197
Crashaw, Richard, 4, 15–16, 31, 33, 36, 47, 69, 154, 203, 212, 216: "Epithalamium," 3; "Hymn to the Name and Honor of the Admirable Sainte Teresa," 5–6, 49; "The Weeper," 5, 150, 153, 155; "Wishes: To his (Supposed) Mistresse," 10
Cupid, 2–3, 39, 46, 127

Dali, Salvador: *Crucifixion*, 212
Daniells, Roy, 34, 221n54
Davril, Robert, 75, 215
Death: as analogous to martyrdom, 29, 36, 51–58, 88–89, 127–28, 190–91; prominence of in Ford's plays, 35; as a transition to the afterlife, 55, 88–90, 97, 101; treatment of in baroque style, 7–8, 21, 29, 56–58, 127–28, 214; treatment of in classicism, 21; treatment of in mannerism, 57–58;

Death: (cont.)
    treatment of in renaissance style,
    6–8, 56–57, 214; see also death-wish
Death-wish, 8, 47–58 passim, 101, 128,
    175–78, 189, 191
Decadence, 198–99, 201, 215
Dekker, Thomas: The Sun's Darling
    (with Ford), 127, 225n27, 229n35;
    The Witch of Edmonton (with Ford and
    Rowley), 225n27
De Rore, Cipriano; see Rore, Cipriano
    de
De Rougemont, Denis; see Rougemont,
    Denis de
Descartes, René, 8
Devereaux, Penelope, 9
Dickens, Charles, 204
Dieussart, François, 32
Dobrée, Bonamy, 234n40
Donne, John, 36, 210, 212: Devotions
    upon Emergent Occasions, 16–17;
    "The Extasie," 15; "The Flea,"
    143–44; Holy Sonnets, 15, 134;
    "A Valediction Forbidding
    Mourning," 15
Dream of the Rood, The, 212
Dryden, John, 11, 20, 170, 186–87,
    189, 194, 205: All for Love, 20;
    "To the Memory of Mr. Oldham,"
    21–22

Edwards, Richard: Damon and Pithias, 95
Eliot, George, 204
Eliot, T. S., 169, 208–209, 212:
    "The Hollow Men," 6; The Waste
    Land, 160
Elyot, Sir Thomas, 58
Empson, William, 2, 206, 208
Etherege, Sir George, 187, 194:
    The Man of Mode, 24, 180

Fames Memoriall; see Ford, John
Fancies Chaste and Noble, The, 212
    INDIVIDUAL CHARACTERS: Castamela,
        45, 70–71, 122–26; Clarella,

123–24; Fabricio, 45, 63, 121,
124, 232n5; Flavia, 45, 121, 123;
Floria, 124; Julio, 45, 121, 123;
Livio, 63, 70–71, 120–24;
Morosa, 63, 121–24, 126;
Nitido, 63, 121–22; Octavio,
63, 70–71, 76, 122–25;
Romanello, 71, 122–24; Secco,
63, 121–24, 126; Silvia, 124;
Spadone, 121–22, 124; Troylo, 71,
120–21, 123, 125–26

MAJOR THEMES: deception, 70–71,
122–24; impotence, 63, 71,
122–23; madness, 63; sexuality,
45, 121

STRUCTURE, 120–24: figure of the
pedant, 125; the masque within
the play, 126; open form, 123–24;
pattern of prostitution, 120–24

Fanelli, Francesco, 32–33
Farquhar, George, 187: The Beaux'
    Strategem, 180
Fenner, Dudley: The Artes of Logike
    and Rethorike, 133–34
Figura serpentinata, 179
Fletcher, John, 11–12, 163, 186, 215:
    The Faithful Shepherdess, 12, 182;
    general relation to baroque style,
    176, 194; general relation to
    mannerist style, 176, 194; invention
    of frustrating situations, 175, 179;
    The Knight of Malta, 180; The Loyal
    Subject, 180, 182; The Mad Lover,
    171–74, 180; principles of dramatic
    structure, 173, 175–76; A Wife for a
    Month, 171, 175–76, 182, 229n31;
    The Wild Goose Chase, 180; Women
    Pleased, 171; see also Beaumont,
    Francis, and Fletcher, John
Fletcher, Joseph, 231n28
Fontainebleau, School of, 171
Ford, John (see also the separate entries
    for individual plays), 8, 12, 186:

Ford: (cont.)
affiliation with Queen Henrietta
Maria's men, 33, 183, 233n27;
affiliation with the King's men, 182,
233n27; as author of dedicatory
verses, 33, 163, 222n77; *Beauty in a
Trance* (lost), 233n27;
biographical data, 195, 234n1; canon
of writings, 195, 224n15, 225n22,
231n28; *Christes Bloodie Sweat*, 34,
151–52, 160, 231n28; collaborative
writings, 127, 225n27, 229n35;
compared with Beaumont and
Fletcher, 171–77, 180–81; compared
with Massinger, 163–65, 167–69;
compared with Otway, 188–94
passim, 234n40; compared with
Shirley, 182–86; ethical values, 40,
196, 198–201, 215; *Fames Memoriall*,
195; general relation to baroque
style and culture, 1, 32–34, 47,
196, 200–201, 205, 213–16; *The
Golden Meane*, 48, 225n22; *Honor
Triumphant*, 38–39, 42, 122;
influenced by Burtonian psychology,
46, 59–62, 125, 132, 224n15,
224n18, 226n35; "On the Best of
English Poets, Ben Jonson,
Deceased," 181; poetic style, 129–61
passim, 196, 203–204, 206–10, 215;
sense of humour, 84, 196; *The
Sun's Darling* (with Dekker), 127,
225n27, 229n35; *The Witch of Edmonton*
(with Dekker and Rowley), 225n27
Forsaken woman characters, 165–67,
177, 185, 187–88
Francis of Assisi, Saint, 4, 9, 28
Freud, Sigmund, 35
Frye, Northrop, 26–27, 77–78,
107–108, 211, 236n30: *Anatomy of
Criticism*, 214
Funeral monuments, 7

Gabrielli, Andrea, 131
Gabrielli, Giovanni, 131

Gascoigne, George, 203: *Supposes*,
117–18
Gaulli, Giovanni Battista, 213
Gentileschi, Orazio, 32
Gero Crucifix, The, 212
Giambologna; *see* Bologna, Giovanni
Golden Meane, The; *see* Ford, John
Greco, El: *The Vision of St. John the
Divine* (pl. 9), 15
Greene, Robert, 198: *Friar Bacon and
Friar Bungay*, 107
Greville, Fulke, Lord Brooke, 203
Grünewald, Matthias, 212
Gryphius, Andreas: *Carolus Stuardus*, 19;
Catharina von Georgien, 127–28

Hemminge, William: *Elegy on Randolph's
Finger*, 195, 234n1
Henrietta Maria, Queen, 199: as
Counter-Reformation symbol, 32;
as patron of poetry, 33; as theatrical
participant, 223n12; as theatrical
sponsor, 32–33; *see also* Queen
Henrietta Maria's men
Herbert, George, 210, 212: "Death,"
57
Herrick, Robert, 10, 31, 70: "To his
Dying Brother, Master *William
Herrick*," 21–22
Herrick, William, 21
Heywood, John: *Johan Johan*, 66
Heywood, Thomas: *A Woman Killed with
Kindness*, 229n31
Holbein, Hans the Younger: *Henry
VIII* (pl. 18), 130
Honor Triumphant; *see* Ford, John
Hooker, Richard, 79, 140: *Of the Laws
of Ecclesiastical Polity*, 30
Hopkins, Gerard Manley, 202, 212
Howell, James, 33
Huxley, Aldous, 4

Iconography: as a method of
interpretation, 2, 26; in relation to
imagery, 151

Idiotes characters, 111, 117

Illusionism: as characteristic of baroque style, 8–10, 18–19, 23, 29, 32, 68–69, 145, 147, 213; as a dramatic theme, 69–76 *passim*, 124, 147

Imagery: in relation to baroque style, 150–57 *passim*, 193–94, 214; in relation to mannerism, 154–55; in relation to renaissance style, 153–54

Incest, 1, 64, 80, 87, 99, 145–47, 164, 183, 188, 196, 199

James I, 213–14

Jesuit order; *see* Society of Jesus

Johnson, Samuel, 143

Jonson, Ben, 120, 168, 181–82, 203, 209: *The Alchemist*, 63; *The Silent Woman*, 63; *Volpone*, 19, 46, 66, 113

Josquin des Prez, 131: *Missa Pange Lingua*, 132

Kaufmann, R. J., 211

Keats, John: *The Eve of St. Agnes*, 204

King's men, 163, 182, 196, 233n27

Knight, G. Wilson, 97, 207

Knights, L. C., 202

Koszul, André, 170–71

Kyd, Thomas: *Soliman and Perseda*, 46; *The Spanish Tragedy*, 12, 57, 67, 82

Lady's Trial, The, 216

INDIVIDUAL CHARACTERS: Adurni, 44, 113, 115–16; Amoretta, 112, 115–16; Aurelio, 61–62, 113; Auria, 44, 61–62, 65, 113–16, 126, 230n18; Benatzi, 113–15; Castanna, 115; Futelli, 115; Levidolche, 112–15; Malfato, 44–45, 62; Martino, 113; Spinella, 44–45, 62, 112–15, 119, 176, 230n18

MAJOR THEMES: chastity, 44–45, 112–13, 115; jealousy, 112–14, 120, 164; madness, 61–62; reconciliation, 113–14, 119; sexuality, 44–45

STRUCTURE, 107, 112–16, 119–20, 126: open form, 115–16; unity achieved through fusion, 114

Lamb, Charles, 208

Langbaine, Gerard, 76

Lanier, Nicholas, 33

Laud, William, 32

Lawes, Henry, 33

Lawes, William, 33

Lawrence, D. H., 204

Leavis, F. R., 202–205

Le Brun, Charles, 22

Leech, Clifford, 34, 200, 208–209

Leonardo da Vinci, 79: *The Last Supper*, 11, 30

Lessing, Gotthold Ephraim: *Laokoon*, 25–26

Levin, Richard, 126

Lewis, C. S., 13, 37

Lillo, George, 205

Loose style in prose, 17, 28

Louis XIV, 10

Lover's Melancholy, The, 174, 224n18

INDIVIDUAL CHARACTERS: Agenor, 108–109; Amethus, 110; Aretus, 109; Cleophila, 60–61, 109–110; Corax, 60–61, 109, 111–12, 125–26, 173, 224n15; Cuculus, 111; Eroclea ("Parthenophill"), 60–61, 69–70, 109–110, 119, 167; Grilla, 111; Meleander, 59–61, 109–110, 125, 173; Menaphon, 61, 69, 110, 167; Palador, 59, 61, 109–11, 167, 172–73, 176; Rhetias, 60–61, 109, 125; Sophronos, 108–109; Thamasta, 60, 110–11

MAJOR THEMES: art versus nature, 69–70; love-melancholy, 59, 61, 109, 112, 120, 164; madness, 60–61, 109, 172

STRUCTURE, 107–112, 119–20: figure of the pedant, 111–12, 125; the masque within the play, 111–12, 126, 173; open form, 108–10; unity achieved through fusion, 111–12

Love's Sacrifice, 183–85, 196, 200, 204
INDIVIDUAL CHARACTERS: Biancha, 41–42, 47–51, 65, 74–75, 91–97, 127, 148–50, 152–53, 157–61, 164–65, 174, 176, 184, 199, 213, 215, 223n12; Caraffa, 41, 48–52, 64–65, 74–75, 91–97, 113, 149–50, 152–54, 157–61, 164–65, 184, 214; Colona, 41, 94; D'Avolos, 41, 64, 74, 96, 159; Ferentes, 41, 94–96, 126, 159; Fernando, 41–42, 47–51, 65, 74–75, 91–97, 127, 148–50, 157–61, 165, 172, 174, 176, 199, 214, 223n12; Fiormonda, 41, 64–65, 74, 94–96, 149; Julia, 41, 94; Maurucio, 65, 95–96; Morona, 41, 94; Roseilli, 95–96

MAJOR THEMES: death and martyrdom, 48–51, 97, 149, 160–61, 174; deception, 74, 149, 159, 161; jealousy, 48–49, 64–65, 74, 92, 158, 164; madness, 64–65; magic, 74–75; marriage versus friendship, 91–93, 159–60; sexuality, 41–42, 92–93, 223n12

STRUCTURE, 90–97: function of humour, 95; the masque within the play, 126–27; open form, 96–97; pattern of vows and perjury, 91–95, 159–61; unity achieved through fusion, 95–96

VERBAL TECHNIQUE: aposiopesis, 158; imagery, 152–55, 157–61, 209; metaphor, 148–50, 153, 160–61, 193, 209; metre, 158

McMaster, Juliet, 122
Magdalene, Saint Mary; see Mary Magdalene, Saint
Mannerism: as distinct from baroque, 14–19; distortion as characteristic of, 15–16, 129, 155, 179; elegance as characteristic of, 171, 174, 176, 180; irony as characteristic of, 14, 17–19, 58, 129, 143–45, 154–55; in music history, 131
Marino, Giambattista, 69
Marlowe, Christopher, 7–8, 105: Doctor Faustus, 29, 77, 126, 153; Edward II, 57, 140; The Jew of Malta, 12, 57, 139; 1 Tamburlaine, 12; 2 Tamburlaine, 148
Marston, John, 120, 168
Marvell, Andrew: "To his Coy Mistress," 150
Mary Magadalene, Saint, 7, 38, 150–51, 153
Masaccio, Tommaso di, 212
Masochism, 1, 7, 48, 50–55, 99, 176–77, 184, 189–90, 192
"Masque of Melancholy," 60–61, 109, 111–12, 126, 173
Masques, 32–33, 127: performed as revels within plays, 67, 94, 126–27, 173, 178; see also "Masque of Melancholy"
Massinger, Philip, 181, 185–86, 215: affiliation with Queen Henrietta Maria's men, 33, 163; affiliation with the King's men, 163; The Bashful Lover, 166–67; Believe as You List, 164; The Bondman, 166; The City Madam, 169; compared with Ford, 163–69 passim; The Duke of Milan, 164–66, 168–69; general relation to baroque style, 194; The Great Duke of Florence, 163; The Maid of Honour, 19, 167–68; middle-class outlook, 169; A New Way to Pay Old Debts, 169; The Picture, 164; principles of dramatic structure,

Massinger: (cont.)
167–68; *The Roman Actor*, 163, 170;
treatment of female characters,
165–67; *The Unnatural Combat*, 148,
164, 166, 169; verbal style, 169,
A Very Woman, 164
Medwall, Henry: *Fulgens and Lucrece*, 205
Melancholy, 1, 17, 111–12, 164, 175:
as analogous to mental disorder,
59–68 *passim*; caused by jealousy,
62–63, 65–67; caused by love, 46,
59–62; *see also* Burton, Robert
Mercer, Eric, 7
Metaphor: definition of, 142–43;
logical interpretation of, 143–45;
psychological interpretation of,
144–50 *passim*; of tearing human
flesh, 144–50, 153, 160, 193
Metaphysical poets, 13, 15, 31, 143,
203, 210
Middleton, Thomas, 171; *Women
Beware Women*, 17, 19, 57, 229n31
Middleton, Thomas, and Rowley,
William: *The Changeling*, 17, 46, 68,
178
Millar, Oliver, 32
Milton, John, 79: *Comus*, 23–25,
202, 221n54; *On the Morning of
Christ's Nativity*, 139; *Paradise Lost*,
30; *Samson Agonistes*, 22
Mincoff, Marco, 170
Misogyny, 1, 43, 45, 62, 76, 116, 118,
120
Montagu, Walter: *The Shepherd's
Paradise*, 223n12
Montaigne, Michel de, 19
Monteverdi, Claudio, 11: *Selva morale e
spirituale*, 132
More, Sir Thomas: *Utopia*, 58
Mucedorus, 107–108, 110–11, 228n23
Multiple plots, 80–81, 94–96, 110,
126, 185
Mytens, Daniel, 32

Neilson, W. A., 197

Neoplatonism, 26, 37–38, 42, 85
Nicoll, Allardyce, 197
Norton, Thomas, and Sackville, Thomas:
Gorboduc, 56, 198

Ockeghem, Jean de, 131:
Missa "Mi-Mi", 132
Oldham, John, 21–22
Oliver, H. J., 215
"On the Best of English Poets,
Ben Jonson, Deceased"; *see*
Ford, John
Otway, Thomas, 163, 215; *Alcibiades*,
186; *The Atheist*, 187; compared with
Ford, 188–94 *passim*, 234n40;
Don Carlos, 186–87, 189; *Friendship
in Fashion*, 187; general relation to
baroque style, 186–87, 189–91, 194;
general relation to classicism, 186–87;
general relation to rococo style,
186–87; influenced by Mrs. Barry's
acting style, 187, 233n34; *The
Orphan*, 186–90, 194, 234n40;
patterns of language, 193–94;
principles of dramatic structure,
191–93; *The Soldier's Fortune*, 187;
special talent for stirring passions,
186–87, 189–90, 194; treatment of
female characters, 187–88; *Venice
Preserv'd*, 186–87, 190–94

Palestrina, Giovanni Pierluigi da, 11
Panofsky, Erwin, 2–3, 8, 26
Paradox, 54: logical interpretation of,
139–40; psychological interpretation
of, 136–42 *passim*
Parmigianino, Francesco, 131, 171, 176
Pascal, Blaise, 19, 59, 68
Pedant characters, 60–62, 99, 111–12,
125
Peele, George, 198: *The Araygnement of
Paris*, 70; *The Old Wives' Tale*, 107
Perkin Warbeck, 33, 90–91, 195–96
INDIVIDUAL CHARACTERS: Astley, 103;
Clifford, 102; the Countess of

Crawford, 44; Crawford, 72;
Daliell, 44; Dawbney, 102;
Durham, 104, 149; Frion, 73,
103–104, 125; Heron, 103; Hialas,
104; Huntley, 44; John a Water,
73, 103; Katherine Gordon, 43–44,
56, 72, 103, 106, 223n13; King
Henry, 67, 72, 76, 102, 104–106,
124; King James, 71–72, 104, 106;
Lambert Simnel, 67, 102; Perkin
Warbeck, 43–44, 56, 67, 71–73,
76, 101–106, 125, 140–41, 149,
215; Sketon, 103–104; Surrey,
102; Urswick, 104; Warwick,
104, 106

MAJOR THEMES: death and martyrdom,
56, 104–106; deception, 71–73,
101–106 passim, 164; madness, 67;
sexuality, 43–44

STRUCTURE, 101–106: departure from
renaissance conventions, 101,
105–106; figure of the pedant,
125; open form, 106; pattern
of pretence, 101–106, 124;
unity achieved through fusion,
105–106

VERBAL TECHNIQUE: metaphor, 102–
103, 149; paradox, 140–41, 209

Petrarchan poetry, 37, 88, 116, 172,
174
Phaethon, 211
Phoenix theatre, 182–83, 196, 233n30
Pinero, Sir Arthur Wing: *The Second
Mrs. Tanqueray*, 165
Platonic love, 95, 122, 125, 199; *see
also* Neoplatonism
Pope, Alexander: *The Rape of the Lock*,
25
Pozzo, Andrea, 213
Poussin, Nicolas, 22: *The Rape of the
Sabines* (pl. 12), 20
Preston, Thomas: *Cambises*, 56–57
Prior, Moody E., 209

Prynne, William, 183: *Histriomastix*,
233n28
Puente, Luis de la, 37–38, 47, 151–52
Puttenham, George: *The Arte of
English Poesie*, 143

Queen Henrietta Maria's men, 33, 163,
182–83, 196, 233n27
Queen, or the Excellency of her Sex, The
ATTRIBUTION TO FORD, 224n15
INDIVIDUAL CHARACTERS: Almada,
118; Alphonso, 45–46, 62–63, 76,
116–19, 176; Bufo, 118; Herophil,
118; Lodovico, 118–19; Mopas,
118; Muretto, 45–46, 62–63, 76,
116, 125, 224n15; Petruchi, 45;
Pynto, 118; the Queen, 45–46,
62–63, 116–19, 126; Salassa, 117,
119; Shaparoon, 118; Velasco,
117, 119

MAJOR THEMES; jealousy, 45, 62,
116–17, 119; madness, 62–63;
misogyny, 45, 62, 76, 116, 118,
120; reconciliation, 119; sexuality,
45–46, 224n15

STRUCTURE, 107, 116–20: battle of
the sexes pattern, 116–17, 119;
figure of the pedant, 62, 125;
open form, 118–19; unity achieved
through fusion, 117–18

Quem quaeritis, 197

Racine, Jean, 22; *Andromaque*, 21
Ramus, Peter, 133
Rape, 98, 136, 147–50, 160–61, 188,
191, 193–94, 209
Raphael: *The Descent from the Cross* (pl. 3),
7, 14; *The School of Athens*, 11, 28, 130
Rebirth: as characteristic of comedy,
108; as characteristic of tragedy, 89;
expressed psychologically in baroque
style, 89–90, 97, 101, 106, 119;
expressed socially in renaissance style,
89–90, 106, 108, 119, 228n20

Renaissance style: absolute clarity of, 2, 8, 30–31, 154; closed form of, 2, 28–29, 31, 78–79, 108; control of pathos in, 6, 132; craftsmanship as an ideal in, 10–13; as distinct from baroque, 1–13; harmony achieved in, 2, 29–30, 79; linear technique of, 1, 8, 27–28, 31, 129–30, 154; logical emphasis in, 28, 129, 131–33, 143; in music history, 11, 131–32; plane surfaces of, 2, 28, 31

Restoration comedy, 23–25, 95, 180, 187

Revenger's Tragedy, The; see Tourneur, Cyril

Rhetoric: definition of, 133–34; in relation to logic, 28, 133–34; in relation to psychology, 28, 134–35

Rhetorical figures: *aposiopesis* 158; *ecphonesis* 134–35; *erotesis*, 134; *pathopoeia*, 134–35

Richards, I. A., 142

Robusti, Jacopo; *see* Tintoretto

Rochester, John Wilmot, Earl of, 186

Rococo style, 2: as distinct from baroque, 22–25; rocaille as touchstone of, 23; social emphasis in, 23–25, 180

Romance: as characteristic of baroque structure, 19, 78–79, 96–97, 119–20; in relation to tragicomedy, 107, 119–20

Rore, Cipriano de, 131

Rosso Fiorentino, 131: *The Descent from the Cross* (pl. 8), 14–15

Rotrou, Jean de, 216: *Saint Genest*, 18–19, 21, 29, 78

Rouault, George: *Head of Christ*, 212

Rougemont, Denis de, 119–20

Rousset, Jean, 10, 27

Rowe, Nicholas: *The Fair Penitent*, 194; *Jane Shore*, 194

Rowley, William: *The Witch of Edmonton* (with Dekker and Ford),

225n27; *see also* Middleton, Thomas, and Rowley, William

Rubens, Peter Paul, 10, 32, 79, 89, 181, 205, 212: *Apotheosis of James I*, 213; *The Descent from the Cross* (pl. 4), 7, 14, 55; *Marie de Médicis Landing in Marseilles* (pl. 17), 27, 70, 130; *The Raising of the Cross* (pl. 6), 7, 14–16, 28, 30, 49; *The Rape of the Sabines* (pl. 11), 20

Sackville, Thomas; *see* Norton, Thomas, and Sackville, Thomas

Salingar, L. G., 201–204

Sanzio, Raffaello; *see* Raphael

Sargeaunt, M. Joan, 231n28

Savage, Sir Thomas, 33

Schelling, Felix E., 197

Schütz, Heinrich: *Johannes-Passion*, 132–33

Senecan prose, 31; *see also* stile coupé

Sensabaugh, G. F., 198–200

Sensationalism, 1, 147, 174, 196

Sentimental drama, 194, 205

Sexuality: expressed in religious language, 36–47; prominence of in Ford's plays, 35, 126, 198; in relation to the distinction between love and lust, 46, 64; treatment of in baroque art, 4, 38

Shakespeare, William, 11, 67, 186, 197, 200, 209, 224n16: *Antony and Cleopatra*, 20, 57, 89, 228n10; *As You Like It*, 111; *Cymbeline*, 203; *Hamlet*, 82, 94–96, 177, 212; *1 Henry IV*, 100, 179; *2 Henry IV*, 12; *Henry V*, 101, 228n20; *Julius Caesar*, 94; *King John*, 179; *King Lear*, 57; *Love's Labour's Lost*, 140; *Macbeth*, 78, 144, 203; *A Midsummer Night's Dream*, 69, 168; *Othello*, 113, 165; *The Rape of Lucrece*, 58; *Richard II*, 105, 140; *Richard III*, 72–73, 106, 228n20; *Romeo and Juliet*, 79–90, 143, 201; *The Sonnets*, 46, 133; *The Tempest*,

Shakespeare: (cont.)
107; *Twelfth Night*, 111, 168; *The Two Gentlemen of Verona*, 115; *The Winter's Tale*, 19, 107, 177
Shaw, Bernard, 165; *Saint Joan*, 160
Shearman, John, 171
Sherman, S. P., 40, 198–200
Shirley, James, 107, 163, 233n28: affiliation with Queen Henrietta Maria's men, 33, 182; *The Arcadia*, 182; *The Cardinal*, 181, 185; compared with Ford, 182–86; *The Constant Maid*, 196; *Cupid and Death*, 127; *The Duke's Mistress*, 182, 184–85; general relation to baroque style, 181, 185–86, 194; *The Grateful Servant*, 182; *Hyde Park*, 182; influenced by Fletcher, 182, 185–86; influenced by Jonson, 182, 186; *Love's Cruelty*, 182–85; skill in plot construction, 185; *The Traitor*, 229n31; *The Wedding*, 182; *The Witty Fair One*, 182; *The Young Admiral*, 182
Sidney, Sir Philip, 31, 36; *Arcadia*, 107; *Astrophil and Stella*, 3, 9; *A Defence of Poetry*, 133, 182
Smith, John, of Montague Close: *The Mysterie of Rhetorique Unvail'd*, 134–35
Society of Jesus, 37
Southwell, Robert, 212
Spencer, Theodore, 7–8
Spenser, Edmund, 13, 15, 31, 79, 204: *Amoretti*, 9; *Epithalamion*, 9; *The Faerie Queene*, 30, 58, 78; *Fowre Hymnes*, 37
Stavig, Mark, 199–200
Stile coupé, 16, 28
Stoicism, 6, 48, 170
Strada, Famianus, 69
Sun's Darling, The; *see* Ford, John
Sutherland, Graham: *Crucifixion*, 212
Swinburne, A. C., 185–86, 208
Sypher, Wylie, 14, 22, 27, 30, 38, 220n42, 220n50

Tancred and Gismund; *see* Wilmot, Robert
Tenebroso painting, 18
Teresa, Saint, 3–4, 5–6, 9, 28–29, 47, 49, 201
Theotokopoulos, Domenikos; *see* Greco, El
Tintoretto: *The Last Supper* (pl. 10), 16
'Tis Pity She's a Whore, 191, 195, 201, 204
INDIVIDUAL CHARACTERS: Annabella, 35–37, 39–40, 54–55, 64, 75–76, 79–90, 125–26, 141–42, 144–47, 149–50, 156–57, 174, 183–84, 200, 207, 228n10; Bergetto, 40, 81, 83–84, 156; the Cardinal, 76, 82, 87–88; Donado, 40, 81, 83, 156; Florio, 64, 81; Friar Bonaventura, 40, 54, 60, 64, 79, 86, 125, 146–47, 156, 206, 228n18; Giovanni, 35–37, 39–40, 47, 54–55, 64, 75–76, 78–90, 126, 141–42, 144–40, 156–57, 183, 199–200, 206, 228n10, 231n22; Grimaldi, 81–83; Hippolita, 64, 126, 156; Philotis, 156; Poggio, 83, 156; Putana, 40, 79, 83–85, 156, 223n9; Richardetto, 82, 156; Soranzo, 64, 81, 83, 126, 141, 145–47, 183, 207; Vasques, 81–82, 156

MAJOR THEMES: death and martyrdom, 35–36, 54–55, 88–89, 147, 156–57; incest, 64, 80, 87, 145–47, 164, 183; jealousy, 64, 145–46; madness, 64; sexuality, 35–37, 39–40, 146

STRUCTURE, 79–90: figure of the pedant, 60, 125; function of humour, 84–85; the masque within the play, 126; open form, 86–90 *passim*; unity achieved through fusion, 81–86 *passim*

VERBAL TECHNIQUE: imagery, 156–57,

'Tis Pity She's a Whore: (cont.)
206–207, 209; metaphor, 144–50,
193, 209; paradox, 141–42

Tomlinson, T. B., 204
Tottel's Miscellany, 85
Tourneur, Cyril, 179, 209–10: The
Atheist's Tragedy, 46; The Revenger's
Tragedy, 17, 19, 57, 78, 143–44,
212, 229n31
Tragicomedy, 12–13, 107, 115–16,
118–19, 166–68, 174, 184–85
Tragic structure: in baroque drama,
19, 78–79, 89, 95–96, 214; in
mannerist drama, 19, 77–78; in
renaissance drama, 77, 89, 95–96,
214
Traherne, Thomas, 203
Trompe-l'œil; see illusionism
Tudor interludes, 197
Tudor myth, 105

Udall, Nicholas: Ralph Roister Doister,
117, 198

Van Dyck, Anthony, 32–33: King
Charles on Horseback (pl. 19), 32,
130, 140
Velázquez, Diego Rodriguez de Silva y,
33
Verberckt, Jacques: Le Cabinet de la
Pendule (pl. 14), 22–23
Vouet, Simon, 212

Waith, Eugene M., 171
Wakefield cycle, 212
Ward, A. W., 197
Warnke, Frank J., 34
Webster, John, 171, 179, 186, 209–10,
220n42; The Duchess of Malfi, 17–18,
57, 68, 121; The White Devil, 154–55,
178, 229n31
Weisbach, Werner, 47
Whinney, Margaret, 32
Wickham, Glynne, 233n30
Wild, Friedrich, 34
Willaert, Adrian, 131
Wilmot, Robert: Tancred and Gismund,
57
Wilson, F. P., 19
Wilson, Thomas: The Arte of Rhetorique,
133, 142; The Rule of Reason, 133
Wimsatt, W. K., 2, 235n18
Wind, Edgar, 26
Winters, Yvor, 203
Witchcraft, 1, 72–74
Wölfflin, Heinrich, 1–2, 8, 27–31, 78,
210
Wyatt, Sir Thomas, 13, 203
Wycherley, William, 187, 194:
The Country Wife, 25

York cycle, 213

Zurbarán, Francisco de, 33